RUSSIAN FOREIGN POLICY TOWARDS THE MIDDLE EAST

T0386312

NIKOLAY KOZHANOV

(*Editor*)

Russian Foreign Policy Towards the Middle East

New Trends, Old Traditions

جـامـعة جـورجـتاون قـطر
GEORGETOWN UNIVERSITY QATAR

Center *for* International *and* Regional Studies

HURST & COMPANY, LONDON

Published in Collaboration with Center for International and Regional Studies, Georgetown University–Qatar. First published in the United Kingdom in 2022 by
C. Hurst & Co. (Publishers) Ltd.,
New Wing, Somerset House, Strand, London, WC2R 1LA
A Cataloguing-in-Publication data record for this book is available from the British Library.

ISBN: 9781787386891

This book is printed using paper from registered sustainable and managed sources.

www.hurstpublishers.com

Printed in Great Britain by Bell and Bain Ltd, Glasgow

CONTENTS

ACKNOWLEDGEMENTS

The chapters in this volume grew out of two working group meetings held under the auspices of the Center for International and Regional Studies (CIRS) at Georgetown University in Qatar. I would like to especially thank Mehran Kamrava, the former Director of the Center, and Zahra Babar, the Associate Director for Research, for initiating, supporting, and guiding this project. Special thanks go to Suzi Mirgani, Assistant Director for CIRS Publications, for her invaluable assistance with all editorial matters. This project also benefited immensely from the assistance of the CIRS staff, Elizabeth Wanucha, Misba Bhatti, and Maram Al-Qershi. I would also like to thank the authors in this volume, Roy Allison, Viacheslav Morozov, Samuel Ramani, Yahia Zoubir, Ghoncheh Tazmini, and Leonid Issaev for their contributions and active cooperation during the publication process. Last, but not least, I would like to thank the anonymous reviewers for their constructive feedback and the team at Hurst Publishers for their editorial input and support.

ABOUT THE CONTRIBUTORS

Roy Allison is Professor of Russian and Eurasian International Relations at the School of Global and Area Studies, University of Oxford. He directs the Centre for Russian and Eurasian Studies at St. Antony's College. His former positions include Reader in International Relations, London School of Economics (2005–11) and Head of the Russia and Eurasia Programme, Chatham House (1993–2005). His ten books (sole-authored, co-authored or edited), include *Russia, the West and Military Intervention* (Oxford University Press, 2013). His recent published articles include "Russian Revisionism, Legal Discourse and the 'Rules-Based' International Order," *Europe-Asia Studies*, Vol. 72, No. 6 (2020). He has provided evidence to UK parliamentary committees on Foreign Affairs, Defence and the European Union. His broad research interests cover the international relations, law, and foreign and security policies of Russia, Central Asia, and other post-Soviet Eurasian states.

Leonid Issaev is Associate Professor in the Department of Political Science and International Affairs in the HSE University. He is also Deputy Head of the Laboratory for Monitoring the Risks of Socio-Political Destabilization in HSE University, Senior Fellow at the Center for Civilizational and Regional Studies in the Institute of African Studies of the Russian Academy of Science. He is a member of the Scientific Council of the Russian Political Science Association. He has published numerous monographs and journal articles, mostly in Russian and English. He is co-author of *Syria and Yemen: Unfinished*

Revolutions (URSS, 2013), *Revolutions and Instability in the Middle East* (Uchitel, 2016), and *Fight for the Middle East: Regional Actors in the Course of Middle Eastern Conflict* (2019), and *Federalism in the Middle East: State Reconstruction Projects and the Arab Spring* (Springer, 2021), among many others. He is a regular contributor to Al Jazeera News.

Mark N. Katz is Professor of Government and Politics at the George Mason University Schar School of Policy and Government. He is also the Chairperson of the Scientific Advisory Council of the Finnish Institute of International Affairs, and a Nonresident Senior Fellow at the Atlantic Council. Katz has been awarded fellowships and grants from the Brookings Institution, the Rockefeller Foundation, the Woodrow Wilson International Center for Scholars, and the United States Institute of Peace. Links to his publications can be found on his website: www.marknkatz.com.

Nikolay Kozhanov is Research Associate Professor at the Gulf Studies Center of Qatar University. Nikolay is also Consulting Fellow at the Russia and Eurasia Programme of Chatham House, where he leads a project on Russia's policy in the Middle East, and non-resident Fellow at the Center for Middle East Studies at the Institute of World Economy and International Relations, Russian Academy of Sciences. His research focuses on the geopolitics of Gulf energy, Russian foreign policy in the Middle East, and Iran's economy and international relations. Kozhanov's recent publications include *Russia and the Syrian Conflict: Moscow's Domestic, Regional and Strategic Interests* (Gerlach Press, 2016), *Iran's Strategic Thinking: The Evolution of Iran's Foreign Policy 1979–2017* (Gerlach Press, 2018), and *Russian Policy across the Middle East: Motivations and Methods* (Chatham House 2018).

Viacheslav Morozov is Professor of EU-Russia Studies at the University of Tartu, Estonia, and Academic Director of the UT's Centre for Eurasian and Russian Studies. His research interests include postcolonial theory and critique, ideology and discourses in Russia (including comparative aspects), and EU-Russia relations. He is a member of Academia Europaea, programme chair of the Annual Tartu Conference on Russian and East European Studies, country editor for USSR/Russia in "The Making Identity Count" project, and member of PONARS Eurasia academic network. He is the author of *Russia's Postcolonial Identity: A Subaltern Empire in a Eurocentric World* (Palgrave Macmillan, 2015). His articles have appeared in *International Theory*, *International Relations*, *Journal of International Relations and Development*, and *Cooperation and Conflict*, among others.

Samuel Ramani is a tutor of politics and international relations at the University of Oxford, where he received his doctorate in March 2021. He is also Associate Fellow at the Royal United Services Institute (RUSI) and non-resident Fellow at the Gulf International Forum. His research focuses on contemporary Russian foreign policy; Russia-Middle East relations; and the dynamics of protracted conflicts in the MENA region, South Asia, and Africa. Samuel is a regular contributor to major media outlets, such as *Foreign Policy* and the *Washington Post*; think tanks, such as the Carnegie Endowment for International Peace and the Middle East Institute; and broadcast media outlets, such as the BBC World Service, Al Jazeera English, and CNN International. Samuel has briefed the US Department of State, NATO Intelligence Fusion Center, UK Foreign and Commonwealth Office, and France's Ministry of Defence IRSEM on international security issues, and he regularly advises these organizations on policy matters. His first book, *Russia in Africa: Resurgent Great Power or Bellicose Pretender?*, will be published by Hurst and Co. in 2022.

Ghoncheh Tazmini is a Visiting Fellow at the Middle East Centre at the LSE, where she conducts research on Iran-related themes. She is the author of *Khatami's Iran: The Islamic Republic and the Turbulent Path to Reform* (I. B. Tauris, 2007, 2009), and *Revolution and Reform in Russia and Iran: Politics and Modernisation in Revolutionary States* (I.B. Tauris, 2012). Ghoncheh is formerly an Iran Heritage Foundation Fellow at SOAS and a British Academy grantee. Her research and publications are positioned at the nexus of modern Iranian history, comparative politics, and global history.

Yahia H. Zoubir is Professor of International Studies and Director of Research in Geopolitics at KEDGE Business School in France. He is the author of numerous books and articles on politics, society, and international relations of North Africa. In 2016, he co-edited with Gregory White *North African Politics: Change and Continuity* (Routledge). In 2020, he published an edited book, *The Politics of Algeria: Domestic Issues and International Relations* (Routledge). He has published articles in the *Journal of Contemporary China*, *Middle East Policy*, *Third World Quarterly*, *Mediterranean Politics*, *International Affairs*, *Africa Spectrum*, *Journal of North African Studies*, *Democratization*, and the *Oxford Research Encyclopedia of Religion & Politics*, among others. His most recent research is on China's health diplomacy and China's Health Silk Road. He is currently preparing an edited volume, *The Routledge Handbook on China and the MENA*.

LIST OF FIGURES

INTRODUCTION

Nikolay Kozhanov

Russia's interaction with the Middle East has shifted during the last decade. Moscow substantially increased its presence in the region after it launched air strikes against groups opposing the regime of President Bashar al-Assad in Syria. This set a precedent. Before September 2015, Russia had tried to avoid full-fledged involvement in conflicts in the region. This was also the first time in the history of Russia's presence in the Middle East that Moscow focused on the use of air power—an approach often applied by the United States—instead of giving priority to ground forces, as was the norm during the Soviet era.

Russia's involvement in Syria made Moscow confident in its ability to affect the behavior of Western and regional powers in the Middle East and beyond, as well as to shape the development of regional events. As a result, Russian policy in the Middle East has become more proactive rather than reactive. The Kremlin has tried its hand at engineering events. After Syria, its second major test was in Libya, where Moscow provided political support and military assistance to General Khalifa Haftar, one of the country's most influential warlords. The Kremlin helped him sabotage the implementation of the UN-led Libyan agreement of 2015, which was aimed at launching a reconciliation process. By 2019, shortly before his failed offensive of Tripoli, Haftar controlled the eastern part of Libya, and his fight against the UN-backed Government of National Accord (GNA) was relatively successful. Moscow's support of Haftar, combined with its activities in Syria, clearly demonstrated Russia's readiness to affect political dynamics in Middle Eastern countries, particularly those politically and geographically closer to the post-Soviet space.

The Kremlin is also keen to maintain Russia's position as an influential external broker in the Middle East. However, Moscow is not confident that Russia would be able to respond effectively if forced into a reactive mode by other players in the region. The Kremlin, therefore, seeks to continue to take initiative and shape the regional agenda according to its own needs and resources. At the same time, Russia's engagement in the Middle East is predominantly driven by changes in its domestic and foreign policy, determined by the ongoing confrontation with the West. However, recent years have also been marked by the appearance of new trends.

All in all, Russia's approach to the Middle East is determined by the Kremlin's agenda of using the region as leverage in its relations with the West; of securing Russia's own economic interests in the Middle East; and of ensuring domestic security, which includes security of the post-Soviet republics of Central Asia. Moscow's involvement in the conflicts in Syria and Libya, as well as its close contacts with the Palestinian authorities and attempts to maintain good ties with the warring sides in Yemen, helps demonstrate to the United States and the European Union Russia's importance as a global player. These main Western powers are thus compelled to take Moscow's opinions into account and keep communication channels with Russia open. In other words, Russia's presence in the Middle East advertises its capacities to project power and helps it avoid international isolation. With regard to the latter, Russia can even play the troublemaker when necessary to show that ignoring its interests is potentially dangerous. Thus, Moscow considers its relations with the Middle East region as another—although very important—bargaining chip in its relations with the United States and the European Union.

By contrast, an economic agenda also drives Russia's decision-makers to treat the Middle East as important, preventing political elites from viewing the region solely through the prism of relations with the West. Russia's economic goals in the region are twofold. First, it considers the Middle East as an important source of investments to spur Russia's broken economy, and as a market for some of its industries—above all, arms manufacturing; agriculture; the nuclear sector; and oil, gas, and petrochemicals, including oil-service companies. Second, the dependence of the state budget on exports of hydrocarbons and the Kremlin's concerns about a potential long-term fall of oil prices compels Russia to cooperate actively with the Organization of the Petroleum Exporting Countries (OPEC) and its informal leader Saudi Arabia. Russia's hydrocarbon producers and service companies have also intensified their attempts to acquire stakes in energy projects in the region.

Finally, the Kremlin's Middle East policy is also driven by concerns regarding the possible impact of the regional situation on radical Islamic movements in Russia and post-Soviet Central Asia. If in 2014–16 these concerns centered on the infiltration of the post-Soviet space by so-called Russian-speaking jihadists with battle experience in the Middle East, nowadays Russia is more worried about potential ideological and financial support provided by Middle Eastern elites to radical Islamists in the country and its surrounding regions. This has led to the intensification of attempts to persuade these elites to support "official" Islam in Russia instead. The Kremlin has allowed more active contacts between the government-supported leaders of Russia's Muslim community, including religious figures and the local governments of the Muslim-populated republics of the Russian Federation (Chechnya, Tatarstan, Bashkortostan, Dagestan, and Ingushetia), with the religious circles and political establishments of Egypt, the United Arab Emirates, Qatar, and Saudi Arabia. Among other goals, these contacts are supposed to convince Middle Eastern elites that Muslims' rights are not being abused in Russia.

More broadly, Russia's domestic situation increasingly determines its approach to the Middle East in two ways. On the one hand, the Kremlin uses Russia's presence in the Middle East for its own propaganda needs, including as a means of shoring up support for President Vladimir Putin within Russian society. The ability to leverage the situation in Syria towards Russia's benefit is portrayed as an achievement of the Kremlin's diplomacy. Trips by Russian officials to the Middle East are often portrayed as proof of Moscow's international recognition as an influential global player. On the other hand, growing domestic unrest and the potential problem of Putin's succession is making Moscow more cautious when taking decisions on the Middle East. The Kremlin would like to avoid any unnecessary problems and complications in foreign policy as the 2024 transition of power from Putin to a successor nears, when the president has to decide whether he stays in power or transfers it.

New Drivers of Russian Policy

New drivers for Russia's approach to the Middle East have also recently emerged. Policymakers are concerned with forecasts issued by Kremlin-funded think tanks about the potential risks leading to the decline of Russia's influence in the Middle East. Russia's leadership believes that its ability to exercise influence there is determined by pragmatically balancing between key regional players. What is more, Russia's military presence in Syria caused some Middle Eastern actors to perceive Moscow as an influential "third power" capable of brokering different deals in the region, which make contacts with Moscow important for both regional and non-regional players. Since 2018–19, however, it began to look as though these "pillars" of Russia's presence might become shaky. With the gradual end of the "hot" phase of the war in Syria, Moscow's military involvement has been losing importance, while the political track of the conflict is becoming more significant. This does not benefit Russia, as it will require additional effort from Moscow to dominate the political track in Syria, where regional powers such as Iran, Turkey, and even GCC (Gulf Cooperation Council) members are able to effectively challenge Moscow. This, in turn, can negatively affect the existing regional perception of Russia as the second-most influential non-regional player, after the United States. A new successful military adventure in the Middle East could potentially help Russia to maintain this image in the region. At the same time, Russia is not prepared for such a move and, as noted above, would prefer to avoid such risky steps.

Russia's ability to play the role of regional broker is also being questioned. Its political efforts in Syria are facing growing challenges created by regional players, including Iran, as well as silent discontent from the regime in Damascus, which is resisting even minimal political changes suggested by the Kremlin. Both Turkey and Iran are questioning Russia's right to determine political and military developments in Syria. Further, Russian relations with Israel are facing difficulties—with Moscow being accused of involvement in Israel's domestic affairs—which makes the Kremlin a less appealing candidate for mediation between Israel and Palestine. Moreover, in Libya, in 2019–2020, Russia is reported to have refused to substantially increase its arms supplies to Libyan National Army leader Khalifa Haftar, which has caused a certain disappointment in the Tobruk-based government. In Yemen, Russia's influence on the Houthis is limited in spite of Moscow's attempts to position itself as a potential mediator between the opposing sides. This, in turn, renders Moscow less important than other international players when it comes to attempts to settle the conflict.

Securing Russia's Position

Any weakening of Russia's ability to exercise power in the Middle East does not imply the immediate diminishing of its presence there. Nevertheless, these difficulties are clearly signaling to the Kremlin that it will need to be more active in securing its positions in the region. Russia is more worried about doing so than substantially expanding its presence. However, even such a holding strategy implies active and aggressive policies by Russia. It is trying to get more involved in regional diplomatic initiatives that do not require much material investment to demonstrate Moscow's importance, as well as seeking to be more active in forming and developing regional alliances. For instance, to advertise Moscow's leading role in the international arena, there have been an abundance of recent multi-level visits by Russian officials to the region, as well as trips by Middle Eastern leaders to Russia.

A recent attempt to demonstrate Moscow's influence in the Middle East was the release of its "Concept of collective security in the

Persian Gulf" by the Ministry of Foreign Affairs in July 2019. The Kremlin believes that it will be able to use this document, not only in the Gulf but further afield too, to flag its status as an important international player. Russia's diplomats believe that current tensions in the Gulf make the international community ready to support this initiative. Russia's Ministry of Foreign Affairs also argues that the publication of the concept is a reaction to similar attempts by Western actors to introduce their own potential solution to defuse tensions in the region. Russia believes that the emergence of a new security system in the Gulf is inevitable. Yet, given its ambitions to play a larger role in this part of the Middle East, Russia does not want this new system to be established without its participation. There are no illusions in Moscow that the concept will be adopted by others as it is. However, it is intended to secure having, in due course, a say in any discussion of the future structure of international relations of the Gulf.

New Domestic Policy Actors

One new factor that can alter Russia's approach to the Middle East is the emergence of domestic actors who can affect the policymaking process with regard to the region or its individual countries. Russian energy companies are reported to have a growing influence on policy decisions. The interests of hydrocarbon producers play a part in motivating the Kremlin to strike a balance between key forces in Libya, keeping Russia away from solely supporting Haftar's forces against the Government of National Accord in Tripoli, led by Prime Minister Fayez al-Sarraj. Thus, Gazprom, one of Russia's leading hydrocarbon producers with strong ties to the Kremlin, also has strong connections to the Libyan National Oil Corporation headquartered in Tripoli. Any evidence of Russia lending massive direct military assistance to Haftar would hurt these ties. Under these circumstances, any information about Russian weapons and ammunition supplies to Haftar should be taken with a grain of salt. Moscow does provide Haftar with ammunition, but it does so very carefully, via third parties and in limited amounts.

The case of Gazprom in Libya is not an exception. The Middle Eastern interests of Russian energy corporations are often associated with members of Putin's inner circle, including Yevgeny Prigozhin and Gennady Timchenko, whose companies enjoy Russia's informal support in Syria, and Rosneft's head Igor Sechin, whose company managed to establish good relations with Iraqi Kurdistan and Iraq's central government with the help of the Russian diplomatic and security establishment.

After Russia began its "return" to the Middle East, it had to deal with numerous non-state and quasi-state structures there, and was forced to use "parallel diplomacy" with formal and informal structures that have no relation to the ways in which the Ministry of Foreign Affairs develops official ties in the region. To communicate with different actors in Libya, Russia relied not only on the ministry but also on individuals not openly associated with the official agencies that deal with foreign matters. Such individuals' personal views inevitably affect policy as they also try to push their own agendas.

For instance, between 2017 and 2020, Lev Dengov, a Belarus-born businessman engaged in the construction business in Libya, helped Russia to establish ties with ex-Prime Minister Sarraj. He received official status as "head of the contact group on Libya at the foreign Ministry of the Russian Federation," although he is not a professional diplomat. Dengov saw the future of his business interests as being connected to Sarraj, and he thus was critical of Haftar. Until recently, his influence in Moscow was strong and allowed him to counter Haftar's supporters there, mostly Defence Minister Sergey Shoigu and officials from his ministry. Even now, after Dengov stepped aside, Shoigu does not have enough means to make his approach to Libya the dominant one in the Kremlin's decision-making. As a result, he has had to concede to the Ministry of Foreign Affairs and Putin's special representative for the Middle East, Mikhail Bogdanov, who previously supported Dengov. Thus, recent fluctuations in the intensity of Russia's support for Haftar reflect the struggle for the Kremlin's attention taking place among different actors in Russia.

The administration at the head of the Chechen republic, Ramzan Kadyrov, is one of the centers of Russia's "parallel diplomacy." In the past, using the connections of the Chechen community abroad, he managed to establish ties with the Misrata forces in Libya. Kadyrov also played a role in improving Russia's relations with Saudi Arabia and the United Arab Emirates—investors in Chechnya—where he was often received as a guest by the administrations of these countries. The Kremlin currently uses Kadyrov to carry messages between Moscow, Riyadh, and Abu Dhabi when it does not want to draw attention to matters discussed. Kadyrov's visits to the two countries usually precede important decisions taken at the official level. For example, in August 2018, he was invited to Saudi Crown Prince Mohammed bin Salman's palace to celebrate Eid al-Adha. It is reported that during this visit, matters discussed included the export of S-400 missile systems to Saudi Arabia, the potential training of Saudi special forces in Chechnya, the future of Syria, and Putin's visit to Saudi Arabia. Only when Kadyrov relayed the message to Moscow that King Salman was willing to host the Russian president in Riyadh did the Kremlin officially declare that it was preparing Putin's visit to the kingdom.

Finally, Middle Eastern countries, above all the Arab monarchies of the Persian Gulf, are forming their own lobbies in Russia at the regional and federal levels. The members of these lobbies have shown themselves to be determined to counter any negative political influence on the development of the Russian-Saudi dialogue. At the level of Russia's regions, as noted, Kadyrov and Chechnya's officials play an important role in developing relations with the Gulf. Apart from securing the interests of Russia's government, these lobbyists also take into account their own priorities, as well as the priorities of the Middle Eastern side.

All in all, by 2020, Russian foreign policy was driven by an intricate mixture of new and old factors, the interplay of which is complicated. This, in turn, makes predicting Moscow's moves in the Middle East a challenging task.

About the Volume

The top priority of this book is to fill a gap in the understanding of Russia's foreign policy towards the Middle East, as well as its drivers and priorities. This gap in understanding is caused by the overconcentration of commentators on those aspects of Moscow's presence in the Middle East that draw the most public attention (such as Russia's vision of the Syrian conflict settlement), thus overshadowing Russia's dialogue with other parts of the region (such as the GCC or North Africa).

INTRODUCTION

This project offers a comprehensive view of the drivers of Russian diplomacy and how their interplay shapes Russia's approaches to the Middle East. These studies demonstrate that, while it plays an important role in shaping Moscow's approaches to the region, Russia's confrontation with the West should not be considered the only factor determining the Kremlin's policy in the Gulf. This research initiative demonstrates that Russia's domestic situation and the heritage of past experiences dealing with the region are no less important. Many underestimate the influence of the struggle for political power within Russia, and ignore the role of the Cold War experience, in determining Moscow's behavior in the Middle East. Many also simplify the role of Russian energy corporations as creating sources for conflict and cooperation between Moscow and Middle Eastern powers. While some authors present Russian oil and gas resources as just another lever through which Moscow exercises its influence in the region, this volume demonstrates that the Russian economy's heavy dependence on the export of hydrocarbons also shapes its policy.

In contrast to most studies of Russia's presence in the region, this book considers Russian involvement in the Middle East from several angles. First, the volume analyzes both global geopolitical risks affecting Russia's Middle Eastern strategy and internal drivers determining Moscow's behavior in the region. Second, special attention is paid to the discussion regarding how much of Russian foreign policy towards the Middle East is based on the principle of continuity. The authors discuss how Moscow's vision of its priorities in the Middle East differs from that of the Soviet Union and how the drivers of Russian presence in the region evolved after 1991. These findings are illustrated by separate case studies analyzing the main trends of Russian relations with Iran, Syria, the GCC countries, Yemen, and North Africa. Third, these studies are not limited by the analysis of bilateral relations between Russia and the selected countries of the region. Instead, they also look into the areas of divergence and convergence between Moscow and Middle Eastern players on a wide range of regional and international issues, including but not limited to the Syrian civil war, Iran's regional activities, and the Yemeni conflict.

Finally, the volume assesses opportunities and challenges faced by Moscow in the Middle East, especially those that motivate the Russian government towards more active cooperation with the region. This book demonstrates that, apart from Russia's confrontation with the West—wrongly acknowledged by analysts as the only key factor determining the context of Russia's presence in the Middle East—there are other no less important issues shaping Russian diplomacy in the region. These include new global challenges as well as Russian economic interests and domestic policies that push Moscow towards greater interaction with the Middle East. All in all, the volume tries to answer the following questions:

- Does the Kremlin have a clearly articulated strategy for developing its relations with key countries of the Middle East? If so, what are the main principles of this strategy and how is it implemented in practice?
- To what extent is Moscow's vision of the region shaped by the crisis in Russia's relations with the West?
- What are the means and limits of Russian influence in the region?
- How does any Middle East strategy fit into Russia's broader conception of its global role in the international arena?
- Who are the main players shaping Russia's approaches to the Middle East, and what are their interests?
- What influence, if any, does Russian public opinion have on Moscow's actions in the Middle East?

The authors contributing to this volume include leading Russian, Middle Eastern, and Western experts on Moscow's relations with the Middle East. This, in turn, provides readers with a rare opportunity to examine Russian presence in the Middle East through different lenses and to compare visions of Moscow's role in the region according to three diverse expert communities.

The first chapter of the book is authored by Viacheslav Morozov, who analyzes the Russian view of the post-Cold War global order and the significance of the Middle East for this image. Morozov argues that Russia's foreign policy outlook has always been West-centric and that its policy in the region and elsewhere has been shaped by a number of factors, including a balance of forces in the domestic political arena. The chapter presents a genealogical account, explaining how Russian foreign policy thinking and practice evolved from seeking an accommodation with the United States in the early 1990s to Russia's more recent annexation of Crimea and intervention in Syria.

The second chapter is authored by Mark Katz and provides a comparison of the strengths and weaknesses of Soviet policy towards the Middle East during the Cold War with Putin's more recent foreign policy towards the region. Katz examines Soviet foreign policy and explores what went well for Moscow as well as what did not, thus, offering an explanation of Soviet gains and misfortunes in the Middle East. A similar examination is provided for Moscow's regional policies during the Putin era. Katz notes that Putin deliberately uses expressions like "what went/has gone well for Moscow" and its equivalent when describing the results of Russian presence in the Middle East, both under his own administration and those of his Soviet predecessors. Thus, he avoids the risk of having Moscow's foreign policy successes and failures viewed as the result solely of Moscow's own foreign policy decision-making. According to Katz, while Moscow's decisions obviously play a role in whether its Middle Eastern policies are successful or not, sometimes Moscow's successes or failures are affected by policies pursued by the United States, by Middle Eastern and other actors, and by events—often unexpected—that affect Moscow's (among others) standing in the region.

A different angle on the main drivers of Russian foreign policy is offered by Leonid Issaev, who examines the domestic factors of Moscow's diplomacy. He argues that the foreign policy of any country cannot be considered in isolation from the processes that occur within the state. This is especially true for Russia, where foreign policy since the times of the Soviet Union has been a service function in relation to the needs of the current political regime. This becomes even more obvious if one looks at Russia during Vladimir Putin's second presidential term. Issaev argues that in the 2000s, Putin managed to capitalize on the public's request for domestic stabilization, and in the 2010s, his public confidence rating was largely based on his foreign policy "achievements." Issaev demonstrates how the Kremlin's more active and, periodically, aggressive actions in the Middle East were a means of building social support at home and diverting public attention away from domestic problems.

This discussion is partially continued in the fourth chapter, by Roy Allison, who concentrates on Russian legal and normative claims for Moscow's intervention in the Syrian conflict since 2015. This dimension of Russia's military presence in the Middle East has attracted little scholarly attention, although it is significant for Russian domestic politics, for regional state conduct, and for the wider international system. Allison argues that the legal and normative claims Russia has advanced to justify this major use of force should not be viewed in realist terms as merely the instrumental language of states in a world governed by geopolitics. Legal and normative arguments seek to legitimize actions internationally and domestically, and the traction they gain is important for states in promoting both their international status and influence.

In the case of Syria, Russian arguments have sought to persuade and attract the support of states in Russia's favor, as part of a wider contestation in the international system over law and norms. This is demonstrated by the way Russia's justifications for its own use of force parallel its diplomatic efforts to refute the legality and legitimacy of Western use of force in Syria, which commenced with air strikes against the Islamic State (IS) in September 2014, followed later by limited punitive strikes against facilities of the Syrian regime.

In the following chapter, Ghoncheh Tazmini explores the nature of Russian-Iranian relations. Russia's interactions with Iran have been ambiguous, manifesting in peaks and troughs, and vacillating between cooperation and contention. Despite regularly colliding geostrategic and geo-economic pathways, the pattern of engagement between these two pivotal states suggests that the Moscow-Tehran strategic partnership is likely to be an enduring feature of the Middle Eastern political landscape. By casting a wide analytical net, Tazmini ascertains that there is a fundamental connective tissue that binds these two pivotal states. She argues that Russia and Iran share a similar geopolitical worldview that is defined by several enduring parameters shaped by historical experience, geographic realities, cultural-civilizational peculiarities, and a similar discursive genealogy in relation to the West. Russia, in particular, challenges the universality of the US-led liberal international order, and, in this pursuit, Iran is a critical partner. Thus, while Moscow's mercurial maneuverings have made it a challenge to decipher the nature of Russian-Iranian relations, Tazmini argues that the Moscow-Tehran alignment is firmly anchored within a broader assemblage of shared principles, priorities, and preoccupations.

In the sixth chapter of the book, Nikolay Kozhanov explores Russia's presence in the Persian Gulf, paying attention to Moscow's relation with the GCC countries. Kozhanov analyzes the drivers of Russia-GCC Relations, trying to understand challenges and prospects for the development of Russia's ties with the Arab monarchies of the Gulf. Since 2015, Russian relations with the GCC have demonstrated a strong tendency for positive development. After the serious cooldown in GCC relations with Moscow in 2012–14 caused by the negative reaction of the Gulf monarchies to Russia's support of the Assad regime, this rapprochement was determined by a complex mixture of factors that include the growing intensity of Moscow's presence in the region; changing dynamics of US relations with Russia, the GCC, and the Middle Eastern powers; evolution of energy markets; existing tensions between Middle Eastern countries; and the transformation of GCC foreign policy vision. This chapter looks into the influence these factors have on the current development of Russia's relations with the GCC. It assesses the prospects for dialogue between these states and Moscow, including the ability of both sides to bring these relations to a new qualitative level.

In Chapter Seven, Samuel Ramani offers his views on Russia's role in the Yemeni conflict. In an apparent contrast to its military intervention in Syria and rising assertiveness throughout the Middle East, Russia has consistently adhered to a policy of strategic nonalignment since the Yemeni civil war began in 2014. According to Ramani, Russia's policy of maintaining cordial diplomatic relations with Yemeni president Abd Rabbuh Mansur Hadi's coalition, the Houthis, and the Southern Transitional Council (STC) has differentiated it from other world powers. Russia has been able to preserve these relationships, while boosting its own geopolitical and status aspirations in the region, without getting mired in Yemen's protracted conflict. The chapter outlines the geopolitical interests and status aspirations that have inspired Russia's strategic nonalignment policy and consistent opposition to the Saudi-led military intervention in Yemen. The chapter analyzes the impact of Russia's approach to the Yemeni civil war on its

13

strengthening relationship with Iran and emerging partnerships with the Gulf monarchies. The chapter concludes with an articulation of how Russia's strategic nonalignment policy translates into a vision for a peace settlement in Yemen and an assessment of Moscow's ability to reconcile its diplomatic relations with the Houthis—a militant non-state actor—with its legal understandings of sovereignty and norms on domestic state order. The chapter extensively cites Russian-language sources and elite interviews to address gaps in scholarship and explores links between Russian conduct in Yemen and broader trends in Russian foreign policy.

The final chapter by Yahia Zoubir examines the evolution of Moscow's relations with the countries of the Maghreb, tracing them from early Soviet times. While Russia is a relatively important player in the Maghreb, the region itself is not vital for Russia's interests. Similarly, the Maghreb did not hold strategic importance for the Soviet Union during the Cold War. However, although Russia did not view the Maghreb as a regional entity, it nonetheless succeeded in building good, lasting relations with the Maghreb states, particularly with Algeria. Moscow seeks to revive those traditional relations to reassert its great power status on the world stage. To do that, Moscow has clearly expressed its intent to defend its political, trade, security, and cultural interests. Indubitably, there are many parallels with the Soviet type of engagement in the region, without the ideological overtone that had characterized Moscow's policy during that era. Today, Moscow's policy in the Maghreb is more pragmatic and more appealing to the incumbent Maghreb governments seeking to balance out or even perhaps distance themselves from Western powers, which they may perceive as too intrusive in their domestic affairs or from which they may be unsure about receiving support.

Overall, this collection of chapters offers insight into the motives behind Moscow's behavior in the Middle East, considering Russia's growing role in the region and its desire to protect its national interests using a wide range of means. The book identifies the various drivers of Russia's regional policy and generates informed prognoses about Moscow's moves in the Middle East.

THE MIDDLE EAST IN RUSSIA'S FOREIGN POLICY, 1990–2020

Viacheslav Morozov

Introduction

This chapter presents a genealogical account of Russia's view of the post-Cold War global order, with a particular emphasis on the factors determining its policy in the Middle East.[1] Russia's decision in 2015 to conduct a military operation in Syria is a major outcome that my analysis seeks to explain by pointing out how Russian foreign and security policy thinking has evolved over the past few decades.

While most scholars agree that Russian foreign policy has been disproportionately focused on the West since the end of the Cold War,[2] there are two main positions with regard to how much the Kremlin's strategic priorities have changed in the post-Cold War period. The most widespread view is that, after the collapse of the USSR, the Russian leadership aimed to rejoin the international community, in the hope that partnering with the United States and the European Union would help Russia achieve both security and prosperity. This attitude began to gradually change from the late 1990s with the more assertive, and eventually anti-Western, foreign policy adopted by the successive administrations of President Vladimir Putin.[3] There are diverging views on the reasons for this change: some blame it on the decision by Washington and its allies to ignore Russia's concerns about the enlargement of NATO and the West-dominated security order in general.[4] Others argue that Russia's apprehensions were ill-conceived, and that ultimately it was Moscow that missed the chance to integrate into the liberal international order.[5]

Another position, most recently spelled out by Dmitry Gorenburg, holds that Russia's strategic priorities have never changed: ever since the Soviet collapse, the country has sought "to restore Russia's great power status while maintaining a zone of influence in states on Russia's border as a buffer against potential security threats."[6] Here, the observed variation in foreign policy was not due to a change in priorities, but to the fact that during Putin's presidency Russia has been able to partially catch up with the West in terms of military power, economic well-being, and global influence. An even more radical version of this perspective is promoted by the pro-Western political elites in Eastern Europe, in particular in the Baltic states, where Russia is considered an expansionist empire that will always threaten its neighbors as long as it has enough power and resources to conduct independent foreign policy.

In this chapter, I do not directly intervene in the debate on the continuity and change in Russian foreign policy priorities, nor do I aim to provide a full overview of Moscow's policies in the Middle East. Rather, what I seek to highlight is how specific interpretations of major trends and events in global politics have resulted in policy choices, and how the relational dynamic between Russia and the West solidified the approach to global affairs that came to drive Russia's Middle East policy from around 2012–13 onwards.

Imperial Legacies and Structural Factors

At first glance, Russia's post-Cold War policy in the Middle East went through an even more dramatic transformation than its relations with the West. A drastically reduced presence under Mikhail Gorbachev and especially Boris Yeltsin was succeeded by a concerted effort by Putin's government to restore Russia's geopolitical influence, leading up to a full-scale military intervention in Syria. An analysis of the evolution of Russian foreign policy thinking in relation to the Middle East helps highlight the key features of Moscow's take on the global order as a whole, and on the relative significance of particular regions and actors.

Russia's outlook continues to focus on the West, perceived as the main subject of world politics, and tends to underestimate local political dynamics, especially on the domestic level. It criticizes the idea of a unipolar world, allegedly promoted by the United States and its allies, and calls upon them to face up to the fact that the world has become multipolar.[7] Paradoxically, Moscow does this from a perspective that still, in a somewhat outdated fashion, sees the world as bipolar, with Russia providing the main counterbalance to US influence.[8] The role of China, BRICS, the G-20, and similar institutions is acknowledged but never brought to the fore.[9] In a further twist of this logic, while criticizing US unilateralism, Russia uses it as a justification of its own selective disrespect for international norms and institutions, which is one of the enabling factors behind Moscow's skillful use of its asymmetrical power vis-à-vis the United States and other Western actors. Last, but not least, Moscow's foreign policy moves are to a large extent driven by domestic factors: any such move is an exercise of balancing between opposing political forces and elite groupings.[10] This exercise has to be conducted with an eye towards the condition of the economy and the need to offset the costs of foreign policy action, both direct and indirect, by securing a favorable economic position now and in the future.[11]

One might question the coherence of the Russian leadership's policy choices in light of the individual criteria outlined above, or even go further and cast doubt on the assumptions on which those priorities are based. However, if one evaluates these decisions as integral elements of a global outlook, one has to admit that they do achieve a certain equilibrium between contradictory imperatives. It is clear that the decision to intervene in Syria, for example, was costly and did not bring any immediate economic benefits. Yet, the resulting increase in Russia's geopolitical profile in the region as a whole is seen as a major investment in securing the country's southern borders, as well as in future economic cooperation not just with Syria but also with Turkey, Iran, and the Arab states of the Persian Gulf.[12]

This perspective provides additional evidence in favor of the argument about continuity in Russian foreign policy since the early post-Cold War period. Indeed, most, if not all, elements of this approach were already present in Soviet policy during the 1990–91 crisis in the Persian Gulf.[13] The decision to back the UN Security Council Resolution 678, authorizing the use of force against Iraq, was the outcome of a domestic political struggle between the old guard—most vocally represented by Evgeny Primakov, then a member of the Presidential Council under Gorbachev—and the proponents of New Thinking. The latter doctrine, proposed by Gorbachev and pushed forward by Foreign Minister Eduard Shevardnadze, included such ideas as interdependence, universal human values, and the need to cooperate in addressing global challenges.[14]

Soviet support of the US position was never unequivocal: in the months between the Iraqi occupation of Kuwait and the start of the US military campaign, Primakov spent a significant amount of time in Baghdad in an attempt to secure a peaceful settlement of the conflict. Already at that time, the scale of the US military deployment and of the campaign itself was seen as disproportional to the declared goal of restoring Kuwaiti sovereignty. Hence, it was aimed at securing long-term dominance in the region. The proponents of New Thinking, in their turn, were not driven by idealism alone: they viewed the Soviet policy of supporting radical anti-Western regimes in the Third World as unsustainable and ideologically bankrupt, and perceived cooperation with the West as the only way to overcome Russia's political isolation and ensure its economic development.[15]

It is also interesting to note that even this lukewarm support for the US-led coalition paved the way towards improving Russia's relations with Saudi Arabia.[16] This, in turn, was the beginning of a new pattern regarding relations between Moscow and the states of the greater Middle East region, eventually producing a situation where Russia, unlike the United States, has reasonably good relations with almost all of them.[17] Importantly, relations with Israel moved beyond the Cold War antagonism, although the radical improvement of economic and cultural relations did not eliminate a continuous diplomatic struggle.[18] All of the above opened up new opportunities both in the field of diplomacy, especially conflict mediation,[19] and the economy, such as the recent cooperation between Russia and the Organization of the Petroleum Exporting Countries, aimed at keeping global oil prices at a comfortable level.[20]

This outcome, however, would have been hard to predict in the early 1990s, when the Russian Federation emerged as a sovereign state and the legal successor of the Soviet Union. Its foreign policy was firmly focused on Europe and the post-Soviet space, and for a while was shaped by the paradigm of New Thinking.[21] This meant that the EU and the United States were considered Russia's main partners, its source of financial aid and investment, and the strategic goal was to join the key institutions of the liberal world order, such as the Council of Europe and the World Trade Organization, established in 1994 on the basis of the General Agreement on Tariffs and Trade.[22]

From the very beginning, however, this liberal foreign policy was challenged by a number of competing approaches. This chapter does not attempt yet another mapping of the foreign policy discourse,[23] but stresses that all these competing positions shared the idea of Russia having a special global and regional role. For the liberals, this role consisted in Russia being a great power alongside the United States, Germany, and Japan, while their rivals defined Russia's mission as being in opposition to the West. The imperial tradition was probably the most powerful in this regard, to a large extent due to the fact that, regardless of the political preferences of individual decision-makers, they all had to deal with the imperial legacies inherited from the Soviet Union. This legacy materialized in a myriad of urgent policy issues, such as the withdrawal of the former Soviet army units from their distant outposts in Central Europe and elsewhere; Russia's involvement in the armed conflicts in Transnistria, Abkhazia, and Tajikistan; the need to design a sensible citizenship policy and deal with migration; and the lack of certainty with regard to Russia's own identity as a multiethnic rump of the former empire, torn apart by multiple separatist movements, most prominently in Chechnya and Tatarstan.[24]

Another key aspect of the imperial legacy was the presence of external constituencies that appealed to Russia as the patron of the homeland, defined in ethnic and cultural terms, in opposition to the dividing lines that were solidifying as part of the new liberal world order.[25] The emergence of these clienteles was the result of a relational dynamic of social construction: the theme of "compatriots abroad" was played up by ethnic entrepreneurs both within Russia and in the new nationalizing states; in the situation of an identity crisis on both sides, the appeals of these entrepreneurs were likely to induce political mobilization and thus provide legitimacy to their claims. This dynamic was strongest in places like Transnistria and the Baltics, but it did influence the political process and bilateral relations in other areas as well, from Ukraine and Belarus to Abkhazia, South Ossetia, and Kazakhstan.[26] The Balkans figure as a special case, but Serbian nationalist leaders were equally eager to play the Russian card.[27]

What is important to emphasize here is that the imperial legacy, first and foremost the historical narratives of "brotherhood" deeply ingrained by Soviet education and mass culture, made it difficult for the decision-makers in Moscow to completely ignore such appeals for patronage. If they chose to do so, nationalists quickly occupied the niche, capitalizing on the preexisting public perceptions of moral responsibility vis-à-vis the "compatriots," "the Serbian brothers," and so on. Thus, the rather erratic course of Russian foreign policy throughout the 1990s was primarily determined by domestic political imperatives, with President Yeltsin, Foreign Minister Andrey Kozyrev, and other key policymakers having to maneuver between the liberals and the nationalists while also trying to manage the still-fragile market economy.

Understandably, foreign policy being an arena of vehement political struggles at home produced a certain myopia in Russia's global outlook, which became mostly limited to its immediate surroundings, aside from managing its key relationship with the world's only remaining superpower. With regard to the Middle East and other remote parts of the world, this basically meant withdrawal: the limited resources available to Russia had to be concentrated in high-priority areas, while the relational dynamic described above did not really work in the case of former clients in the Arab world and other culturally and geographically remote areas.

At the same time, it would be wrong to perceive Russian foreign policy of the 1990s as completely compartmentalized: on the contrary, the relational dynamic that drove Russia's engagement in its "near abroad" also worked elsewhere. This was not solely because of the rhetoric of geopolitical responsibility in relation to these former clients that was maintained by people like Primakov, especially after his move in early 1996 from the position of chief of external intelligence to head of the Foreign Ministry.[28] As Bobo Lo points out, during this time, Moscow neglected both the "far" and the "near abroad" by conducting a reactive policy driven by a West-centric outlook: "Resources were invested not in developing productive bilateral and multilateral relations, but in responding to individual events and/or actions by outside, predominantly Western, parties."[29] The key aim, according to Mark N. Katz, was not to compete with the United States but to make Russia, backed up by its allies, an indispensable player capable of keeping US unilateralism in check.[30]

The best way of achieving this goal was indeed to try and build good, or at least non-conflictual, relations with key stakeholders. While Russia did not have the capacity to actively engage in the Middle East, it was at least trying to build up trust and capitalize on the history of mutual engagement, where available. Thus, as early as the 1990s, Russia advocated a gradual phasing out of sanctions against Iraq, arguing that isolation of Saddam Hussein's regime would not make the region more secure. It strongly condemned the 1998 air strikes on Iraq by US and UK forces and worked with other states— most notably China and France—on alternative solutions in the UN framework.[31] Similarly, it was the only significant country that did not choose sides in the 1994 Yemen civil war, trying instead to mediate between various factions. All of that pointed to what were to become the key principles of Russian diplomacy in the early twenty-first century: the primacy of sovereign statehood and a strong preference for what it calls "universal and comprehensive" security arrangements based on equally respecting the interests of all parties. Explicitly or implicitly, this "universal" approach was presented as a direct alternative to US unilateralism.[32]

To sum up, Russia's foreign policy from the early 1990s onwards demonstrates the key features that define its evolution in the subsequent decades. In its disproportionate focus on the West—seen either as the key partner or the main rival—it follows the logic of domestic political competition among actors playing on various elements of Russia's imperial legacy, encapsulated by the idea of great power.[33] It is also opportunistic, meaning that its policy moves and its choice of tactics are largely determined by the resources available. In the prolonged crisis of the 1990s, this meant focusing on Russia's immediate surroundings in an attempt to prevent the geopolitical expansion of the United States and the EU into what Moscow increasingly came to see as its sphere of influence. The same logic applied to the Middle East and other areas of the "far abroad," which came to play a much more central role in the transformation of the foreign policy doctrine and practice in the Putin era.

From Disillusionment to Balancing

The two inaugural events of the Putin era were NATO's military campaign against Milošević's Yugoslavia in 1999 and the 2001 terrorist attacks in the United States. The Kosovo crisis severely damaged Russia's trust in the United States and its allies: the intervention was widely interpreted as a cynical abuse of human rights driven by *realpolitik* considerations, primarily by the West's desire to expand its sphere of influence in a key region of Europe.[34] The 9/11 attacks, in turn, refocused global politics on the Middle East, a region that had been one of Russia's key concerns for a number of years. Since late 1999, Russia was fighting its second war in Chechnya, precipitated by a series of terrorist attacks in Russia in August–September 1999, which included blowing up several residential buildings and killing hundreds of people. The war made both the security services and the general public acutely aware of the spread of transnational radical networks operating under the banner of Islam.[35]

In the aftermath of the 2001 attacks, the Kremlin demonstrated full solidarity with the United States: Putin was the first among the world leaders to call President George W. Bush to express his sympathy for the American people. The calculation in Moscow was that the Western world would now fully understand the reasons for Russia's involvement in Chechnya and engage in a concerted effort to eradicate terrorism from the Middle East.[36] Washington, however, chose to act unilaterally, which in Moscow's eyes continued the pattern already on display during the first Gulf War and, even more blatantly, in Kosovo.[37] In addition, in 2001, the Bush administration chose to withdraw from the 1972 Anti-Ballistic Missile Treaty—a move that Russia saw as having the potential, in the long term, of undermining parity between the two nuclear superpowers.[38] Despite these concerns and the pain of being ignored by Washington in its own War on Terror, Russia was ready to tolerate the United States' actions in the Middle East so long as it concentrated on fighting the radicals. The turning point in this respect was the 2003 campaign against Saddam Hussein's Iraq.

For Washington's critics, in Russia and elsewhere, the Iraq War stood out in two key respects. Firstly, it was a unilateral military intervention conducted in defiance of the UN Security Council as well as of key NATO allies, France and Germany. Secondly, its central aim, disguised poorly if at all, was to remove Iraq's leader, whose despotic rule was incompatible with the rather simplistic version of a democratic peace theory that was increasingly influential as the background for US global engagement. Saddam Hussein was to be removed from power not because he posed a direct threat to the United States, but for the sake of promoting a more stable and peaceful world order that would supposedly go hand in hand with the spread of democracy in the Middle East and other parts of the world.[39]

Saddam's Iraq could hardly be described as Russia's ally, but, as pointed out above, Russia had still cultivated this relationship, partly as a counterbalance to US dominance. Saddam's removal provoked indignation in Moscow because it was seen as both illegitimate and irresponsible. Russian politicians and experts drew direct parallels between the invasion of Iraq and the events in Kosovo and concluded that the US War on Terror was in fact a much more ambitious enterprise, aimed at establishing unilateral hegemony in global affairs.[40] Against this background, the EU and NATO adding to their ranks countries in Eastern Europe provoked only muffled reactions from Moscow: Russian elites continued to view NATO's move east as a violation of promises given to Gorbachev at the time of German reunification, but it had been a gradual decision, coming into play in the mid-1990s when Russia could do little to reverse the course of affairs.[41]

The 2003 Iraq War happened under different circumstances. It prompted a decisive turn in Putin's foreign policy towards the promotion of "multipolarity."[42] In the context of Russia's foreign policy doctrine, the latter term needs to be understood as referring to the emergence of alternative centers of power capable of limiting US influence in key regions, including the post-Soviet space, greater Eurasia, and South America.[43] Once again, this policy continued to exploit new opportunities opened by the abandonment of the rigid Soviet approach to alliances under Gorbachev. It was, however, much more successful, not least because of the economic rise of the "emerging powers," among which Russia used to proudly count itself before the 2008–09 economic crisis.[44]

This was indeed a multi-vector diplomacy that sought to establish partnerships all over the world. Russia heavily invested in BRICS, which developed from the vague idea of lumping together Brazil, Russia, India, and China—selected because of their equally impressive economic growth in the 2000s—into a loosely institutionalized but highly visible organization, and expanded in 2010 to include South Africa. Since 2009, BRICS has held regular summits and, since 2015, boasts its own multilateral bank (the New Development Bank).[45]

Russia has also established a number of bilateral partnerships, each featuring a different proportion of economic and geopolitical cooperation. Thus, relations with Turkey, a NATO member, warmed up in the 2000s on the basis of mutual economic interest and only came to include security cooperation in the subsequent decade, as a reflection of the growing tension between Recep Tayyip Erdoğan's government and the Western powers.[46] Russia's relations with countries like Syria and Venezuela, on the contrary, were predominantly driven by geopolitical considerations: in both cases, Russia's key interest consisted of using them as military and geopolitical outposts in key areas of the world, while economic interests, with all their undisputed significance, could not in and of themselves have provided enough ground for mutual engagement. The opposite logic drove Russia's relationship with Israel: it had a solid foundation in trade and people-to-people contacts—around 15 percent of the Israeli population are Russian-speakers, mostly immigrants from the former USSR—which helped the two countries stay on speaking terms even at times of severe diplomatic tension.[47]

This foreign policy course consolidated in subsequent years, mostly due to events that, in Moscow's eyes, provided additional evidence of the United States' hegemonic ambitions. The "color revolutions"—popular uprisings that brought down the ruling regimes in Georgia (2003), Ukraine (2004), and Kyrgyzstan (2005)—were perceived by the Russian establishment as indications that the promotion of US democracy was moving ever closer to Russia proper: indeed, Moscow interpreted these uprisings as a direct threat to domestic political stability. The 2004 Ukrainian "Orange Revolution," named after the color associated with the winning political party, was particularly significant in this context. Popular protests against large-scale fraud in the second round of presidential elections in November 2004 forced the Supreme Court to annul the victory of Viktor Yanukovych, the candidate who was considered pro-Russia. The January 2005 re-vote brought a clear victory for Viktor Yushchenko. Moscow was deeply suspicious of the unequivocal support for the revolution expressed by the United States, the EU, and nearly the entire Western world: the events were thus interpreted as being orchestrated from Washington and Brussels. This conspiratorial view, which came to dominate the Russian discourse, did not allow for any grassroots initiative in matters of "high" politics: if political protesters were not being manipulated by Moscow, they had to be paid and otherwise motivated by the West.[48]

This went hand in hand with the consolidation of the historical narrative in which the political turmoil of the 1990s was presented as a key historical Other, along with such events as "the time of troubles" of the early seventeenth century and the Civil War of 1917–1922.[49] In other words, it was assumed that a Western intervention in Russian domestic politics was not only possible but in a certain sense already ongoing, and that letting it continue unchecked would unleash another domestic crisis with potentially catastrophic consequences for Russian statehood.[50]

This thinking was summarized in Putin's speech at the Munich Security Conference in February 2007, meant as a warning to the United States and its allies not to continue with their interventionist policies.[51] This was also the time when Vladislav Surkov, then deputy head of the Presidential Administration, a person who is widely believed to be the main ideologue of Putin's authoritarian rule, came up with the slogan "sovereign democracy."[52] The main idea was that democracy can exist in a wide range of culturally specific forms, maintaining that Russia is no less democratic than the United States or Western Europe but that it develops democracy in its own unique way.[53] The primary purpose of this discursive move was to provide an ideological defense against critique of the Russian political system as non-democratic—at that time, most people would prefer formulae like "hybrid regime" or "illiberal democracy"—while at the same time preserving a claim to an equal status among developed countries, and thus a place in the liberal world order dominated by the West.[54]

The stage for the final act of the drama that led to the annexation of Crimea, the war in Donbas, and the Syrian intervention was set at the end of the decade. The conflict with Georgia, which escalated steadily for more than a decade, spilled over into a five-day war in August 2008. A key consequence of this conflict was the proclamation of the so-called "Medvedev doctrine"—a set of five principles formulated by then President Dmitry Medvedev. It reiterated some of the key principles already put forward by Putin as well as by official doctrines such as the Foreign Policy Concept.[55] Thus, Medvedev reasserted the primacy of international law and the need for a multipolar world as opposed to a global order dominated by one power—presumably the United States. The most important points of the doctrine consisted of clearly affirming Russia's right to protect its citizens everywhere in the world, as well as the claim that, "as is the case of other countries, there are regions in which Russia has privileged interests."[56]

As a sign that Russia was taking this claim seriously, it also drew painful lessons from the military experience itself: its army was poorly prepared for regional conflicts, insufficiently mobile, and in want of modern communication equipment and intelligence capabilities. However, a radical military reform, implemented by Minister of Defense Anatoly Serdyukov, was able to address the most crucial shortcomings, leading to what Bettina Renz has described as "Russia's Military Revival."[57]

The West, however, was unmoved by the Russian leadership's proclamations. At their April 2008 Bucharest summit, leaders of the

NATO countries committed themselves to eventually admitting Georgia and Ukraine into the alliance.[58] The EU, in turn, boosted its Neighborhood Policy in 2009 by adding the Eastern Partnership as a new institutional framework specifically targeted at six European post-Soviet states. In a few years' time, this led to negotiations on Association Agreements with Armenia, Georgia, Moldova, and Ukraine. All these decisions were explicitly framed as affirming the sovereign right of Eastern European nations to choose their own geopolitical orientation, in explicit defiance of Russia's claim to a sphere of privileged interest.[59] Partly in response to this, Vladimir Putin started his reelection campaign in October 2011 by declaring his goal to create a Eurasian Union.[60]

Russia's View of the (Post-)Liberal World Order

As Russia entered the 2011–12 parliamentary and presidential election cycle, its foreign policy elites were already firmly entrenched in their world outlook. The genealogical account presented above can now be reframed as a set of specific points that define this worldview. Its first, and most important, feature is Eurocentrism: Russian foreign and security policy is primarily focused on relations with Western countries and on the challenges that Russia faces in "wider Europe," including the South Caucasus. The importance of other regions and countries is determined by what Russia perceives to be the key geopolitical conflict of the post-Cold War era: the struggle between US hegemonic ambitions and the will of non-Western nations (Russia included) to preserve their sovereignty. This is not to say that opportunities and threats not directly related to this struggle are ignored, but they rarely enjoy priority and/or are approached through the prism of competition with the West.[61]

Secondly, in Russia the world order is seen through the prism of such concepts as sovereignty and multipolarity. The crucial significance of sovereignty stems from the Hobbesian view of the state as the only guarantee against total chaos—something that Russia allegedly has experienced many times in the past, most recently in the 1990s. The West, led by the United States, has the ambition to establish a unipolar liberal order in which the United States would remain the only fully sovereign power. Meanwhile, everyone else would have to follow rules imposed from outside, and Western-style liberal market democracy would remain the only legitimate political regime. In trying to achieve this goal, the West behaves irresponsibly, repeatedly destroying sovereign statehood in key regions in order to establish friendly regimes. This is being done regardless of the consequences: in the cases of Afghanistan and Iraq, US interventions have led to the emergence of failed states, unable to provide basic security to their populations. Russia's mission is to ally with other non-Western countries in an attempt to resist this self-defeating policy, defend sovereign statehood everywhere in the world, and ensure multipolarity.[62]

Thirdly, in its promotion of a unipolar world order, the West mobilizes its supporters in non-Western countries. Acting as a fifth column, these supporters undermine their own sovereign national statehood and open the way to Western intervention. Generally, ordinary people value stability and have a strong sense of patriotism, so they would never revolt against their own rulers for the sake of externally imposed values such as liberal democracy.[63] However, moral decay and corruption can lead to some elements of an otherwise healthy body politic defecting and allowing themselves to be used as foreign agents.

Fourthly, Russia has to keep its sphere of "privileged interests": this is not an imperialist whim but a geopolitical imperative. It is determined by a number of factors—geographical, historical, and rooted in the very nature of the international system. Russia is a continental country with poor access to seas, open to potential military invasions from nearly all directions. A friendly neighborhood is a must if Russia wants to feel secure both from military threats and from sudden interruptions to its trade flows. In addition, its neighbors have historically been part of a single economic space, so if they reorient towards other trading blocs, such as the EU, it hurts Russia economically. Finally, total isolation would be dangerous for any state, so keeping up good relations with nearby states is essential for Russia's survival in an anarchic international environment.[64]

The fifth point, which can be deduced from all of the above, is that Russia actually feels weak and dependent on the West, not just economically but also normatively and in terms of identity. Dependence on Western technology and investment is a deep-seated structural condition of the Russian economy, but it is exacerbated by the fact that Russia has no way of defining its own identity other than by relating it to the West, either positively or negatively. If some consider Russia as not a European country, or as European in its own unique way, Russia still has to be defined in contrast to some idealized image of Europe. There is simply no other way of postulating Russia's uniqueness: all attempts to emphasize the Eurasian dimension remain superficial as they cannot relate to any established cultural tradition.[65] This one-sidedness means that the Russian perception of international anarchy and of the threats it conceals is skewed against the West: the latter is seen as dangerous by definition, whereas China, for example, is generally viewed in much less alarmist terms, despite its growing power.

As a sixth and final point, a tentative qualification needs to be added to all of the above: to be sure, Russia does appreciate the formidable threat of international terrorism in general, and the radicalization of Islamic groups in particular. This is a major reason why the Greater Middle East, from North Africa to Afghanistan, has never entirely disappeared from Russia's list of foreign and security policy priorities. However, in the same way as its perception of international anarchy is skewed westwards, Moscow's approach to the Middle East has always been defined in the shadow of its relations with the United States and other Western powers. External factors in the second Chechen War, for instance, were an extremely serious concern for the decision-makers, but there was always a suspicion that the radical Islamists who provided assistance to the separatists were in various ways encouraged, if not directly supported, by the Americans and their allies in Tbilisi, Riyadh, and elsewhere.[66] Similarly, Moscow's cooperation with Washington on the issue of military transit to Afghanistan (the so-called Northern route) always was as much a matter of the US-Russia bilateral relationship as it was a policy aimed at securing the southern borders of the post-Soviet space.[67]

The Road to Damascus

The foreign and security policy outlook summarized above also provided essential background to Russia's interpretation of the Arab

Spring events. Moscow's original response to the spread of popular unrest against authoritarian governments throughout the Arab world was in line with President Medvedev's previous course towards an accommodation with the West: as part of the US-Russia "Reset," he had already withdrawn from a deal to sell S-300 air defense systems to Iran and supported a tougher sanctions regime at the UN. In 2011, Medvedev ordered the Russian representative to abstain from the vote on the UN Security Council Resolution 1973 introducing a no-fly zone over Libya—a move that proved extremely controversial within Russia and might have cost Medvedev his second term as president. The subsequent large-scale intervention by NATO powers was seen by many in Russia, including Putin, as a violation of the terms of the resolution and as another attempt by the West to unilaterally impose the rules of the game. The execution of Libyan leader Muammar Gaddafi was particularly shocking as an archetypal expression of an externally provoked state collapse that would bring disorder.[68]

This shockwave was pronounced enough to affect the perception of the domestic movement for fair elections, heralding a large-scale nationwide protest that broke out in December 2011 and continued until May 2012. The context of the Arab Spring was conducive to the suspicion that these protests were externally induced to affect the outcome of the March 2012 presidential elections by preventing Putin from coming back to the top leadership position, or at least undermining his legitimacy. The protests resulted in a number of important readjustments both in domestic politics and foreign policy, the main thrust of which was in the direction of securing Russian domestic political space from any kind of outside influence and intensifying support for the existing anti-Western regimes all over the world, but with a special emphasis on Russia's immediate surroundings.[69]

It is easy to see that the Euromaidan revolution in Ukraine, which broke out in late November 2013, was a challenge to Russia on a number of counts. Its immediate cause was President Yanukovych's decision to renege on his earlier promise to sign an Association Agreement with the EU, opting instead for an intensified cooperation with Russia, which was pushing its Eurasian Economic Union project. The protests were explicitly supported by the EU and the United

States, which, for Moscow, was an indication of external meddling in Ukraine's domestic affairs. The overthrow of Yanukovych in February 2014 and the coming to power of a pro-European nationalist government was interpreted as an illegal coup, which was not just a challenge to the principle of national sovereignty, but also an immediate and acute security concern.[70]

It was widely believed in Moscow that the new government would be quick to bring Ukraine into NATO, which, *inter alia*, would put an end to the Russian naval base in Crimea. There was also fear that the Ukrainian turmoil would spread into Russia. The Kremlin perceived the situation as requiring an urgent reaction, and the annexation of Crimea probably resembled the most logical decision. The decision to support the local, and rather disorganized, separatist riots in Donbas was less self-evident, but might have been taken as an extra precaution to ensure a permanent destabilization of Ukraine as a counter-measure to its NATO membership.[71] Obviously, "strategic denial of Ukraine to NATO" and the EU was not the only rationale behind the Kremlin's action,[72] but it was certainly a crucial one since even hypothetical enlargement of NATO into Ukraine was considered an existential threat. The Western sanctions that followed were certainly expected, although some analysts believe that the Kremlin was unpleasantly surprised by the degree of cohesion that the EU, the United States, and other Western nations exhibited in response to what they saw as a blatant violation of international law on Russia's part.[73]

The significance of these events for Russia's Middle East policy consisted primarily of the fact that by intervening in Ukraine, Russia finally broke with the decades-long tradition of avoiding an open confrontation with the West. Even the Russian-Georgian war of 2008 and the recognition of Abkhazia and South Ossetia occupied something of a gray area, as many in the West agreed that Russia was provoked into action by the confrontational moves of then Georgian President Mikheil Saakashvili. Annexing a piece of another state's territory clearly crossed a red line and was bound to elicit a hostile response from Western powers.[74]

Another key consequence of the Ukraine crisis was that it gave the Russian military one more chance to test its capabilities in a relatively small-scale regional conflict, in particular, when it came to rapid deployment, intelligence gathering, and covert operations. Although exhibiting mixed results, this experience was probably deemed satisfactory by both military planners and the political leadership.[75]

Finally, the rallying-around-the-flag effect produced by the "return" of Crimea to Russia was impressive, with Putin's approval ratings skyrocketing to above 85 percent. This indicated to policymakers that taking a bold position in dealing with Western "partners" struck a chord with the majority of Russians and helped them to feel proud about their country.[76]

With all this in mind, Syria was the perfect arena for what the Russian leadership probably saw as developing its geopolitical success achieved in Ukraine. The US intervention in the Syrian civil war was seen as yet another case of illegitimate violation of the state sovereignty of a country that had historically been allied with Russia. In addition to such general considerations, Russia also felt the need to secure its diplomatic investment in the region, and in Syria in particular. The 2013 chemical weapons deal, in whose negotiation and implementation Russia had played a central role, was of particular importance here. The naval supply point in Tartus had always been a tangible asset for Russian operations in the Mediterranean. Too small to host deep-sea ships, it was nevertheless essential for Russia's ability to maintain a permanent naval presence in the theater, which it reestablished in 2013.[77] There was also a tangible threat of terrorism and radicalism, whose existence had been acknowledged by the Western powers. At the same time, Moscow disagreed with Washington as to which specific movements were to be classified as terrorist: in particular, it was inclined to regard as dangerous many forces that the Americans accepted as legitimate representatives of the anti-Assad opposition.[78]

Legally, a Russian military operation could not be interpreted as yet another blatant violation of international law, since the United States and its allies were already operating in the country and Russia had been invited to intervene by the internationally recognized government. Hence, there was a chance to frustrate yet another American scheme and earn extra points with Washington's international critics, while also keeping up a degree of political mobilization at home. The Russian military was eager to test its new capabilities in an operation that would, in comparative terms, be large-scale and conducted outside of Russia's immediate region.

Despite a few setbacks, all of these goals have been achieved. A friendly regime was saved from imminent failure, and the United States had to grudgingly accept the fact that its plans for regime change in yet another Arab country had been thwarted. Moscow has not just secured its naval presence in Tartus, but also established an air base in Khmeimim, thus ensuring a sustainable, if limited, military presence in the Eastern Mediterranean. The Russian military has demonstrated its capability to cope with the immense logistical challenges of conducting an intensive air campaign from a remote location, as well as to limit losses to a reasonable minimum.[79]

Russia has also emerged as a major diplomatic player in the wider region by developing a working cooperation with all key regional actors, in particular Iran and Turkey. Its role as a mediator has acquired an entirely new quality—largely due to the fact that, in many cases, Moscow is now able to serve as a power broker and mobilize its allies from outside of the Middle East, as exemplified by the Astana process and the role played by the first Kazakh president Nursultan Nazarbaev in this endeavor. These goals were achieved despite a few moments where relations between Moscow and Ankara were on the brink of a total breakdown, especially after the downing of the Russian Sukhoi 24 jet by the Turkish air force. Notably, Russia has also managed to achieve all of this without alienating Israel, whose adversarial relations with Syria and Iran, and their proxies, continue to affect the conflict structure in the region.[80]

The apparent success of the Syrian mission has emboldened Moscow in promoting its own view of the international order at the level of general principles. The document entitled "Russia's Security Concept for the Gulf Area" was published in July 2019 and widely promoted by Russian diplomats as a way to ensure the elimination of international terrorism and the creation of a stable security system at the regional level. It spells out the principles described above, in particular that any such security system "should be universal and comprehensive; it should be based on respect for the interests of all regional and other parties involved, in all spheres of security, including its military, economic and energy dimensions."[81] Further, "Exclusion of any stakeholder for any reason" is declared "inadmissible," and it is highlighted that "peace-making operations can only be conducted on the basis of relevant resolutions of the UN Security Council or upon request of the legitimate authorities of the attacked state."[82] Thus, respect for sovereignty and territorial integrity is the central principle, while "double standards" must not be tolerated.[83] Russia would eventually like to see these principles being applied everywhere in the world. In this sense, Russia regards the Gulf region as the building ground for a future international order, where the principles of sovereignty and multilateralism will take precedence over the promotion of democracy and human rights.

Conclusion

This chapter has presented a genealogical account of Russia's understanding of the present-day global order and analyzed its significance for Moscow's conduct in the Middle East. As my analysis suggests, there is a significant degree of continuity in the Russian approach to global affairs in general and to the international issues in the Middle East in particular. Russian foreign and security policy continues to focus predominantly on its relations with the West, which Russian society regards as both a key partner and main rival. Consequently, domestic political struggle over the choice of trajectory for Russia—Europeanization versus a unique Russian path—has always been a major determinant of foreign policy choices. The domestic hegemony of pro-Western forces during the first Gulf War resulted in Russia's support of the United States then, whereas in 2015 the clear dominance of the anti-Western position was a major factor behind Russia's decision to support President Bashar al-Assad against the US-backed opposition.

Ever since the early 1990s, Russia has been concerned about its status in the world. During the Yeltsin and early Putin periods, this concern was mostly about recognition, but around the mid-2000s it acquired a distinct security dimension. The traditional feeling of inferiority vis-à-vis the West evolved into a sense of vulnerability in the face of the policies of regime change and/or Europeanization pursued by the United States and EU in both the post-Soviet space and in the

Middle East. The Russian leadership's attempts to articulate these concerns to their Western counterparts did not have much impact, as Russia's position was interpreted, rightly or wrongly, as imposing its will on neighboring countries and protecting dictatorships further afield. The annexation of Crimea was in response to a perceived Western expansionism and, most probably, was not pre-planned in its entirety. However, the Syrian intervention reflects a more systematic approach to the post-Crimea geopolitical reality on the part of the Russian leadership, and, as such, it is indicative of the kind of policies that Russia is likely to conduct in the future.

This conclusion should not be interpreted to the effect that Russia is likely to engage in yet another military operation in the Middle East or elsewhere, nor does it exclude such a scenario. Syria was obviously a unique case, in many respects distinct from other countries unsettled by the Arab Spring that had been supported by Moscow throughout the post-Soviet period, in particular after Assad's regime came under growing Western pressure in the mid-2000s. At the same time, the recent developments in Libya suggest that some form of military intervention, perhaps on a smaller scale or by private subcontractors, is a possibility elsewhere in the region.[84]

In any case, the same general logic is likely to apply to any future situation of geopolitical significance. Moscow will assess any such challenge from the point of view of the basic principles of the international order that it is trying to uphold, and in particular from the perspective of its impact on state sovereignty, understood through the prism of non-intervention. Russia will also take into account how prominent any given issue is for various domestic political forces, and what resources are available for dealing with the issue. What Russia will not take into account is any potential Western reaction short of outright military confrontation. Russia will not risk a direct military conflict with NATO, but it will not think twice before initiating another diplomatic row with the West, if the end goal is deemed to be worthwhile.

This logic, even if clever and beneficial in the short to medium term, might prove to be risky in the longer-term perspective. As Russia's experience in both Donbas and Syria has demonstrated, disengagement from the conflict occurs under circumstances significantly different from the moment when the decision to engage was taken. In particular, the economic situation can change to Russia's disadvantage: indeed, the current state of the Russian economy is already putting serious strain on its social security system and its entire public sector, leading to multiple protests and political debacles at the regional level. This might require a political settlement with the United States and its allies that would allow Russia to stop pumping resources into the separatist entities in eastern Ukraine and produce a more cooperative security solution for Syria. However, as pointed out by Andrej Krickovic and Yuval Weber, such a new "grand bargain" would be hard to achieve due to commitment problems: the level of mistrust on both sides is so high that any deal would eventually hinge on the short-term distribution of power, which would make it inherently unstable.[85] As a result, Russia will end up with a long-term engagement in a number of multidimensional conflicts, which will be an investment with diminishing returns.

2

DIFFERENT BUT SIMILAR

COMPARING MOSCOW'S MIDDLE EAST POLICIES
IN THE COLD WAR AND PUTIN ERAS

Mark N. Katz

Introduction

In comparing Moscow's Soviet-era foreign policy towards the Middle East with its current foreign policy under the administration of Vladimir Putin, it appears that President Putin has been far more successful at spreading Moscow's influence in the region than the Soviets were. While the Soviets mainly had good relations with anti-Western revolutionary regimes in the region (though not always even with them), Putin has good relations with all Middle Eastern governments. During the Cold War, the United States largely excluded the USSR from playing a meaningful role in the Arab-Israeli peace process. Not only has Putin's ability to talk with all parties allowed him to play an active role in all the region's conflict-resolution efforts, but it has often allowed him to play a more active role than that of the

United States. Finally, while the Soviet Union lost two important Middle Eastern allies, Egypt and Somalia, Putin's Middle Eastern diplomacy has succeeded at simultaneously building and maintaining good relations with opposing sides in the region's many disputes.

Soviet foreign policy toward the Middle East certainly had its failures, but it also had many successes. Moscow maintained close allied relations with several important governments, spanning from their coming to power until the end of the Cold War. Like Putin, the Soviets managed to have good relations with opposing sides in several disputes, including those between Syria and Iraq, Iraq and Kuwait, and North and South Yemen. Further, both the Soviets and Putin were able to take advantage of regional opposition to American foreign policy. The decline of Soviet influence in the Middle East was the result not so much of the failure of its policy towards the region, but of the failure of the Soviet Union itself.

This chapter seeks to compare the strengths and weaknesses of Soviet policy towards the Middle East during the Cold War with Putin's more recent foreign policy in the region. I will first examine Soviet foreign policy, with attention to what went well for Moscow and what did not. A similar examination of what has and has not gone well for Moscow during the Putin era will follow. The expressions "what went/has gone well" and their negatives are used here deliberately in order to avoid viewing Moscow's foreign policy successes and failures as being solely the result of its own foreign policy decision-making. While Moscow's decisions obviously have played a role in whether its Middle Eastern policies are successful or not, sometimes the successes or failures of policies pursued by the United States, by Middle Eastern and other actors, and by events—often unexpected—have strongly affected the standing of Moscow (among others) in the region.

I will argue that some of the factors contributing to Putin's Middle East foreign policy successes also contributed to the success of Cold War-era Soviet foreign policy towards the region. Further, it will also be argued that some of the factors that contributed to Soviet foreign policy setbacks in the region are either nascent or actually in evidence at present. The Soviet experience also suggests that the ultimate success or failure of Putin's Middle East policy may depend on factors that Moscow cannot fully control.

Cold War-Era Soviet Middle East Policy

Moscow's foreign policy towards the Middle East did not begin with the Cold War. Due to space limitations, it must suffice here to note that Tsarist Russia pursued an active foreign policy in the Middle East, especially vis-à-vis the Ottoman and Persian empires, and the early Soviet state also had ambitions in the region, though these were sidelined when Moscow became increasingly focused on Soviet internal and European affairs during the interwar years.[1] By the end of World War II, in 1945, the Soviet Union had very little influence in the region. Most Middle Eastern countries either remained under British or French control or had recently been restored to it after the defeat of German and Italian forces. The few "independent" countries of the region were closely allied to the West. Further, Stalin's own threatening actions towards Turkey and Iran in the immediate aftermath of World War II pushed these two countries closer to the West. It is not difficult to understand, then, how Stalin may have hoped that the new state of Israel—where Jewish nationalists had fought against British rule—appeared to be a greater prospect for Soviet influence than conservative Arab states, protectorates, or colonies that were closely linked to the West.[2]

This situation changed dramatically, though, in the 1950s and 1960s when anti-Western Arab nationalists came to power in Egypt, Syria, Iraq, North Yemen, Algeria, Sudan, and Libya. A somewhat Marxist but definitely anti-Western regime also came to power in Somalia. Although not an Arab country, Somalia became a member of the Arab League, and so will be considered as part of the Middle East here. In addition, a self-proclaimed Marxist regime came to power in South Yemen after the British departed in 1967. Moscow's support for the Arabs against Israel also served to burnish Moscow's relations with the Middle East's anti-Western regimes as well as public opinion of Moscow throughout the Arab and broader Muslim worlds from the mid-1950s through the early 1970s.[3]

Moscow's relations with revolutionary regimes in the Middle East, however, were often difficult. Many Arabs complained that the USSR did not give as much support to them as the United States gave to Israel. Shortly after the 1973 Arab-Israeli War, the United States came to dominate the Arab-Israeli peace negotiations, in which Moscow played only a marginal role. In the mid-1970s, Egypt and Somalia not only ended their alliances with the USSR, but they made new ones with the United States. And although Saddam Hussein was firmly anti-Western at the time, Soviet-Iraqi relations experienced a severe downturn in the late 1970s. Further, unlike the "revolutions" that led to the downfall of conservative regimes (or outright Western colonial rule) and the rise of revolutionary regimes aligned with Moscow in the Arab world, the 1979 Iranian revolution that overthrew the US-aligned shah gave rise to an "Islamic Republic" that was not just anti-Western, but anti-Soviet and anti-communist as well.

Finally, the Soviet invasion and occupation of Afghanistan led to genuine fear in some Middle Eastern states about what Moscow intended for them, and to a more negative view of the Soviet Union throughout the region.[4] Mikhail Gorbachev's withdrawal from Afghanistan contributed to an improvement in Moscow's overall relations with the Middle East (including the establishment of ties with several Arabian peninsula monarchies). However, this improvement also came at a time when Gorbachev was pursuing good relations with the United States and so was not challenging American influence in the region. The collapse of the Soviet Union in 1991 ushered in a period in which Moscow was largely, though not completely, inactive in the Middle East.[5]

What Did and Did Not Go Well for Moscow during the Cold War

Among the factors that served to advance Soviet influence in the Middle East was the fact that the 1950s–60s were an era in which conditions in the Middle East, especially the Arab countries, were ripe for an increased Soviet role there. Britain and France were unpopular not just due to their past colonial rule, but because of their forceful efforts to continue it in some places—notably in Algeria and South Yemen for France and the United Kingdom, respectively. The United States was unpopular, too, due to its support for the creation of the state of Israel, something that Arabs in particular viewed as an act of European colonization at a time when the European colonial powers were in retreat everywhere else. Further, the poor showing of the Egyptian monarchy in the 1948 Arab-Israeli War led to its loss of legitimacy even among its own officers, who fell increasingly under the sway of Arab nationalists. They came to see the Soviet Union as a potential ally despite Moscow's initial support for Israel.[6] Moscow did not create these conditions, but it certainly benefited from them.

Another factor that enhanced Soviet influence in the region was the mutual appreciation between the Soviet Union and the Arab nationalists. Since the inception of the Bolshevik rule, and at the Second Comintern Congress in 1919 in particular, Soviet leaders had acknowledged that while there were communist movements in the developing world, there were also nationalist movements that were not communist, and were sometimes even anti-communist. The pros and cons of supporting communists as opposed to nationalists—or the extent to which the Soviets could support both simultaneously—was a subject of debate in the USSR for decades. After World War II, while Joseph Stalin had come to take a dim view of anti-communist nationalist forces in the developing world, Nikita Khrushchev took a more positive view of them in general, and of Arab nationalism in particular. Indeed, when Arab nationalist governments brutally suppressed Arab communist movements in Egypt, Syria, and Iraq, Moscow looked the other way. Khrushchev in particular adopted this "patient" attitude in the belief that the anti-Western Arab nationalist movement was a halfway point on a path that would eventually lead to Marxism-Leninism, in which he was ultimately proved to be mistaken.[7]

Similarly, the Arab nationalists valued the Soviet Union because they regarded the Soviet economic model based on central planning as superior to the Western model based on capitalism. By the 1950s and 1960s, it still seemed to many that the Soviet Union had pursued economic development more quickly and successfully than the capitalist West, which had recently experienced the Great Depression. Further, Soviet-style central planning offered Arab nationalist regimes much greater control of their economies than did Western-style capitalism, with its multinational corporations that Arab nationalist governments saw as adversaries and exploiters.[8]

However, it was American support for Israel—especially after the 1967 Arab-Israeli War—that gave Moscow its biggest opening into the Arab world. The United States had sought to have good relations with both Israel and Arab governments (even Gamal Abdel Nasser's Egypt), but Washington's disagreements with them over Israel and other issues resulted in the Arab nationalist governments turning to Moscow for support. Khrushchev and Leonid Brezhnev seized this opportunity to offer assistance to Arab states seeking an alternative source of support. This process advanced farthest with Egypt and Syria—two states that had lost territory to Israel in 1967. Moscow not only provided them with weaponry, but also sent large numbers of military advisers and even established military facilities on their territories.[9]

The USSR's willingness to provide military and economic support initially allowed Moscow to expand its influence with Arab nationalist regimes. Over time, however, Moscow did not provide as much as some of these governments wanted or expected, which caused friction in relations with some, especially Egypt. Indeed, Nasser's successor, Anwar Sadat, came to view the USSR's large military presence in Egypt as not advancing Cairo's aim of winning back the territory it lost to Israel in 1967, but rather for pursuing Moscow's own military aims unrelated to Israel.[10] Similarly, while the USSR's breaking of diplomatic relations with Israel in 1967 won admiration from Arab governments and publics alike at the time, this decision helped the United States to exclude Moscow from playing a lead role in the disengagement negotiations between Israel on the one hand and Egypt and Syria on the other after the 1973 Arab-Israeli War. This was also the case with the Egyptian-Israeli peace agreement, as well as subsequent Cold War-era Arab-Israeli peace efforts. Russian observers later acknowledged that the USSR's breaking of diplomatic relations with Israel in 1967 had been a mistake.[11]

Moscow's Cold War policy towards the Middle East, of course, was about more than just the Arab-Israeli conflict. In a move presaging Putin's reaching out to America's Middle Eastern allies, the USSR also sought good relations with many of these countries during the Cold War. While not without some degree of discord, Moscow succeeded at this in some cases, including with the monarchies in Morocco, Jordan, and Kuwait, as well as those in North Yemen and Iran before their downfalls.[12] It did not, however, succeed with the monarchies of the Arabian peninsula, with the exception of Kuwait, until the Gorbachev era. For the Gulf Arabs in particular, Soviet professions of friendship were severely undercut by Moscow's support for radical regimes hostile to them, including Nasser's Egypt, Saddam Hussein's Iraq, and Marxist regimes in Ethiopia and South Yemen. Nor did they appreciate Soviet propaganda and material support for groups seeking the downfall of Gulf monarchies, such as the Popular Front for the Liberation of the Occupied Arab Gulf (PFLOAG) and its successor, the Popular Front for the Liberation of Oman (PFLO), the Bahrain National Liberation Front, and the Saudi Arabian Communist Party.[13]

For Middle East monarchies in particular, the problem with responding positively to Moscow's calls for improved ties was that the Soviets always seemed to enthusiastically support the downfall of monarchies whenever they occurred, and they would then seek good relations with their anti-Western successor regimes. One of the most blatant examples of this was in North Yemen, where the monarchical government trusted Moscow sufficiently to allow in Soviet military advisers. These same advisers were later present when Moscow's ally Nasser (with Soviet logistical support) backed the Yemeni Arab nationalist officers who overthrew the government in 1962. This gave rise to the fear in other conservative Arab governments that Moscow's protestations of friendship were less than genuine.[14]

Conservative Middle Eastern governments were not the only ones who feared that Moscow would welcome their downfall. Even Moscow-aligned Arab nationalist regimes sometimes suspected this. In May 1971, the new Sadat government arrested one of Nasser's top lieutenants, Ali Sabry, who advocated close Soviet-Egyptian ties, on charges of plotting to overthrow Sadat.[15] Shortly thereafter, in July 1971, there was an abortive communist coup against Sudan's Arab nationalist regime, which the Soviet Union was accused of being involved in.[16] Similarly, Soviet-Iraqi relations deteriorated in 1978, when Saddam Hussein's regime launched a massive crackdown on the Iraqi Communist Party, which Hussein accused of plotting a coup with Moscow's support.[17] Moreover, as in other Marxist-Leninist Third World regimes, Moscow played a role in South Yemen's deadly leadership struggles in the 1970s and 1980s.[18] These and other instances illustrated why even Middle Eastern leaders allied to Moscow feared that the Soviets might be willing to replace them with "someone better."

Another way in which Soviet policy towards the Middle East presaged Putin's policy was Moscow's practice of supporting or balancing between opposing sides in various Middle Eastern antagonisms (except, of course, the Arab-Israeli case). Although the countries involved always resented this, Moscow sometimes managed to maintain good, though not always smooth, relations with both sides simultaneously. In some cases, this was managed for quite some time, despite the animosity towards each other, as with Iraq and Kuwait, North and South Yemen, and rival Ba'thist regimes in Iraq and Syria. This practice, though, contributed to losing Somalia as an ally when Moscow tried to develop close ties to the new Marxist regime in Ethiopia while tensions between the two countries were increasing.[19]

In some cases where Moscow sought good relations with both sides in a conflict (such as Tehran and Baghdad prior to the 1980–88 Iran-Iraq War, or Baghdad and Kuwait prior to the 1990 Iraqi invasion of Kuwait), one side (Iraq in both 1980 and 1990) sought to "force Moscow's hand" by launching a surprise attack, assuming Moscow (as well as others) would have little choice but to accept the "new reality." Such efforts, though, tended not to achieve the intended aims, instead causing complications in Moscow's relations with both sides. For example, the USSR cut off arms supplies to Iraq in the initial phase of the 1980–88 Iran-Iraq War. Later, Moscow actually approved a UN Security Council resolution authorizing the use of force against Iraq after its 1990 invasion of Kuwait.[20] And just as in 1980 and 1990, when Iraq blamed Moscow for not providing the support Iraq expected and believed it deserved, in 1980 and 1990 both Iran and Kuwait (along with its allies) respectively blamed Moscow for having provided their opponents with the means to launch an attack in the first place (as did Israel in 1973). The risk that an ally will make use of external military support to engage in military adventures that the great power providing it does not approve of is inherent to arms-supply relationships, and is one that Moscow encountered in the Middle East several times during the Cold War.

As noted earlier, the Soviet invasion and occupation of Afghanistan had a hugely negative impact on Moscow's image in the Middle East and beyond. The Brezhnev leadership may have genuinely seen the invasion as a defensive one; according to some Russian sources, Brezhnev had become convinced that the Marxist president of Afghanistan was actually an American ally who was going to allow the United States to build a base there.[21] Western and conservative Arab governments (as well as others), however, saw the invasion as the beginning of a Soviet offensive ultimately aimed at the Gulf.[22] While both views may have reflected exaggerated fears rather than reality, the Soviet military presence in Afghanistan allowed Saudi Arabia and the United States in particular to capitalize on Muslim disapproval and turn Afghanistan into a *cause célèbre*. Saudi Arabia, the guardian of Islam's two holiest cities, had long been criticized by Moscow's Middle Eastern allies for its alliance with the United States, Israel's strongest supporter. The Soviet occupation of Afghanistan allowed the Saudis to draw the attention of the Muslim world to a situation in which Muslims were being oppressed not by the United States, nor by Israel or any other American ally, but by the USSR.[23] Moscow obviously did not want this to happen, but its occupation of Afghanistan created an opportunity for Saudi Arabia, the United States, and many others who feared the USSR would exploit the situation; and they did.

While the Soviet/Russian withdrawal from the Middle East at the end of the Cold War and immediately afterward has been portrayed as a setback for Moscow, including by many Russian observers,[24] it must be remembered that this resulted not just from diminished capacity but also from conscious choice. In the late Gorbachev and early Yeltsin years, Moscow saw cooperation with the West as being its most important foreign policy priority. This being the case, support for anti-Western regimes in the Middle East and elsewhere was now seen as counterproductive; not only did it hinder the cause of cooperation with the West, but it also did not provide compensating benefits for Moscow. The revolutionary allies that Moscow previously regarded as assets were now considered liabilities. Under these circumstances, Moscow's decision to distance itself from these regimes was rational.

During these years, Moscow did succeed in improving relations with several Western-aligned governments in the region with which it had previously had poor relations: Turkey, Israel, Saudi Arabia, and the other Arabian peninsula monarchies besides Kuwait. Moscow also managed to improve relations with Iran during this period. But as Moscow's ties with Washington began to deteriorate over the course of the 1990s, the Yeltsin administration—under the guidance of Soviet Middle East hand Yevgeny Primakov—sought to rebuild relations with Moscow's Soviet-era Arab nationalist allies.[25] However, Moscow's pressing internal problems, including its deteriorating economy and its war in Chechnya, limited Yeltsin's ability to focus on or take action in the Middle East. Unwilling to see how Moscow's policies both in the Soviet era and in the subsequent Yeltsin era may have contributed to the rebellion in Chechnya, Russian officials and observers often blamed it on foreign sources. In particular, they blamed Saudi Arabia for supporting the Chechen rebels in the same way Riyadh had previously supported the Afghan *mujahideen*.[26]

Putin-Era Russian Middle East Policy

Just like the Soviet Union at the end of World War II, Russia had very little influence in the Middle East at the dawn of the Putin era. However, just as Soviet influence in the region grew in subsequent years, Russian influence has also grown over the course of the Putin era. From the very beginning of his reign, Putin placed great emphasis on pursuing economic relations with the Middle East. He at first sought to get traditional allies in the region to repay their Soviet-era debts to Moscow, but when they proved unwilling to do this, he pragmatically agreed to reduce their debts substantially and instead sought trade and investment agreements with them. Putin's interest in pursuing profitable economic ties also led him to seek improved relations not just with Moscow's Soviet-era allies, but also with America's richer allies, which were in a much better position to trade with Russia, and to invest in it.[27]

Indeed, pursuing improved relations with all Middle Eastern governments would quickly become a hallmark of Putin's Middle East policy. At first, though, Moscow's ties with Saudi Arabia were noticeably cool. Putin even sought to take advantage of the 9/11 attacks to ally with the United States against Saudi Arabia, which he portrayed as a common threat to them both. However, as Russian-American relations soured during the lead-up to and aftermath of the US-led invasion of Iraq, Saudi-Russian relations improved, partly on the basis of both countries' common unhappiness with US policy towards Iraq.[28] By 2010, when Medvedev was president and Putin was prime minister but still in charge, Moscow had developed good relations with all governments in the Middle East, including Israel, Iran, and the post-Saddam government in Iraq, as well as Fatah, Hamas, Hezbollah, and the Kurdish Regional Government.

Moscow's initial response to the outbreak of the Arab Spring and the downfall of longstanding authoritarian regimes linked to the West—in Tunisia and Egypt—was, like that of Western governments, to adjust to the situation by accepting the new governments that arose. However, when the Arab uprisings of 2011 spread to two countries with governments that were more closely linked to Russia—Libya and Syria—Moscow became uneasy. While Russia (and China) abstained on the UN Security Council resolution authorizing a no-fly zone to protect Muammar Gaddafi's opponents (thus allowing the resolution to pass), Moscow objected to the subsequent military intervention in support of the Libyan opposition by the United States and some of its Western and Arab allies. This led not only to the downfall of the regime, but also to the death of Gaddafi himself.

Determined not to let the same scenario unfold in Syria, Moscow blocked Western efforts to pass a UN Security Council resolution authorizing a no-fly zone to protect the Syrian opposition. Moscow also stepped up its military support of the beleaguered Bashar al-Assad regime, which was also being supported by Iran.[29] The Syrian opposition—with support from Saudi Arabia, Qatar, Turkey, and even to an extent the United States—appeared to be close to overwhelming the Assad regime when Russian forces directly intervened in September 2015 and turned the tide of battle in Assad's favor.[30]

Interestingly, while Russia and Saudi Arabia were on opposite sides in Syria, Moscow expressed support for the Saudi-backed Bahraini government against its internal opponents during the Arab Spring, which began in 2011. Moscow additionally supported the Saudi-backed power transfer in Yemen from President Saleh to Vice President Hadi, intended to defuse the many conflicts there.[31]

With regard to Turkey, Russian-Turkish relations nosedived in November 2015, when Turkish forces shot down a Russian military aircraft flying in the vicinity of the Turkish-Syrian border. The relationship was revived in mid-2016 when Turkish President Recep Tayyip Erdoğan apologized for the incident, and again when Putin expressed support for Erdoğan more quickly than Western leaders did during the July 2016 attempted coup against him. Russian-Turkish relations have grown friendlier since then despite their continued differences over Syria, Libya, Nagorno-Karabakh, and Ukraine. [32]

In an even more dramatic development, President Donald Trump's announcement that he was pulling out US troops from northeastern Syria—troops who had worked with the Syrian Kurdish forces there against IS—was followed immediately by Turkish intervention in the Syrian Kurdish-controlled region along the Syrian-Turk border. This quickly led to the Syrian Kurds finally acceding to Russian calls, which they had previously resisted, to allow Syrian government forces into their zone. This then led to a Russian-Turkish agreement to remove Syrian Kurdish forces from the border region and to allow joint Russian-Turkish patrolling of it. [33] What was especially amazing was that the Trump administration lost influence both with the Syrian Kurds, as his actions had made them vulnerable to Turkish intervention, and with Turkey due to his criticizing Ankara for its intervention that the US withdrawal had facilitated. Russia, meanwhile, was able to improve its relations with the Syrian Kurds and the Turkish government, at least initially.

Unlike the Soviets during the Cold War, Putin has succeeded in building good relations with every government and major opposition group (except the jihadists) in the Middle East despite their antagonism towards each other. Putin, for example, has good ties with Iran and Israel; with Turkey and the Syrian Kurds; with Israel and the Palestinians; with Qatar and its (now former) opponents Saudi Arabia, the United Arab Emirates, Bahrain, and Egypt; and with opposing forces in both Libya and Yemen. However, unlike at the end of the Cold War, when Moscow deliberately chose to prioritize cooperating with the West over continuing to support its anti-Western allies in the Middle East, pursuing good relations with the West is not a priority for Putin.

What Has and Has Not Gone Well for Moscow during the Putin Era

Soon after he first became president, Putin began trying to rebuild Russian influence in the Middle East by visiting numerous countries in the region. As was the case with the Soviets, it was not Moscow's actions alone that benefited Russian efforts to boost ties in the region. Regimes at odds with the United States had regretted the collapse of the USSR and Moscow's withdrawal from the region, and so they welcomed Putin's renewed interest. In addition, many Middle Eastern actors had previously regarded the Soviet-American rivalry as an opportunity to derive benefits from both sides, by encouraging Washington to provide more by indicating that they might "turn towards Moscow" otherwise. They welcomed the opportunity to start doing this again.[34] Also, as before, regional unhappiness with American foreign policies provided opportunities for Moscow to show how its foreign policy positions were more aligned with the interests of Middle Eastern governments than Washington's have been.

Common opposition to the US-led intervention in Iraq that began in 2003 helped to improve Russian ties to several Middle Eastern (and other) governments, especially Saudi Arabia. The image of an aggressive, blundering United States that had intervened in Iraq to bring about regime change—and might well attempt to do so elsewhere—helped Putin boost the image of Russia as a more responsible partner that did not interfere in the internal affairs of sovereign states in the Middle East, and that was willing to work with all governments there.

During the Arab uprisings, several Middle Eastern governments supported and even encouraged the United States and other Western nations to bring about the downfall of Gaddafi in Libya and Assad in Syria, both of whom Moscow regarded as partners. Even so, Moscow was able to exploit the concerns of many Middle Eastern governments over how the Barack Obama administration had "betrayed" its "loyal ally" Mubarak in Egypt by calling upon him to step down. It further stressed how US intervention in Libya, as in Iraq, had replaced a dictatorial regime that Washington did not like with chaos, rather than democracy.

Russian military intervention in support of the Assad regime—while Turkey, Saudi Arabia, and Qatar in particular were supporting its opponents—hurt Moscow's influence in the region briefly, but not for long. Indeed, even while those countries wished to see Assad fall, Putin benefited from being seen as loyal to his allies in the region while the United States was not. In addition, Middle Eastern governments appreciated that Putin accepted them as they were and did not press them on issues such as democratization or human rights like post-Cold War US presidents (except Trump) and the US Congress (even under Republican leadership during the Trump administration) have done. This has enhanced the Russian narrative that Putin is a reliable ally when it comes to defending the Middle East status quo, whereas the United States is not.[35]

In addition, just as the Bush administration's interventionism helped drive Middle Eastern governments and Russia together, so too did the Obama, Trump, and Biden administrations through the actions they took to reduce US involvement in the region. Indeed, the willingness of some US allies in the Middle East to cooperate with Moscow may be an attempt on their part to exploit growing US-Russian animosity as a way of encouraging Washington to remain engaged in the region. It may also be a pragmatic reaction: if US interest in the Middle East is declining, then growing Russian interest there makes it essential for governments to work with Moscow somehow.[36]

Concerns about petroleum have also enhanced cooperation between Russia and certain Middle East oil producers, especially Saudi Arabia. For many years, the Kingdom and other OPEC members were unhappy with Russia for not cooperating with OPEC in limiting oil production to bolster prices. Russia instead maintained and even increased its oil production while OPEC was limiting its own. Then, in December 2016, the threat of increased US shale production led to increased Saudi-Russian coordination both on a bilateral basis and through the new OPEC+ format.[37] In March 2020, Saudi-Russian oil cooperation broke down spectacularly when Riyadh and Moscow disagreed over oil production quotas. Saudi Arabia punished the Kremlin by flooding the market, resulting in drastically lower oil prices. After this episode, however, Saudi-Russian oil cooperation via OPEC+ resumed.[38]

Further, while Russia lacks the economic resources to provide large-scale economic assistance to poorer Middle Eastern states where

Moscow hopes to become or remain influential, its partnership with China may compensate for this. The Middle East appears to be part of Beijing's Belt and Road initiative, which is essentially the provision of Chinese loans to countries for the development of economic projects linking them to China. Just as they already do in Central Asia, Moscow and Beijing may be able to work out a mutually advantageous division of labor in which Russia provides security assistance and China provides economic assistance.[39]

Besides all these factors that have served to help Putin expand Russian influence in the Middle East, there have also been several that might have been expected to limit it but have not (at least so far). Already mentioned was the fact that Russia provided support for the Assad regime. Now that the regime has been stabilized, several Arab governments have recently improved ties with Syria, or have indicated their openness to doing so. Saudi Arabia and Israel in particular object less to the Assad regime or Russian support for it than to the presence of Iranian and other outside Shi'a militias in Syria. Previously, they had seen the potential downfall of Assad as a way of eliminating Iranian influence in Syria, and perhaps even in Lebanon. Although disappointed that Russia allied with Iran in Syria, Arab governments now appear amenable to Moscow's claim that Iran can be kept in check more successfully if Russian forces are present in Syria.[40]

Unlike during most of the Soviet period, when Moscow vociferously expressed its support for the Palestinians and Arabs in the conflict against Israel, the Russian-Israeli relationship has grown remarkably close under Putin. In addition to the two countries' extensive trade and security cooperation, Putin has visited Israel three times, and Israeli leaders—especially Prime Minister Benjamin Netanyahu—have visited Russia on numerous occasions to meet with Putin.[41] While Israel remains as unpopular as ever with the Arab and Muslim publics, this close Russian-Israeli relationship does not seem to have hurt Russia's relations with Arab governments. This is partly because several Arab governments see Iran as their main threat and even regard Israel as a tacit ally against it. Four Arab governments (the UAE, Bahrain, Sudan, and Morocco) even signed normalization agreements (known collectively as the "Abraham accords") with Israel in 2020.

All Arab governments, of course, express verbal support for the Palestinian cause, as does Russia. In 2018, Moscow joined the Arabs in denouncing the Trump administration for moving the US embassy in Israel from Tel Aviv to Jerusalem, as well as for recognizing Israel's annexation of the Golan Heights less than a year later.[42] However, Moscow remained neutral during the May 2021 conflict between Israel and Hamas, during which it mainly issued calls for an end to the fighting.[43] The lack of Russian material support for the Palestinians against Israel, though, has not caused problems in Russia's relations with Arab governments, for which the Palestinian cause has become much less of a priority than Iran and/or their own self-preservation.

Further, while there have been serious tensions in Russian-Turkish relations (as previously noted), President Erdoğan's growing animosity towards the United States and Europe has helped Moscow overcome these. Erdoğan's determination to purchase Russian S-400 air defense missile systems—despite Washington declaring that they are incompatible with NATO security and subsequently halting the sale of F-35 fighters to Ankara—only furthers Putin's goal of weakening the NATO alliance.[44] Russian-Turkish security cooperation in northeastern Syria in the wake of Trump's withdrawal of US forces from the region has raised the prospect of deepening cooperation between Moscow and Ankara at a time when their relations with Washington are under increasing stress.

Still, while many factors have helped Moscow increase its influence in the Middle East since the rise of Putin, there have also been factors that limit and may even reduce this. To begin with, while Putin has succeeded in building and maintaining good relations with opposing sides in the region, various Middle Eastern actors are hoping to persuade Moscow to switch from hedging its bets to supporting them against their adversaries. Moscow's reported suggestion that Russia's presence in Syria contributes to checking Iranian ambitions there has raised expectations in Israel and Arab Gulf countries about this. However, now that the Assad regime (with the assistance of Russia, Iran, and Hezbollah) has largely prevailed over most of Damascus's opponents, Moscow does not seem to be either willing or able to reduce Iranian influence in Syria. This being the case, Israeli forces have struck at Iranian and Hezbollah positions in Syria even though this has sometimes caused tension with Moscow.[45] Further, Moscow's continued close ties to Tehran gives both Israel and the Arab Gulf states strong incentive to continue their security cooperation with the United States.

Just as Moscow's close ties to Iran have caused concerns about its reliability in Israel and the Arab Gulf states, so have its close ties to Israel and the Arab Gulf states caused concerns about Russia's reliability in Iran. There have even been reports about Russia and Iran acting at cross purposes in Syria. Russian- and Iranian-backed enterprises appear to be in competition with each other for reconstruction contracts in Syria. Moscow and Tehran reportedly back rival elements within the Syrian security services.[46] And while Russian forces cooperate with their Iranian counterparts in Syria, Chechen forces loyal to pro-Putin strongman Ramzan Kadyrov, sent to Syria by Moscow, reportedly do not. And some observers have noted that while Russia is unwilling to do anything to challenge Iran in Syria directly, Moscow has done little to stop Israel doing so.[47] Iran (unlike Israel and the Arab Gulf states) does not have the opportunity to turn to Washington for support if threatened by Moscow's actions. Growing Russian-Iranian competition does not bode well for the two countries' ability to continue cooperating with each other.

As noted earlier, Saudi-Russian relations improved in 2016 when Moscow began cooperating with Saudi Arabia in the OPEC+ format, deteriorated in March 2020 during their brief "oil war," and then improved again afterward. Moscow, though, could revert to its earlier practice of "free riding" on the higher oil prices resulting from Saudi/OPEC restraint in production to maximize Russia's profits. Russia's economic exigencies, exacerbated by Western sanctions, could make this understandable. However, Russia suggesting that it might cooperate with the Arab Gulf in restraining oil production and then dashing those hopes will not give Saudi Arabia and other OPEC states confidence in Russia as a partner in the oil market; in fact, Russia remains their competitor in this realm.

Finally, while Moscow succeeded in increasing its cooperation with the Syrian Kurds and Turkey, despite their mutual hostility, after Trump announced he would pull US troops out of northeastern Syria, US forces have remained in the region and continued cooperating with the Syrian Kurds, thereby limiting Moscow's ability to pressure them into accepting Assad regime "protection."

Conclusion

At present, Putin's policy towards the Middle East seems more successful than that of the Soviets. While the Soviets had good relations with some Middle Eastern governments and hostile relations with others up until the Gorbachev era, Putin has established good relations with all Middle Eastern governments and other major actors— including Hezbollah, Fatah, and Hamas—even though these governments and actors are often bitterly opposed to one another. However, Putin's policy of supporting opposing sides simultaneously has inherent risks, as the USSR's earlier experience in the region showed. Now, as was the case back then, some Middle Eastern states might retain or even strengthen their ties to the United States if they feel threatened by Moscow's relations with their regional adversaries. Anti-Western actors like Iran, as Moscow knows, are usually not in a position to turn to the United States for support if they are unhappy about Russia's close ties with America's Middle Eastern allies. Still, as the Soviet experience with Egypt and Somalia demonstrated, this can happen.

A greater danger in supporting opposing sides simultaneously is the likelihood that one of the opposing sides will launch a surprise attack or initiative intended to create a *fait accompli* in hopes that Moscow (and others) will be forced to accept it. Even if the surprise move fails to achieve its objective, as is often the case, such an action undertaken by one of Moscow's partners would complicate Russia's relations with the target of such a move. Saddam Hussein's 1980 attack on the Islamic Republic of Iran, with which Moscow had initially hoped to collaborate on the basis of their common hostility towards the United States, and Hussein's 1990 attack on Kuwait, with which Moscow had long had cooperative, profitable relations, are examples of this occurring during the Soviet era. Recent hostilities in Syria between Israel on the one hand and Iranian and Hezbollah forces on the other are parallel examples in the Putin era. The propensity for surprise moves by Middle Eastern actors, of course, does not affect just Russia, but other external actors as well—including the United States. Moscow's attempts to avoid choosing sides and to maintain good relations with all risks damaging its ties to one side or even both.

This risk could be mitigated, though, if Moscow could succeed in resolving or at least reducing conflict between opposing sides. Indeed, successful Russian-led conflict resolution efforts could enhance Moscow's position in the Middle East while diminishing Washington's. After the 1973 Arab-Israeli War, the ability of the United States to work with both Israel and the Arab states—while the USSR could not, after it broke diplomatic ties with Israel in 1967—allowed Washington to manage Arab-Israeli peace negotiations, from which it largely excluded Moscow for decades. By contrast, the United States has been unwilling to work with either Iran (except on the nuclear issue during the Obama and Biden administrations), the Assad regime in Syria, or Hezbollah. Moscow's friendly relations with these actors, as well as with their Washington-aligned adversaries, has allowed Putin to play a much larger role than the United States in diplomatic efforts aimed at resolving the conflict in Syria. Further, Moscow's ability to work with opposing sides in Yemen and Libya—while Washington sided with some actors against others in the former, and has been relatively inactive after 2011 in the latter—has allowed Russia to play an important role in the diplomacy over these two conflicts as well. Russian commentators have noted that Moscow's ability to work with all sides in the Middle East, while Washington cannot or will not, now puts Russia in a position similar to that of the United States in the latter part of the Cold War, when Washington dominated the Arab-Israeli peace process.[48]

While the ability to talk to opposing sides may be a necessary condition for an external power to resolve a conflict, it is not a sufficient one. The United States was able to negotiate the Camp David agreement between Egypt and Israel not only because it could talk with them both, but because the United States was willing and able to provide massive economic assistance to both—which it is still paying—as an inducement for both countries to sign and abide by the agreement. By contrast, despite Putin's ability to talk with opposing sides (including the opposition to Assad in Syria) in many Middle Eastern conflicts, Russia is neither willing nor able to provide large-scale economic assistance as an inducement for them to come to an agreement. Indeed, in the one conflict that Russia is most heavily involved—Syria—not only is Moscow unwilling to pay for large-scale reconstruction efforts; it has instead sought to persuade Western nations and Arabian peninsula monarchies to provide the funds needed to pay Russian firms to undertake this work.[49] Nor is it clear that closer Sino-Russian partnership along with Beijing's much greater capacity to provide economic assistance will result in its doing so in Syria. China seeks profitable opportunities to invest its economic resources in, and it does not appear to view conflict-ridden Syria as one of these.[50]

Moscow's efforts to bring about a peace settlement between the Assad regime and its internal Arab opponents, then, have not yet succeeded—nor are they likely to until the regime offers significant concessions to its opponents and allows for the safe return of Syrian refugees. However, Putin's success in helping the Assad regime recapture much of its lost territory has only hardened Assad's resolve not to make any concessions needed to reach a peace agreement.[51] Further, the strong presence in Syria of Iranian and Hezbollah forces—which support Assad's recalcitrant position—means that Russia's ability to persuade or coerce Assad into making concessions is limited. Thus, while Russia along with Iran may have succeeded in propping up the Assad regime militarily, the lack of a peace agreement means that the situation in Syria is likely to remain unstable and require an indefinite Russian military presence to ensure both the regime's continued survival and Russia's continued influence. If, however, Moscow's efforts can prevent outright conflict between Turkish and Syrian Kurdish forces, or if they can keep Turkish forces contained behind the immediate border area that Moscow was willing to let them occupy in October 2019, Russia's reputation for being able to mediate (if not resolve) conflict in the Middle East will be greatly enhanced.

In other Middle Eastern conflicts where Russia is less directly involved militarily, Moscow's ability to talk to opposing sides has not translated into any success in actually resolving conflict. With regard to one of the most serious potential conflicts in the region—between Iran and Israel—Moscow is not even trying to mediate. Washington, of course, is not doing so either. In the absence of conflict resolution efforts by any external party, the possibility of heightened tension between Iran and its regional opponents will persist. If conflict does occur, it is highly likely that the United States will lend its support to Israel and/or the Arab Gulf states against Iran. This might confront Moscow with some difficult choices. If it sides with Iran, it could lose influence with America's Middle East allies that had previously hoped to draw Moscow away from Tehran. If Russia instead sides with America's Middle East allies, it could lose influence with Iran—and support from Russia would not be as important to the United States' Middle East allies as support from Washington.

If Russia continues an "even-handed" policy of balancing between both sides, while the United States sides with one side against the other, Russia risks disappointing them all and possibly losing influence over the outcome of the conflict. Moscow may succeed in balancing between opposing sides simultaneously for quite some time, but unless it can ameliorate these conflicts, such a policy involves substantial risk over the long term. While Moscow initially succeeded in getting the Syrian Kurds to accept Assad's forces into their territory, and in limiting how far into northeastern Syria Turkish forces could go in the wake of the partial US withdrawal from the region, Russia's ability to prevent and contain them is likely to be tested by one or more of the antagonistic parties in this fractious region.

Putin's Middle East policy faces still other risks. As noted earlier, Putin has been far more successful in cooperating with Western-aligned Middle Eastern governments than the Soviets were because, unlike the Soviets, Putin is not seeking their downfall or supporting their internal opponents. The Soviets were usually able to benefit from the downfall of Western-aligned governments and the subsequent animosity between their "revolutionary" successors and the United States, but Russia under Putin is so closely tied to authoritarian status quo governments in the Middle East that Putin may be unable to avoid losing influence if any fall to popular uprisings. This, of course, is also a problem for America and the West, but that may be little consolation to Moscow if this occurs.

Yet another problem Putin faces that the Soviets did not is that while the United States and the USSR were the only two superpowers strong enough to play the role of great power in the Middle East during the Cold War, this is not necessarily the case now. It is possible that Russia and China will pursue common aims in the Middle East, just as they do in Central Asia, but Russian and Chinese interests in the Middle East may also differ. Indeed, their interests are already different in one very important way: while Russia, along with OPEC, exports petroleum and therefore wants it to be priced higher, China is one of the world's largest petroleum importers and wants the price to be lower.

If and when China decides to exert its influence in the region, Russia will not be in a position to stop it, especially if Moscow's economic dependence on China continues or grows. India may also be able to play a great power role in the region. Further, there are states in the region that would welcome its doing so.[52] Even in the unlikely event that the United States withdraws from the region, the rise of these two Asian great powers means that Russia will be unable to replace America in the Middle East—and perhaps even in regions closer to Moscow, such as Central Asia and the Caucasus—as the predominant external power in the region, like the United States was in the 1990s and 2000s.

Further, while Putin's improved relations with Middle Eastern governments has meant that none of them has sought to support Muslim opposition in Chechnya or elsewhere in Russia, as Saudi Arabia and others were doing at the turn of the century, opposition activity inside Russia's Muslim republics could still be revived due to internal causes. If this occurs, Middle Eastern governments that have good relations with Moscow are unlikely to help Russian Muslim opposition groups. On the other hand, they are unlikely to be willing or even able to help Moscow suppress them. And, of course, if such movements really did grow strong and their secession from Russia seemed likely, certain Middle Eastern states might ally with some of these groups, if only to limit the ability of their Middle Eastern rivals to do the same.

Finally, just as the Soviet withdrawal from the Middle East at the end of the Cold War was not caused by the failure of Moscow's Middle East policies but by dramatic change in the USSR itself, Russia's ability to remain influential in the region now may depend less on the policies it is pursuing there than on events in Russia itself. Should Russia perceive China as an increased threat, whether this occurs during Putin's administration or more likely that of his successor, this might lead Moscow to de-emphasize competition with the US in the Middle East and elsewhere. Other changes—such as increased conflict involving Russia in Ukraine or elsewhere in the former Soviet space, elite infighting and domestic unrest at the end of Putin's fourth term as president in 2024 (whether he seeks to cling to power or not), the rise of Muslim opposition in the North Caucasus and elsewhere in Russia, and/or a severe economic downturn—could necessitate Moscow focusing more on these issues and less on the Middle East.

Russian influence in the Middle East has expanded greatly during the two decades that Putin has been in power. However, the same could be said about either of two twenty-year periods of Soviet policy towards the Middle East—either from the end of World War II in 1945 (i.e., 1945–65), or from 1953, when Khrushchev first rose to power and began a concerted effort to expand Soviet influence in the region (i.e., 1953–73)—especially since even the defeat of Moscow's Arab allies by Israel in 1967 at first led to expanded Soviet influence in the region. It is not foreordained, of course, that Putin's foreign policy towards the Middle East will experience the same trajectory as Soviet foreign policy towards the region did in prior years. However, what Soviet experience in the Middle East demonstrates is that even two decades of expanding influence in the region does not guarantee continued success for the following twenty to twenty-five years.

3

DOMESTIC FACTORS IN RUSSIA'S MIDDLE EAST POLICY

Leonid Issaev

Introduction

A country's foreign policy cannot be viewed in isolation from the processes that occur within the country itself. This is especially true for Russia, where foreign policy, since the times of the Soviet Union, has been a function of the political regime's domestic policymaking. This becomes even more obvious if one looks at Russia under Vladimir Putin, a president whose popularity among Russians is largely based on his foreign policy. Despite several of his unpopular social and economic policy decisions and a protracted economic crisis, the share of Russians positively assessing Russia's stature on the world stage reached 72 percent during his administration.

Since the Ukrainian crisis in 2014, Moscow has largely forsaken the international norms established after the end of the Cold War by posing a challenge to the United States and its allies. Over time, this stance has proven increasingly draining on the Russian economy, society, and the regime itself. A vivid example of this effort has been in the Middle East, which objectively is not a region of high importance from the point of view of Russian national interests. The EU and the post-Soviet space as well as China present more immediate challenges—and opportunities—than the Middle Eastern region. Despite this, the Middle East—together with Afghanistan, Venezuela, and North Korea—began playing a more prominent role in Russian foreign policy, if only because of Russia's conflict with the West.

Within the framework of this study, an attempt will be made to reveal, on the one hand, exactly how the Middle East agenda is used by the Russian leadership to accomplish its internal political objectives, and, on the other, how the situation inside Russia affects its policy in the Middle East region.

The "Stable" 2000s

Russia's return to the Middle East is largely associated with the name of Vladimir Putin, calling to mind his severe position on Libya in 2011, the beginning of the military campaign in Syria in 2015, the open confrontation with Turkey after a Russian fighter-bomber was shot down, and Russia's support for Libyan Field Marshal Khalifa Haftar. Nevertheless, such active involvement in Middle East politics was not always typical of the Russian president.

The Middle East was on the periphery of Vladimir Putin's attention during the early terms of his presidency. The most vivid evidence of this is the fact that Putin's first visit to the region took place only during his second presidential term. In 2005, the Russian leader visited Egypt, Israel, and the Palestinian territories. During his meeting with Ariel Sharon, the Russian leader asked the Israeli prime minister: "I am new to the Middle East. What would be your primary advice?" Ariel Sharon responded: "Never trust anyone."[1]

There are at least two explanations for why the Middle East occupies such a modest consideration in Russian foreign policy thinking. In the first half of the 2000s, Russia aimed to avoid confrontation with the United States by building dialogue with Washington, NATO, and the European Union. After the 9/11 terrorist attacks in 2001, Russia and the United States managed to develop cooperation along certain lines. Russia supported NATO's military campaign in Afghanistan and began an arrangement of exchanging information through special services channels. The Russian leadership also provided NATO with its air space for the delivery of shipments to Afghanistan.

The Russian leadership's reluctance to aggravate relations with the United States over Middle East issues became most evident in 2003 when the American authorities announced the launch of a military operation against Saddam Hussein's regime. Russia had its own interests in Iraq. At the start of the 2000s, Baghdad had promised to start paying part of its considerable debt to Russia after the abolition of sanctions.[2] In 1997, a contract for the development and production of the second stage of the Iraqi West Qurna oil field (West Qurna-2) was signed between the Iraqi Ministry of Oil, the company "Lukoil," and the Russian foreign economic associations "Zarubezhneft" and "Machinoimport." Moreover, about 40 percent of Iraqi oil exports went to Russia, where it was subsequently resold.[3]

Nevertheless, while choosing between confrontation with Washington or a war in Iraq, Moscow preferred the latter. After the meeting between Vladimir Putin and George W. Bush in Saint Petersburg in November 2002, the Russian leader delegated former foreign minister Yevgeny Primakov to Baghdad to convince Saddam Hussein to resign. Primakov recalled:

> Fearing that Saddam's resignation could cause inner destabilization in Iraq, Putin ordered me to tell Saddam Hussein that he could, for example, keep his post in the party. ... It was a face-to-face conversation, as I had requested. ... After this, Saddam Hussein invited some members of the government to join us to let them hear the essence of Putin's message and to gauge their reaction. ... Saddam silently patted me on the shoulder and left. And while Saddam was leaving, Tariq Aziz spoke loudly, so that Saddam could hear, saying: "In ten years, we shall see who turned out to be right, our dear president or Primakov."[4]

Another explanation for Moscow's limited interest in the Middle East (and in foreign policy, in general) in the 2000s is that at that time the Russian authorities were mainly focused on the country's domestic issues and securing full control of the country's political system. This was a typical feature of Putin's regime in his first two presidential terms (2000–8). Moreover, in the 2000s, the ruling regime fully secured its power. Russians were fed up with the 1990s and looking forward to the 2000s with renewed hope.[5]

Putin took full advantage of the overwhelming societal demand for peace and stability. Before the global financial crisis of 2008, tens of millions of Russians had reasons to praise Putin's presidency.[6] In the eyes of the Russian population, Putin was not responsible for the domestic upheavals of the 1990s, and his popularity was also unexpectedly boosted by a growing global demand for hydrocarbons. A near-constant increase in oil and gas prices from 1999 to 2008 spurred economic growth in Russia and greatly contributed to a major consumer boom.

It was at this time that new urban areas began to grow rapidly, the number of cars on city streets increased, and large shopping centers opened, among other developments, all of which were associated with the policies of the new president. Former Russian prime minister Yegor Gaidar and privatization chief Anatoly Chubais, seen as the founding fathers of Russia's modern economic system, noted: "Over the past 8 years [since 2000], the income of the population [in real terms] has been growing by more than 10% per year … [which] is the basis for the stability of the political structure that has developed in Russia in recent years."[7]

Russian economist Dmitry Travin points out that "many nations throughout their history have shown that they have no problems with living under monarchical and authoritarian regimes, if these systems ensure a normal life. Under Putin, thanks to oil, life was even more than normal until 2008."[8] In this regard, the interest of the Russian authorities in foreign policy issues (except for the post-Soviet space, which the Kremlin perceived as its sphere of exclusive interests) during Putin's first two presidential terms was low. Moreover, in the 2000s, the Russian leadership was interested in developing integration projects with Western countries, which were the principal source of investment, modern technologies, and industrial best practices in Russia. In this regard, the Middle East, with its diverse problems and conflicts of interest, was of little concern, or indeed value, to Moscow.

The Era of Changes

During Dmitry Medvedev's presidency, the situation started to change both in Russia and globally. In 2011–12, the world in general and the Arab countries in particular experienced a surge of protests.[9] Although the protests in Algeria began earlier, it has become practice to pinpoint the start of the Arab Spring events on December 17, 2010, when the young, unemployed Mohamed Bouazizi committed self-immolation in the provincial Tunisian town of Sidi Bouzid. The ensuing wave of protests resulted in the unexpectedly rapid fall of the Ben Ali regime, primarily due to the intra-elite conflict between the non-privileged army and the privileged security forces who came under the special care of the president.[10] Consequently, the army sided with the protesters, which determined the fall of the authoritarian regime in Tunisia.

This surprisingly quick (and rather bloodless) fall of Ben Ali pushed secular leaders of youth movements in Egypt to attempt to stage large-scale protests in their country. Due to considerable internal stress in Egypt,[11] this caused a political avalanche that led to the fall of Mubarak's regime. All of the above set off a wave of destabilization throughout the Arab world, the signs of which were already visible immediately after the quick victory of the Tunisian revolution. The scale of destabilization in each country depended on a number of factors, such as the extent of internal elite conflict, intermediate regime type (half-democratic/half-authoritarian), the presence of disadvantaged groups, a high proportion of unemployed young people (especially those with higher education), etc.[12] In some cases (especially in Libya and Syria), external destabilization was a factor.

Under the influence of the Arab uprisings, the rest of the world experienced a non-trivial upsurge of protest activity as well, including the "Occupy" movements, from Occupy Wall Street to Occupy Abay. The truly outstanding nature of these events is emphasized through quantitative empirical data. In order to better understand the scale of the Arab uprisings and their global echo, consider Figures 3.1 and 3.2.

As we see, in 2011, the protest activity in the Middle East experienced a staggering leap by two orders of magnitude.[13] In this global protest movement, Russia was no exception: after the falsifications in

Fig. 3.1: Dynamics of the total number of major anti-government demonstrations registered in the world annually as recorded in the Cross-National Time Series (CNTS) database (1920–2012).

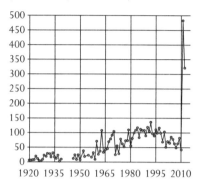

Source: Cross-National Time Series (CNTS), "Data Archive Coverage," Databank International, 2015, www.databanksinternational.com.

Fig. 3.2: Dynamics of the total number of major anti-government demonstrations registered in the Middle East and the rest of the world annually as recorded in the CNTS database (2002–12).

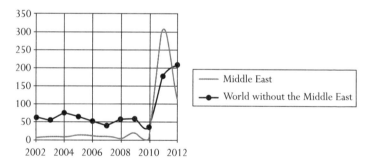

Source: Cross-National Time Series (CNTS), "Data Archive Coverage," Databank International, 2015, www.databanksinternational.com.

the parliamentary elections in September 2011, street protests broke out against the rigged elections for the State Duma and policies pursued by Vladimir Putin and the "United Russia" party (of which he was also chairman).

The protests at Moscow's Bolotnaya Square in the winter of 2011–12 were hardly the first manifestation of citizens' dissatisfaction with the policies pursued by the authorities. The pension benefits reform of 2005 led to massive protests by retirees across the country. However, due to high oil prices at the time, Russian authorities could de facto "bribe" the protesters into standing down. After that, the country's budget was increasingly spent on financially placating the so-called "Putin majority" to maintain his and United Russia's high polling numbers.

The protests of 2011–12 were distinct from the events of 2005 in that they took place under completely different conditions and were perceived differently by the authorities. First, the sharp drop in oil prices in 2008 produced a sobering effect on the Russian authorities, who realized that a favorable world market situation was a temporary phenomenon.[14] In addition, the resources spent after 2008 to mute social discontent, because of Russia's falling GDP, failed to suppress the political crisis at the end of 2011.

Secondly, the Arab uprisings led to the fall of several Middle Eastern leaders: Egypt's Hosni Mubarak was arrested and Libya's Muammar Gaddafi was brutally murdered. In this context, Russian authorities viewed the ongoing domestic political protests from a rather alarmist perspective. As a result, the Kremlin tried to denigrate them through a massive propaganda effort while simultaneously increasing expenditure on law enforcement agencies—the so-called *siloviki*—to have enough reliable forces to suppress any discontent when necessary.[15]

At the initial stage of the Arab uprisings, the Russian leadership generally believed that the discontent in the Middle East was justified, but following the protests in Moscow in 2011–12, and especially after the events in Ukraine at the turn of 2014, the narrative changed significantly.

At first, the Russian Ministry of Foreign Affairs gave the following assessment of the events in Egypt in 2011:

> From the very beginning of the Arab Spring, Russia sincerely supported Egyptian people's desire for freedom and for a fair solution to the socioeconomic and sociopolitical problems that had accumulated over the preceding decades. The results of the election of a new composition of the National Assembly of Egypt held in the country at the end of last year confirmed the sentiments of most of the country's

voters in favor of the country's development on a pluralistic and democratic basis.[16]

Mikhail Bogdanov, who was Russian ambassador in Cairo at the start of the Arab uprisings, also commented on these events in July 2011:

> As for the root causes of the current turmoil in the Arab countries, in my opinion, they lie both in the socioeconomic and political spheres. Of course, with all the specifics of the development of events in different countries, there is much in common—in many countries, the crisis of the authoritarian political system was long overdue. Unchanging leadership and political elites in general, low degrees of social mobility, belated or even absent reforms, high unemployment, corruption, and other social diseases were all internal conflict factors that accumulated for many years and detonated at the beginning of this year. In addition, we must not forget that in the Arab countries, youth predominate. They are modern, educated people who have mastered the internet, blogs, and social networks, and who do not see a future in the existing coordinate system. It is not by chance that they became an important mobilizing element of the "Arab revolutions."[17]

However, after the protests in Moscow and subsequent events in Ukraine, the Russian authorities' assessment of the Arab uprisings changed considerably. Thus, in 2013, Russian Deputy Foreign Minister Grigory Karasin gave the following assessment of the situation: "The 'Arab Spring' has by no means brought about qualitative positive changes. If we analyze the events, they basically led to chaos, unrest, and the transformation of individual political groups into others, with incomprehensible, sometimes dangerous consequences."[18]

This statement is of special interest, because it allows us to understand the ideology formed by the Russian political elite regarding the Arab uprisings. "The United States first supported the anti-Russian 'color revolutions,' then the Arab Spring events unfolded according to this 'scenario,' after which the likely 'scenario' was conceived to weaken Russia and potentially make it disintegrate."[19] In other words, in the context of confrontation with the West and the need to strengthen its grip on the country, the Russian leadership chose to weaken the anti-regime opposition by linking it directly to the damaging events in the Arab countries.

This narrative coincides with a supposed dichotomy between democratization and stability, which has gained an important place in Russian social and political discourse after the mass protests in Moscow in 2011–12. Since then, the Russian political establishment began actively promoting the idea that stability should serve as a key criterion for the effectiveness of any political regime. The events of the Arab uprisings only confirmed this thesis. For example, the authoritarian but stable dictatorship regimes of Bashar al-Assad of Syria or Abdel Fattah al-Sisi of Egypt were believed to have opposed the projects for democracy that resulted in different radical groups like the Islamic State gaining power.

For this reason, Russia's political solutions are top-down and aligned with dictatorships, rather than bottom-up or siding with the revolutionaries that aim to change the status quo. Moscow has effectively saved Assad's regime in Syria, and has supported Sisi in Egypt and Haftar in Libya. Russia is actively promoting conflict-resolution scenarios in the UN Security Council that serve the interests of Middle Eastern dictatorships. This, in Moscow's view, suits Russia's interests better than supporting popular struggles for political rights. However, it appears that Russia's interventions tend to exacerbate the causes that triggered these uprisings in the first place.

A New Source of Support for the Russian Regime

The Russian people voted for Putin in his first two presidential terms, largely because they associated his government with the socioeconomic upswing of the 2000s. By Putin's third term (2012–18), the reasons for supporting the government were becoming less convincing, and votes for the opposition were growing. As Dmitry Travin rightly points out, "in such a situation, he [Vladimir Putin] needed to come up with some effective ways of strengthening his personal power. And it was necessary to build a new political system so that it does not depend on economic prospects."[20] On the one hand, the Russian political regime became more ideologically consolidated. On the other hand, Putin's personal governing style became characterized by his preference for intra-elite conflict, so that he could serve as the chief arbiter of the ruling class.[21] In the 2010s, Putin became all but indispensable in this role.

The state of conflict inside the ruling elite is a favorable environment for the Russian leader: it does not "undermine Putin's position, but, on the contrary, only strengthens it."[22] Putin generally savors conflict. During his first two presidential terms, the primary conflicts were those occurring within Russia, such as the struggle between the president's ex-KGB entourage with Yeltsin-era oligarchs, or the war in Chechnya. However, during Putin's tenure as prime minister (2008–12), as well as during his third presidential term (2012–18), the concept of using conflict as a tool for wielding political power acquired a new foreign policy dimension, and he put it to use in wars with Georgia and Ukraine, conflicts in Syria and (partially) Libya, and a continuing confrontation with the United States. Real and perceived victories in these conflicts carried Putin to the top of public opinion polls and helped him avoid unpleasant surprises during elections.

It is from this perspective that the Russian invasion of Syria in September 2015 should be analyzed. By mid-2015, Putin's regime was badly in need of a new wave of patriotic mobilization, which was achieved through successful military operations abroad. Thus, there was increased public support for the Russian leadership's foreign policy after the war in South Ossetia in 2008 and the conflict in Crimea in 2014 (see Figure 3.3). A similar positive public effect was achieved within the framework of the Syrian campaign. While the events in South Ossetia and Ukraine had a high degree of positive influence on Russia's internal political processes, the country's involvement in Syria shifted the focus from domestic problems towards a renewed patriotism—especially since this was the first time since the collapse of the USSR that the country had begun a military campaign far from its own borders.

The actions of Russian Aerospace Forces in Syria generated positive reactions from the Russian population for many years. President Putin's popularity skyrocketed, even when the country entered a period of economic crisis with falling standards of living. One of the main reasons for Putin's popularity was his "we do not give up our friends" policy, his firm position on Crimea, and Russia's actions in Syria.

Figure 3.3 shows that the patriotic mobilization of Russians occurs in waves and has a limited effect. A decrease in popular support can be observed in 2015, when the effect of the Crimea annexation began

Fig. 3.3: Russian citizens' attitude towards government policies, 1996–2017. (*The gray line means "the country is heading in the right direction" and the black line means "the country is heading in the wrong direction."*)

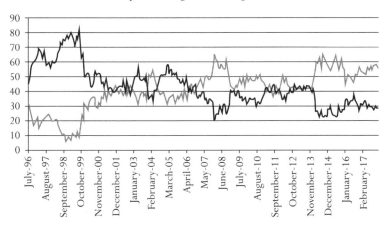

Source: Travin and Gudkov, *After Crimea: Opinion Polls in 2017.*

to evaporate, which predetermined the need for another push to mobilize public opinion in support of the Kremlin's policy. This was especially true ahead of the parliamentary elections in the autumn of 2016. Moreover, it was vitally important for Russian authorities to prevent the repeat of the late-2011 and early-2012 events, when the State Duma's rigged elections resulted in mass protests in Moscow.

While there are internal conflicts within the Russian regime, there is generally an ideological consolidation, which allows us to better understand the logic of Russia's foreign policy, particularly in the Middle East. Eurasianism fits well with the idea of Russia's unique stature. According to the Eurasian concept of Russian history, the Euro-Atlantic world is historically alien, even inimical to Russia, which is destined to be at the center of its own separate civilization, and includes most of the ex-Soviet states and even some European countries.

It is in the categories of its own exclusiveness that the Russian leadership is inclined to interpret its presence in the Middle East. For instance, at the Moscow International Security Conference in 2019, Valery Gerasimov, Chief of the General Staff of the Armed Forces of

Russia, assessed Russia's military operation in Syria by claiming that "Russia arrived just in time to prevent a final catastrophe that could threaten the entire Middle East."[23]

The Kremlin's position is that Russia played an important role in stabilizing the situation in the Middle East. During his 2015 speech at the 70th session of the UN General Assembly, Vladimir Putin noted that "the power vacuum that has arisen in several countries of the Middle East and North Africa led to the formation of zones of anarchy that immediately began to be filled with extremists and terrorists."[24] Similarly, summarizing the results of Russia's 2015 foreign policy, the minister of foreign affairs, Sergey Lavrov, said that "Russia's response to the Syrian leadership's appeal had really helped to change the situation in the country ... It became clear who fights terrorists and who supports them."[25] The Russian president noted that Russian Aerospace Forces successfully completed their assigned tasks, preserving the sovereignty of Syria and preventing the spread of extremism. He argued that, with Russia's support, "Syria is preserved as a sovereign, independent state. Refugees are returning to their homes. Conditions have been created for a political settlement under the auspices of the UN."[26]

Moreover, a typical feature of Russian exceptionalism is its opposition to the "destructive" actions of the West, primarily the United States. The dangers of Washington's policies in Yugoslavia, Iraq, Syria, Libya, and Ukraine have been an integral feature of Russian political discourse over the past twenty years. Russian Federation Council (upper chamber of parliament) member Alexei Pushkov once tweeted that "The United States has already destroyed Iraq, Libya, Syria, has given rise to an 'Islamic state.' This is the US leadership."[27]

The Russian president maintained a similar assessment of the results of US policy in the Middle East in 2015:

> Aggressive external intervention led to the fact that instead of reforms, state institutions and the way of life itself [in the Middle East and North Africa] were completely ruined. Instead of the triumph of democracy and progress, there is violence, poverty, and social catastrophe. Human rights, including the right to life, are not respected. One would like to ask those who created such a situation: "Do you at least realize now what you have done?"[28]

The Eurasian doctrine fits this vision of the world in which Russian leadership offers stability and state sovereignty as the alternative to Western concepts of liberal democracy and human rights. Both narratives have become deeply rooted in the larger discourse of the Russian authorities and Putin personally. This ideology is meant to make the Russian people believe that nearly any serious change in society or politics inevitably leads to destruction. In this sense, "people see their life becoming more difficult, but they tend to compare it not with previous successes, but with hypothetical catastrophes."[29] This trend was set by Putin when, during the final meeting of the 5th State Duma, he appealed to the opposition "not to rock the boat."[30]

Russian state-owned media incessantly depicts the chaos and devastation allegedly brought by the West-backed anti-governmental demonstrations in the Arab countries, while the years preceding the Arab uprisings tend to be shown with nostalgia. Perhaps the most common illustration used is Libya during Muammar Gaddafi's rule. According to the Russian state-controlled media, although lacking democratic institutions, Libya was the embodiment of the "welfare state," offering free education and medicine, low taxes, and financial support for families.

All Russian state propaganda narratives depict a dramatic drop in the living standards of the Arab countries that deposed their dictators. The average Russian media consumer is compelled to favor preservation of the status quo over radical change. At the meeting of the Presidential Council for Civil Society and Human Rights in 2018, Putin encouraged such thinking, this time citing the protests in France: "You and I do not want to have events like those in Paris, where the paving stones are overturned, everything is on fire, and the country plunges into a state of emergency."[31]

The narratives of "stability" and "state sovereignty" promoted by the Russian authorities were adopted by the new Arab governments that emerged after the Arab Spring, which were faced with the task of concentrating power in their own hands and preventing further anti-government protests. The discourse of new Arab leaders, including Sisi and Mohammed bin Salman, as well as representatives of an older generation of leaders, such as Assad and the Algerian ruling elite, increasingly elevated "stability" as a political virtue.

Moreover, from the Kremlin's point of view, the concepts of stability and state sovereignty contradict human rights, democracy, and liberalism. Ultimately, the latter are declared not only alien, but also destructive for non-Western societies, including the Russian people. This discourse quickly found adherents in the Middle East, which is confirmed by Sisi's statements that always stress Egypt's need for stability.

The results of this political and ideological strategy are ambiguous. On the one hand, it fully satisfies the Russian population's domestic demand for Russia's "great power" rhetoric and status (Figure 3.4). It was Putin who contributed to this demand early in his first presidency, noting that "the collapse of the USSR became the main geopolitical catastrophe of the twentieth century."[32] In its confrontation with the United States, the Kremlin positions itself as Washington's peer, challenging what is seen by Moscow policymakers as the US-dominated "unipolar" world. Speaking at the UN General Assembly a few days before the start of the military campaign in Syria, Putin declared that Russia had regained its "superpower" status, which it had lost after the collapse of the Soviet Union. The intervention in Syria was supposed to demonstrate this. Indeed, for the average Russian citizen—Putin's core electorate, still largely beholden to the Soviet political mythology—the idea of being a "superpower" entails military conquests. In fact, in the eyes of the Russian public, the ability to conduct effective military operations, including air strikes, around the globe is indeed its main characteristic.

Fig. 3.4: The percentage of Russians who consider Russia a "superpower."

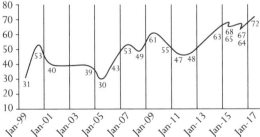

Source: Travin and Gudkov, *After Crimea: Opinion Polls in 2017.*

On the other hand, Russia's status as a superpower carries numerous risks for the country's foreign policy in general, and for its position in the Middle East in particular. Russia's presence in the Middle East is less about establishing stability in the region or fighting terrorism and more about challenging Washington. Moscow is attempting to force the United States into a negotiation regarding the "Middle Eastern assets" Russia acquired in recent years, with the intention of exchanging these for more important concessions like Russian domination of the Ukraine and ex-Soviet space, as well as the lifting of US sanctions.

However, as Russian political analyst Grigory Golosov notes, "the whole series of enchanting foreign policy failures will only benefit the Russian ruler. Foreign policy is lost outright, but domestic policy is won."[33] Russia did not and cannot become a strategic ally for economic reasons. While Russia was able to play a decisive role in Syria, realistically it cannot do the same all over the Middle East, due above all to its economic circumstances. Russia's main areas of economic cooperation are the United States, Western Europe, China, and rising India. Therefore, the desire to find common ground with the West remains the primary vector of all its foreign policy.

Russian involvement in the Middle East is less associated with the "revival" of Russian influence, and more due to changes in the United States' policies towards the Middle East after the events of the Arab Spring, and Washington's change of priorities towards this region. This created a geopolitical vacuum that both regional and global actors are trying to fill, and Russia is no exception. Nevertheless, it remains obvious that the countries of the region, albeit to a lesser extent than before 2011, still prefer to maintain friendly relations with the United States. In this regard, local elites often use the development of relations with Russia as an additional trump card in an attempt to negotiate for themselves more favorable conditions in cooperation with Washington. As a result, we are dealing with a situation in which, in the long run, Russian activity in the Middle East, as well as attempts by local elites to flirt with Moscow, occurs ultimately in hopes of normalizing or strengthening relations with the United States.

The strategy for resolving the Syrian conflict has been on Moscow's agenda from the very beginning of its intervention. The Russian leadership feared that it might get bogged down in the Syrian civil conflict, just as the Soviet Union—which did not initially plan to launch a full-scale military operation—was held hostage by the circumstances in Afghanistan in 1979; the way out of the Afghan war was extremely painful for both the Communist Party and for the whole of Soviet society. In 1989, the USSR's Congress of People's Deputies concluded that "the decision to send Soviet troops to Afghanistan deserves moral and political condemnation."[34] The Russian authorities do not want a similar fate for themselves in Syria, and this explains the Kremlin's desire to minimize casualties in the conflict.

Nevertheless, the problem of withdrawing from Syria turned out to be more complicated than Moscow had assumed at the beginning of the intervention in 2015, and this is not limited to Syria. This is demonstrated by the fact that Putin has repeatedly announced the withdrawal of Russian troops from Syria, and Sergey Lavrov has similarly reiterated that Moscow's main task—the fight against terrorist structures in Syria—has been successfully implemented.

The Syrian conflict has allowed Moscow to achieve recognition of its significance in the Middle East, including the Gulf, contributing to improved relations between Russia and the Gulf countries (at least, those that were themselves affected by the Arab Spring). Russia understands the importance of the current moment. Opportunities for cooperation—primarily in the economic, energy, and military-technical spheres—were the result of Russia's active military-diplomatic participation in Middle Eastern affairs. In this regard, the Russian leadership reasonably fears that a reduction in its military presence in the region will result in a decline in the Middle East's, and especially the Gulf's, interest in Moscow.

Does the Middle East Hold Foreign Policy Potential for Russia?

An important aspect that determines Russia's presence in the Middle East and North Africa is the domestic mood in Russia. The Kremlin's foreign policy takes into account Russian public opinion and sympathies with or antipathies towards one or another sociopolitical or religious movement, and towards one or another country or regime. It is thus clear that Russia's Middle East policy is only important for

Putin's regime insofar as it contributes to the growth of his domestic popularity. Therefore, how ordinary Russians perceive the Kremlin's actions abroad plays and will continue to play an important role in the Russian leadership's calculations vis-à-vis the Middle East.

It is necessary to clarify how the majority of Russians understand the essence of Russia's foreign policy. According to Denis Volkov, a polling expert at the Levada Center, the majority of Russians believe that the Russian government is protecting Assad's legitimate regime from terrorists in Syria, while in Ukraine, Moscow is helping the Russian-speaking citizens in the Donbas region. In the eyes of the Russian population, Russia is helping other countries and peoples, only to be unfairly treated by the West in return. However, such policy is a heavy burden for the country's finances. Russia badly needs resources for long-overdue salary and pension increases and an overall improvement in living standards.[35]

The effects of Russia's "small victorious wars" are short-lived. Moreover, in mass-media terms, the "plot" of each subsequent war should always be more fascinating than that of the previous one. For instance, Russia's latest row with Georgia—ignited by a Russian delegation's controversial but official visit to Tbilisi in June 2019—failed to arouse any interest among the Russian population. The challenge to keep the public interested makes Russian operations in the Middle East even more complex. Prime-time television shows and numerous video conferences with Russian military personnel in Syria were new phenomena for the Russian public. Videos released by the Russian General Staff, which showed the destruction of alleged Islamic State terrorist bases by the Russian Aero-Space Forces, were perceived by Russian audiences as an unprecedented media-based thriller.

However, people's interest in the Syrian operation faded quickly, forcing the Russian authorities to announce the end of the military campaign several times.[36] Russia's potential military operations in other parts of the Middle East will have similar limited effects. This fact largely determines the balancing strategy that is being increasingly used by the Russian leadership in the Middle East; the Kremlin's policy of maintaining active relations with all regional actors being the most effective means of preventing Moscow from involving itself in any regional conflict. Syria has almost ceased to contribute to domestic Russian policy, and the costs of participating in yet another conflict are likely to overweigh any potential advantages. In this regard, Moscow would hesitate to be drawn into any new conflicts in the Middle East.

Russia's current geopolitical position is beginning to lose domestic support. According to Public Opinion Foundation (FOM) surveys presented in June 2019, the Russian people's interest in foreign policy has noticeably decreased.[37] For the first time since the survey was first taken in 2015, the percentage of those not interested in Russia's foreign policy slightly exceeded the percentage of those who followed it (see Figure 3.5).

Russian youth are those most skeptical of Russia's foreign policy. Among 18–30-year-olds, 38 percent of respondents see Russian foreign policy as a failure rather than a success, while 32 percent believe the opposite. The percentage of those who consider Russian foreign policy successful has decreased from 60 percent in 2017 to 48 percent in 2019, and the share of those who called it unsuccessful has increased from 17 to 23 percent.[38]

According to the FOM survey, Russian people tend to view their country's involvement in "the military operation in Syria" positively. Russia's other perceived achievements include a "return of the Crimea," "improving relations with other countries," and "strength-

Fig. 3.5: Do you follow Russian foreign policy? (in %).

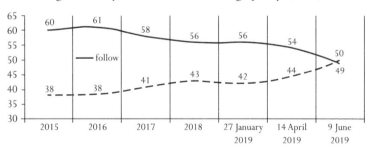

Source: Public Opinion Foundation (FOM), "Vneshnyaya politika: monitoring" [Foreign policy: Monitoring], June 20, 2019, https://fom.ru/Politika/14223; Public Opinion Foundation (FOM), "Interes k vneshney politike. Uspekhi i neudachi" [Interest in foreign policy. Successes and failures], May 20, 2019, https://fom.ru/Politika/14209.

ening Russia's defense capabilities." Russia's failures include such notions as "Russia cannot deal with Ukraine," "Russia fell out with all the European countries," "international sanctions," and, curiously, "Russia is too much involved in Syria."[39]

The FOM survey also reflects ordinary Russians' growing skepticism with regard to the mainstream media coverage of Russia's achievements abroad. The Russian public's own economic, social, and environmental problems take precedence over news of Russian troops in Syria, sales of S-400 anti-missile and anti-aircraft technology, or Japan's claims to the Kuril Islands. Russian people are more concerned with how the Russian leadership, especially the president, will address their more pressing issues, solutions for which were postponed for the sake of victories abroad.[40]

Fatigue on the part of Russian citizens with regard to the Syrian agenda is further confirmed by polls conducted at the end of 2017 by the Levada Center. Even though it was one of several withdrawal announcements by the Kremlin over the years, the majority of those

Fig. 3.6: The most important events of 2017 in the opinion of Russian citizens.

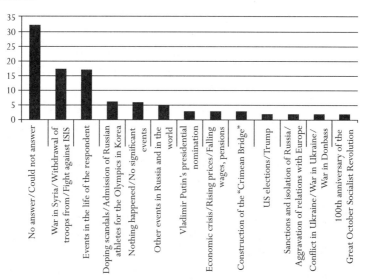

Source: Levada Center, "Siriya i doping" [Syria and Doping], February 1, 2017, www.levada.ru/2018/02/01/siriya-i-doping.

surveyed called "the withdrawal of Russian troops from Syria" the most important event of 2017 (Figure 3.6), outranking "US presidential elections," "construction of the bridge to Crimea," and even Putin's announcement that he would run for president in 2018.

Conclusion

Since the collapse of the Soviet Union, the key problem of Russian foreign policy has been the ruling elite's inability to suggest a viable alternative to Western models, both domestically and in the realm of foreign policy. During Soviet times, communist ideology and party leadership managed to provide a strong alternative to Western narratives, foreign policy included. Ultimately, the Soviets lost the ideological competition. In the contemporary era, Russian foreign policy is adrift. "Eurasianism" and "multipolarity" are concepts favored by the Kremlin, but they have failed to provide Moscow with long-term allies or soft power in the traditionally close post-Soviet space, let alone in the Middle East.

The Putin regime often resorts to conspiracy theories to blame Washington for the woes of the world, constructing an image of Russia as a fortress besieged by the hostile West in order to secure the loyalty and support of the Russian population. However effective these depictions are domestically, they are incapable of serving Russia's long-term foreign policy goals, including in the Middle East. In his speech at the Valdai Discussion Club in 2018, Putin tried to provide some rationale for this state of affairs, noting that "Russia is ready for dialogue … but so far there has been no chance for that to happen … All we can do is wait."[41] The term "strategic patience" has already been coined to describe the Russian leader's view of the country's foreign policy.[42] This term is especially effective, considering that the attitude of the West towards Russia is unlikely to change substantially any time soon. It seems that easing international tensions and rejoining the rules-based international order will be back on the agenda in the post-Putin Russia.

In the mid-term perspective, Russia will continue to formulate its own policy in the MENA region and maintain its rivalry with Washington in order to act in its own national interests. In the long-term perspective, due to its current economic strains and limited resources, Russia will not be able to sustain regional competition with the United States, China, or even the European Union, its military presence in the MENA region notwithstanding. Perhaps the most favorable option for Moscow, given its capabilities and intentions, could be the role of an "honest broker" aiding resolution of regional conflicts, as former Russian foreign minister Andrei Kozyrev once proposed.[43] However, this will require a serious revision of the Kremlin's basic ideas about Russia's role in the world in general and in the MENA region in particular.

4

RUSSIAN LEGAL AND NORMATIVE CLAIMS FOR ITS INTERVENTION IN THE SYRIAN CONFLICT SINCE 2015

Roy Allison

Introduction

Scholarly analyses of Russian military intervention in the Syrian conflict since September 2015 have focused mainly on explanations for this unprecedented post-Cold War case of Russian power projection beyond former Soviet borders. Russian motivations have also been examined, as well as Moscow's complicated diplomacy around the conflict with other regionally influential states. However, one dimension of this intervention has attracted little scholarly attention, although it is significant for Russian domestic politics, for regional state conduct, and for the wider international system: the legal and normative claims Russia has advanced to justify this major use of force.

This chapter argues that such claims matter and should not be interpreted simply in terms of realist theory, as the instrumental language of states in a world governed by geopolitics. Legal and normative arguments seek to legitimize actions internationally and domestically, and the traction they gain is important for states in that it promotes both their international status and influence. Russian arguments have sought to attract the support of states in its favor, as part of a wider contestation in the international system over law and norms. This is shown by how Russia's justifications for its use of force parallel their diplomatic efforts to refute the legality and legitimacy of Western use of force in Syria, which commenced with air strikes against the Islamic State (IS) in September 2014, followed by limited punitive strikes against facilities of the Syrian regime.

For years, Moscow had denounced the unraveling of legal restrictions on the use of force, reflected in the earlier use of force by Western powers in Kosovo, Iraq, and Libya. Russia feared this could empower groups and embolden states intent on overturning regimes. In particular, ever since the NATO intervention in Kosovo in 1999, Russia guarded against Western nations' use of "humanitarian emergency" as a potential justification—providing legitimacy, if not clearly legal support—for military intervention without a UN Security Council mandate, thus bypassing Russia's veto in the UNSC. In 2011, Russia exceptionally acceded to a UN resolution, in the context of a humanitarian crisis, by abstaining from voting, which enabled NATO military action in Libya. Russia later regretted the outcome. All this was in contrast, however, to Russian legal and normative claims over conflicts in the Commonwealth of Independent States (CIS) region; Russia asserted regional entitlements and even used humanitarian claims to justify its interventions in Georgia in 2008 and Crimea in 2014. Therefore, Russia's understanding of the acceptable legal and normative standards for use of force applied to the international system at large was sharply at odds with the same when it came to Russia's post-Soviet neighborhood.

Among the latter, the annexation of Crimea is the most egregious modern case of a state violating Article 51 of the United Nations Charter, which provides strict conditions on the use of force, which is permissible in individual or collective self-defense, or as a decision of the Security Council, acting under Chapter VII, in response to threats to international peace and security. Russia had previously emphasized the overriding role of Article 51, known in legal terms as a "restrictionist" interpretation of the use of force. As the Ukraine crisis continued to sour Russian-Western relations, Russia sought to redirect international attention concerning the principles governing the use of force away from regions in Russia's immediate neighborhood to regions where Article 51 would most likely restrain American rather than Russian power.

At the launch of its military campaign in Syria at the end of September 2015, Moscow hoped to reclaim some legal high ground by presenting the operation as one of collective self-defense, in response to an invitation from the Syrian government and promoting a set of important wider norms. Equally, Russia hoped to coordinate a coalition of states to resist "unjustifiable" Western military action in Syria. Legal claims were bolted onto broader Russian claims for legitimacy derived from appeals around counterterrorism. Its aim was to bolster the sovereignty, integrity, and stability of the Syrian state, and its eventual goal was mediation and conflict resolution. With these arguments, Moscow sought to attract follower states, especially in the "non-West." Legal and normative discourse was crafted to support wider Russian diplomacy around Syria. The response of Middle Eastern states and elites was understood to be especially important. Russian leaders certainly were aware of the Middle East's history of resistance to heavy-handed external military intrusions.

However, the Syria operation is an unprecedented case of Russia's use of force beyond the borders of the former USSR in the post-Cold War period.[1] It is the first such military intervention since the humiliating failure of the ten-year Soviet debacle in Afghanistan, another Muslim state. It does not require a great leap for Russian citizens to view this as an unhappy parallel. In February 2013, Foreign Minister Sergey Lavrov, referring to the Middle East and North Africa, proclaimed, "We will not fight for our positions by sending an expeditionary force to the region and creating our next 'Afghanistan.' Never, no way."[2]

In the case of Afghanistan, the great majority of the international community had rejected Russian justifications for intervention, and the Afghan entanglement contributed to the dissolution of the Soviet state itself. This precedent reinforced the necessity for Russia to craft a contrasting narrative of legality and legitimacy over its action in

Syria, both for states at large as well as to persuade domestic elites and public opinion (assisted by controlled media messaging) to support the deployment of Russian military assets and personnel to Syria. This had to be done quite quickly, since less than two months before Russia began its operation in Syria, President Vladimir Putin's spokesperson still claimed there was no discussion about using Russian military aviation in Syria. The task was to present the surprise military operation as lawful and rightful.

Responding to Invitation by the Syrian State

From the outset of Moscow's operation in Syria, Russian officials claimed it was lawful, on the grounds that Russian action took place at the invitation and with the explicit authorization of the Syrian state, represented by the government led by President Bashar al-Assad.[3] This had a mixed reception. Some states close to Russia explicitly approved Russia's claim. For example, the then chair of the Senate of the Kazakh Parliament, Kasymzhomart Tokayev, declared, "The military operation by Russia is being conducted at the request of the legal government of Syria, under international law."[4] Most states simply refrained from disputing the legal basis of intervention by invitation in this case, which could be interpreted as tacit acceptance.

Indeed, Russia has employed the invitation claim to dispute the legality of other states' strikes or potential interventions in Syria, especially as regards the US-led counterterrorist coalition. Shortly after Russia began its air operations in Syria, Lavrov disputed the justification of the US-led coalition's strikes on Syrian territory based on "the right of preventive self-defense" under Article 51 of the UN Charter. He complained, "I haven't heard of any preventive self-defense concept" in their actions, so "the legal basis of the coalition's activities in Syria is really flawed."[5] Russian operations would remain separate from those of the coalition, he stressed, since "We cannot be part of the coalition, which operates without the Security Council mandate and without the request from one of the countries on whose territories they operate." That would be Syria, since Iraq had made this request.[6]

In April 2017, after the United States struck a Syrian air base in retaliation for the Syrian state's alleged use of chemical weapons against civilians, the Russia-dominated joint command center in Syria issued a statement deploring the US for crossing "red lines." It threatened, "From now on we will respond with force to any aggressor or any breach of red lines from whoever it is and American knows our ability to respond well."[7] However, in practice, the threat was more to give teeth to Syrian air defense, which is technically equipped by Russia and assisted with Russian intelligence, rather than risking a direct Russian-US military clash. Thus, a senior Russian parliamentarian clarified that Russian air defense would not shoot down incoming missiles in the event of another US strike, but it would not prevent Syria from defending itself.[8]

Likewise, the possibility that Saudi Arabia and Turkey might be emboldened by US air operations in Syria to commit their own forces in February 2016 met a scathing response from the head of the international affairs committee in the Federation Council (the upper chamber in Moscow). "The air campaign by the so-called US-led coalition, which includes the Saudis, is illegitimate under international law," he argued, "unlike the Russian military operations there." Indeed, "the deployment of any ground forces by the Saudis and Turks would be all the more so illegitimate. ... It would mean the use of force to overthrow a country's lawful authorities."[9]

This rhetorical barrage failed to stop Turkey from eventually deploying its forces in regions of the Idlib province close to the Turkish border, and Russia even reluctantly assented to that reality in an effort to draw Turkey into Russia-led conflict management in Syria. More dramatically, Presidents Putin and Erdoğan negotiated directly to limit the scale of Turkey's invasion of the Kurdish-controlled sector of northern Syria in October 2019. As a result, Moscow introduced its own military police patrols close to the Turkish border. In this case, Russian officials refrained from joining Syria in officially condemning Turkish aggression, although fully aware this was an illegal offensive with potentially serious territorial implications. A Russian Academy of Sciences researcher was prepared to spell it out: "of course, this is a violation of international law and a violation of the integrity of Syria, insofar as the Turkish army has neither a mandate from the UN nor a request from the Syrian government."[10]

By contrast, the Russian authorities accept that Iran's operations and its ground presence in Syria, to the extent that Tehran acknowledges this exists—in addition to Hezbollah and other non-state Shi'a militias—are covered by an invitation by the Syrian state. This is the legal justification for Iran's various forms of military assistance to the Assad government, whatever political rhetoric about countering American hegemonic ambitions in the region or talk of the need to counter terrorist threats may be heard in Tehran. Moscow is well aware of an agreement on military cooperation signed in August 2018 by Damascus and Tehran, which provides for Iran's assistance in rebuilding the Syrian defense industry and the country's infrastructure.

In parallel, a joint command center set up to coordinate Russian and Iranian forces, as well as other militias fighting for the Assad regime, reinforces Russian-Iranian alignment in the Syrian conflict. The legal dimension of this alignment was expressed in a joint declaration on enhancing the role of international law, signed in June 2020 by Foreign Ministers Sergey Lavrov and Javad Zarif.[11] Speaking from their shared platform, Zarif accused the West of "abusing humanitarian efforts and international rules to see to their purposes" with respect to Syria, and stated that Iran would solicit Russia's help "when it comes to transparency" of any intervention in that region.[12] Given this common front, it seems that Russia also accepts that the military role of Hezbollah and other non-state Shi'a militias in Syria is also covered by an invitation from the Syrian state, although Moscow refrains from spelling this out.

There is some juridical debate, nevertheless, on the legal standing of the "response to invitation" claim, even with regard to Russian military operations.[13] Certain Western lawyers have agreed that such an invitation to Russia by the Syrian state amounts to collective self-defense, is permissible, and does not breach the obligation to refrain from the threat or use of force specified in Article 2 (4) of the UN Charter. It can be pointed out in this context that the International Court of Justice and the International Law Commission of the United Nations have both accepted this interpretation.[14] In the Syrian case, this particular intervention by invitation does not involve one state's use of force against another state, but rather represents the combining of military forces to reestablish peace and security within the territory of the inviting state. So it may be argued that this falls outside the scope of Article 2 (4).

For Russia to invoke the precept of intervention by invitation, however, a core requirement is the consent of the Syrian state and the validity of that consent. The International Court of Justice, the main judicial organ of the United Nations, has been insistent on the prohibition of intervention without state consent in international law, and in this respect the landmark *Nicaragua* case of 1986 and that of *Democratic Republic of Congo v. Uganda* of 2005 remain highly influential.[15] On the face of it, this seems to support the Russian case over Syria. However, the validity of such consent still has to be established.

In this respect, it is relevant first in legal terms that the Syrian government was indisputably under threat by September 2015. It confronted a multifaceted military campaign prosecuted by various armed groups and non-state actors. It had lost control of much of eastern Syria and, most tellingly, Damascus itself was increasingly vulnerable to this resistance. Secondly, the intervention was characterized by clear, multilevel coordination between Russian and Syrian government forces. In the field of air defense and military intelligence, this had commenced already before autumn 2015. Further, the intent of the two sides is expressed in a contract they drew up on August 26, 2015, which outlined the terms of Russian air combat support for the Syrian president. Moscow signed up to an open-ended time commitment for its military deployment in Syria, which either side could terminate with a year's notice.

This agreement resembles in a rather abbreviated way the purpose of status of forces agreements that the United States has signed with countries in which it has military bases. However, the Russian-Syrian agreement maximizes Russian prerogatives and flexibility. For example, Article 2 permits the transfer "without charge" of "Hmeimim airbase in Latakia province, with its infrastructure, as well as the required territory agreed upon between the parties," for the use of the Russian aviation group to be deployed in Syria.[16] Russia has not publicized an official document specifying the invitation for military assistance, but the August 2015 contract and ample proof of coordination structures for Russian and Syrian operations since autumn 2015 confirm Syria's consent to Russia's actions.

It was also highly relevant, as previously noted, that when the Russian air forces began their operations, no state formally contested the legality of this intervention, whatever their criticisms of it. As a state response, this has political consequences, but it also suggests that, despite the Syrian government's loss of control of large swathes of its territory to opposition groups by September 2015, this did not, in legal terms, remove the validity of its consent to the intervention. This is significant when compared to Cold War conflicts, when governments that invited external military assistance in certain civil wars had only controlled part of their national territory. At the time, this had given rise to the legal proposition that the authority and standing of such an invitation would decline and perhaps be lost as territorial control was ceded.

More recent state practice and juridical opinion has not tended to uphold such a sliding scale. However, some legal specialists have changed this qualitative evaluation of the party issuing the invitation (here the Syrian government's control of territory) in an interpretation of the traditional principle of effective control. This is control determined by the "test of acceptance" of governmental authority. Effective control is represented by an authority's ability to govern and enforce public law (note: in itself, this disregards the political nature of the regime). The absence of effective control as it is understood here, it could be argued, delegitimizes the Syrian government, and so calls strongly into question Assad's authority to petition other states for assistance.[17] This, it is suggested, arises from the broader development of international law on statehood.

In practice, states have tended not to apply the above definition of effective control in terms of governability with regard to evaluating the Syrian government's invitation for Russia to intervene. However, the evolution of law on statehood has led to another more significant qualitative evaluation of the Russian intervention—which reprises earlier Russian-Western controversies over interventions in the Middle East—based on the political legitimacy of state authority.

Syrian Government Legitimacy and Russian Intervention

The central issue in this evaluation is the rise of principles of democratic legitimacy in disputes over the recognition of governments. For our case, it gives rise to the question: "Should an invitation by a government or rebel group be judged, at least in part, by the democratic bona fides of the issuing party?"[18] Applying such a legitimacy criterion, or a similar standard of representativeness, renowned legal scholar Marc Weller argued in 2017 that a "very large number of states have determined that the Assad government can no longer fully claim to represent the people of Syria." This group of states, influenced by principles of democratic legitimacy, had not gone so far as in the Libyan case in 2011 where they considered the Libyan Transitional National Council to be the government of Libya. Still, this demonstrated that the Syrian government "no longer has the right to claim full and unfettered international representation of Syria."[19] Therefore, "having been disowned by such a large segment of its population, and over such a long period, it can no longer lawfully invite foreign military force to intervene and fight on its behalf."[20] In Weller's view, a government so disenfranchised is not entitled to keep itself in power through armed intervention by external forces.

A comparison could be made with Ukrainian President Viktor Yanukovych's call for Russian armed intervention in February 2014. This was "without legal effect" since "it occurred after he had lost the power to represent the state due to the public uprising against his rule."[21] Russia called this an unconstitutional coup but did not try to reinstate Yanukovych in response to his plea. Weller criticizes Russia's response in the Syrian case as relying on a "conservative interpretation of international law." This "would hold that a population is trapped within a state and whoever can claim to be the established government has the exclusive right to control what happens to that population." This claim could extend to "the exclusive right to call for foreign military intervention in support of its armed campaign against its own people." In contrast to this conservative interpretation, the more modern view is that international law exists "to protect the people and is vested in the people, rather than in abusive governments."[22]

This dichotomy has not been clear in actual state practice, however, during the extended Syrian crisis. In general, the legitimacy of the Assad government has remained a rather gray area, even for Western states. Various Western governments have consistently called into question the legitimacy of President Assad's government, but none of them has formally recognized the opposition coalition or any element of it as representing the Syrian state. Some states have "recognized" the main opposition group, the Syrian National Coalition, as "the legitimate representative of the people"; however, this was "merely meant as political support for the Syrian people, not as legal recognition of a particular legitimate authority."[23] This contrasts, for example, with official Western state recognition of the authority of the political opposition in Venezuela under Juan Guaido early in 2019, after the presidential elections which Nicolás Maduro claimed he won were disputed as being fraudulent.

Pragmatic concerns influenced the responses of Western leaders as to legal recognition of the Assad regime. From at least 2013, they were increasingly concerned about the growing political influence in Syria of powerful Islamist insurgent groups outside the opposition coalition. Western powers sought an elusive process towards a more inclusive government. In the absence of this outcome, giving full recognition to an alternative to the Assad regime would raise significant political risks of an anti-Western (and anti-Russian) Islamist coalition rising to exert dominant political control in Syria. In this context, President Putin, well aware that most countries were reluctant to formally withhold recognition of Assad's regime, argued rather tortuously before the UN General Assembly—just before the Russian air campaign commenced—that states had the right to determine their own legitimacy. He defined state sovereignty and "the question of the so-called legitimacy of state authority" as "basically about freedom and the right to choose freely one's own future for every person, nation and state."[24] It is the state here, rather than the individual, that counted.

This dominance of the Syrian state, as represented by the government led by Bashar al-Assad, is clearly present in Russia's political narrative justifying its intervention—counterterrorism—though this is also presented as consistent with international law. Russia's claim that it is essentially conducting a counterterrorist campaign with Damascus seeks to bolster the international legitimacy of the action of the Assad regime (still representing the Syrian state) as well as Russian operations. This claim draws on the more fluid post-9/11 global script validating state actions against transnational terrorist groups. Secondly, it is supported by the more recent global revulsion specifically directed toward the acts of IS in Iraq and Syria. Thirdly, it gains support from the readiness of various authoritarian Middle Eastern states that escaped the 2011 Arab Spring uprisings to define resistance to local regimes in the language of terrorism.

Putin appealed to the UN General Assembly with this support base in mind on the cusp of Russia's military intervention. "On the basis of international law," he proclaimed, "we must join efforts to address the problems that all of us are facing and create a genuinely broad international coalition against terrorism." He proposed a Security Council resolution "aimed at coordinating the actions of all the forces that confront the Islamic State and other terrorist organizations."[25] Foreign Minister Lavrov specified that such an anti-terrorist front should operate with the consent of and in close coordination with the region's states. The resolution should work towards shaping "a common understanding of how to approach the war on terror."[26] The call for states to rally behind Russian efforts, in a UN framework, aimed in advance to position Russia's campaign at the center of a legitimate global struggle, with Russia center stage in shaping potential new norms.

This did not transpire. Few states were convinced that Russia was focused primarily on the terrorist challenge once its air force went into action in Syria. Despite Lavrov's claim a couple of weeks into the operation that "we are willing to coordinate our actions with the patriotic Syrian opposition" to recapture territories from the terrorists, Russian strikes primarily targeted the Syrian resistance, rather than IS or more extreme Islamist groups. Lavrov now sought to juxtapose Russia's proposed counterterrorist coalition, "subject to consent from the countries where military action should take place" (that is Syria), with the existing multinational US-led coalition in action against IS, whose legal foundations for operations in Syria were extremely shaky.[27] In polarizing language, Lavrov blamed the terrorist challenge on Western states themselves, arguing, "Ultimately, the problem of terrorism spreading in the Middle East is due to the fact that statehood in Iraq, Libya, and now Syria is being destroyed."[28] This rhetoric returned to Russia's core statist concerns, but it also showed that the vision of Russia leading and championing a counterterrorist front and developing norms around such statist principles had quickly dissipated.

This analysis of state responsibility to invite armed assistance and the related issue of the legitimacy of such state authority assumes that the military forces deployed are acknowledged as representatives of the state they come from. This acknowledgment makes it necessary to justify the use of such forces by their parent state. However, Russia has relied quite heavily on "private" military and security contractors (PMCs) to provide armed personnel—which are in effect mercenaries—on the ground in Syria, often for frontline roles. The Wagner private military company in particular has been notorious for its role in Syrian operations, as well as operations in Ukraine. It is reportedly secretly overseen by Russian Military Intelligence (GRU) and armed by the Russian state, though it has revealed no official links with Russian forces on paper. Such PMCs recruit mercenaries, but could also provide a thin cover for Russian special forces and other entities whose combat role and casualties Moscow would prefer not to have to own up to. PMCs offer Russia plausible deniability in sensitive operations. They have been analyzed by Western specialists as part of a spectrum of Russian activities that occur in a gray area between coercion and open combat.[29]

However, the operation of PMCs in Syria weakens Russia's legal and normative narrative. It might appear that these unacknowledged forces are implicitly covered by the collective self-defense invitation issued by Damascus to the regular Russian forces, since the presence of the PMCs seems to be accepted by the Syrian government as part of the wider Russian military contribution. From this perspective, their role is similar to that of the irregular Shiʻa militias that augment the Iranian ground forces present in Syria. However, the invitation Syria extended was to the Russian state, and Russia has demonstrably avoided state accountability for the actions of its PMCs in Syria, including for the significant casualties they have incurred. This is in part to camouflage Russian military operations; indeed, Putin's first acknowledgment that Russian PMCs were active in Syria came only in June 2019, when he claimed they were there "in their private capacity" and that "it has nothing to do with the Russian state or the

Russian army and, therefore, we do not comment on this subject."[30] When the Wagner Group suffered heavy casualties alongside pro-Syrian government forces in a firefight with US troops in February 2018, Russia shrugged off accountability. This avoided the risk of a serious escalation in the crisis vis-à-vis Washington. Also, by suppressing news of the deaths of Russian citizens in this clash, the Russian authorities hoped to prevent an erosion of support for Russia's military role in Syria.[31]

In short, Russian PMCs in Syria have operated in a legal limbo. With this shadow presence, many states would regard them as less legitimate actors in the Syrian civil war than armed indigenous opposition groups that attracted widespread domestic support fighting the Syrian regime. Yet, referring to the latter, Putin has claimed that the "provision of military support to illegal structures runs counter to the principles of modern international law."[32] In this assessment, Putin focuses on the sovereign authority of the Damascus regime, which alone has the legitimacy to issue an invitation for assistance. However, his claim clashes with Russia's clandestine support for PMCs in Syria.

International Humanitarian Law, Human Rights, and the Russian Intervention

Russia's view that sovereignty remains in the hands of a recognized government repudiates the notion that the population is the true sovereign. This position is reflected in Moscow's approach to the humanitarian dimensions of the Syrian crisis. This firstly weakens the Russian claim for lawful intervention in support of the Syrian government. Secondly, it has encouraged a lax or dismissive Russian attitude to the separate body of international humanitarian law (IHL) throughout the Syrian crisis. Using this corpus of international law and norms, based on the Hague and Geneva Conventions, as criteria, it is difficult to claim that Russian actions have been lawful.

In the first place, the argument might be made that the Syrian government's consent to Russian military intervention is rendered invalid if subsequent Russian actions enable acts (by Syrian or Russian forces) which violate obligations that are mandatory for all states under a peremptory norm of international law. In other words, consent is invalid if it enables the use of force in a way that would be viewed as illegal under international law.[33] Such generally acknowledged peremptory norms, or "intransgressible principles of international customary law," include prohibitions of genocide, crimes against humanity, and torture.[34] In international law, the obligation to prevent these atrocities is *jus cogens* (a peremptory norm): it cannot be avoided by any state irrespective of whether they are signatories to their respective conventions. This directs attention to the effect of Russian air strikes on the human population in Syria, both as a direct result and in terms of the precedent such strikes set for what the Syrian government is enabled to do to its population, as we consider below.

In practice, the especially grave charges of genocide or crimes against humanity require a high threshold of proof. States have been reluctant to accuse Russia, it being a UNSC member, directly of such offences, or even to formally charge the Syrian regime, despite evidence of atrocities. This reluctance has been reinforced by evidence of crimes of this nature undoubtedly committed by IS and its affiliates, which Russia has identified (albeit unconvincingly) as the primary target of its strikes.

Therefore, there has been more focus by Western states, Turkey, Gulf states, and human rights organizations (such as Amnesty International, Human Rights Watch, and the Syrian Observatory on Human Rights) on more easily determined violations of international humanitarian law by Syrian and Russian forces. Evidence of the Syrian government's complicity in the use of chemical weapons—especially the use of sarin in Eastern Ghouta in 2013 and of chlorine in Douma in 2018—and Russia's disavowal of such evidence has been especially controversial. The Syrian regime's use of sarin bombs in April 2017 on the town of Khan Sheikhoun, killing ninety people, even prompted retaliatory strikes from the United States, raising the risk of a wider clash with Russia.

However, Russian culpability in violations of IHL has been easier to confirm in the case of the large numbers of Russian air strikes against supposed "terrorists." Conducted in civilian areas controlled by Syrian opposition groups of various political hues, they regularly targeted civilian infrastructure, such as hospitals, in violation of

IHL. This in itself has resulted in a large civilian death toll in the bombing campaign, especially in the final assault for control of Aleppo in December 2016.[35] Amnesty International has repeatedly called on Russian forces and authorities "to abide by the rules of war, ensure humanitarian access to civilians in need, and stop hampering international efforts to investigate and prosecute crimes under international law."[36]

This appeal to Russia extends beyond the separate operations of its own forces. According to the Geneva Conventions (1949), states engaged in multinational operations (in this case Russia, Syria, and arguably Iran) are required to opt out of operations that are expected to violate the Conventions, whether by a knowledge of facts or a past pattern of action; otherwise, this is defined as assisting the violations. Russia has acceded to or facilitated the Syrian regime's heinous use of barrel bombs, cluster munitions, and phosphorus bombs within cities, and in this sense Moscow cannot evade responsibility under the framework of IHL for such actions. Indeed, Russian forces seem to have operated in close coordination with their Syrian counterparts, with an extensive command and control presence across Syria allowing them to link up in this way. This includes a Russian coordination and advisory network with the Syrian military, as well as the Coordination Centre for Reconciliation of Opposing Sides, based at Khmeimim airbase, which has had a role in humanitarian aid and support as well as, reportedly, a significant role in intelligence gathering and combat operations.[37]

To consider this further, Russia is bound by IHL to protect civilians and civilian objects and to restrict the means and methods employed by its military. Therefore, it should be bound by the principles of distinction, proportionality, and precaution: including, in essence, the need to distinguish between civilians and combatants, as well as between civilian objects and military targets, and to take all feasible precautions in choosing weapons and methods of warfare so as to avoid excessive loss of civilian life or damage that would outweigh the projected military advantage. The protection of civilians was placed at the core of the protocols added to the Geneva Convention in 1977.

Russia has signed and ratified these protocols and is a party of further major IHL treaties, including the 1980 Conventional Weapons

Convention and its five protocols, and the 1993 Chemical Weapons Convention. Thus, Russian actions fall under the legal purview of these treaties. By contrast, the competence of the International Criminal Court (ICC) and its ability to launch investigations are restricted since Syria has not signed the ICC's Rome Charter and Russia has not ratified it; indeed, Moscow withdrew from it in 2016. Therefore, a case on Russia can only be opened through a referral from the UNSC, which Russia would veto. Nor is it likely that a separate court will be established to prosecute war crimes in Syria through an authorization of the Security Council—as was the case, for example, with the International Criminal Tribunal for Yugoslavia—given that Russia holds veto rights.

Russia has repeatedly acknowledged its legal obligations to protect civilians in its Syrian operations, arguing: "The Russian party does everything possible in order to prevent victims among civilians and does not assign targets located in towns."[38] From early in its campaign in Syria, the Russian UN envoy condemned "the politicization of human rights and humanitarian topics" in the Syrian conflict and "specious observations" on alleged civilian deaths from Russian air strikes.[39]

However, as the campaign developed, there were many credible reports of Russian violations of IHL, such as the use of concrete-piercing unguided "bunker busting" bombs in Aleppo and other urban areas that caused entire buildings to collapse. Such actions continued late into the campaign, including during efforts to regain control over Idlib province in 2019. Citing first responders, witnesses, and open-source material, Human Rights Watch accused the Syrian-Russian "military alliance" of using a "cocktail of internationally banned and indiscriminate weapons."[40] Attacks on civilians in northwestern Syria reportedly used cluster munitions, incendiary weapons, and barrel bombs. In August 2019, the UN Secretary General authorized an investigation into a surge of Russian and Syrian air strikes against hospitals and clinics in northwestern Syria, an area where only Russian and Syrian warplanes were operating, amid growing concerns that Russia had been using UN-supplied data to deliberately target medical facilities.[41]

In November 2019, Federica Mogherini, the EU foreign policy chief, condemned "indiscriminate attacks on critical civilian infrastructure, including health and education facilities, by the Syrian regime and its allies." All parties to the conflict, she insisted, "are bound to respect and uphold international humanitarian law and international human rights law."[42] Nevertheless, a UN report, based on the board of enquiry set up, found a number of cases in the battle for Idlib province where it was plausible or probable that air forces of "the regime and/or its allies" attacked hospitals or clinics whose coordinates had been shared to ensure they were not hit.[43]

Western military analysts have even claimed that Russian and Syrian forces have implemented a strategy to depopulate rebel-held areas in order to prevent insurgents from reinfiltrating any civilian population that remains. This is effected through the use of weapons designed to inflict physical damage and terrify the population into leaving.[44] In this way, the bombing of civilian targets was closely tied to military strategy on the ground.[45] Chemical weapons attacks by the Syrian armed forces in areas of civilian populations, of which there were credible reports, could represent an extreme variant of this strategy. The UN-affiliated Organization for the Prohibition of Chemical Weapons (OPCW) reported on a number of cases where there were reasonable grounds to believe the Syrian regime had used sarin and chlorine on civilians.[46] In response, Moscow has obstructed independent investigations into such reports, accusing Syrian resistance groups and "terrorists" of these grave violations of IHL.

Russia's approach to these IHL claims relies on deniability and contestation over facts, as is the case with aspects of its military policy in Ukraine since 2014.[47] Unlike US-led coalition forces operating over Iraq and Syria, Russia lacks a civilian casualty-monitoring cell. It has also failed to engage with NGOs documenting civilian casualties, even disparaging them with accusations of political partiality. The Russian Ministry of Defense has argued that allegations of civilian casualties at Russian hands are manipulations to distract attention from civilian casualties caused by US-led actions in Syria and Iraq. It has also published alternative narratives and information, much of which has been exposed as false by investigative monitoring organizations, such as the online collective Bellingcat.[48]

Russian leaders expect this effort to deflect IHL claims against Russia to have some discursive traction in the wider international community, especially in the Middle East, as well as in the controlled media environment in domestic Russian politics. For one matter, the US-led antiterrorist coalition 'the Global Coalition to Defeat ISIS' itself ratcheted up civilian casualties in its final major offensives against the Islamic State. President Putin has especially emphasized the high civilian death toll from the coalition's four-month aerial bombardment campaign to liberate Raqqa in 2017. In response, an Amnesty International official called on the coalition to conduct meaningful investigations and reparations over hundreds of civilians killed in the campaign. Nevertheless, she condemned Putin as "beyond cynical" in using "civilian deaths in Raqqa to deflect attention from Russia's own role in horrific violations contributing to the deaths of tens of thousands of civilians and the displacement of millions during Syria's war."[49]

The scale of the casualties caused by Russian actions is not so easily overshadowed by pointing the finger at the events of Raqqa. Putin relies more heavily on a consistent broader Russian narrative about the destructive human consequences of Western military interventions in the Middle East, especially Iraq in 2003 and Libya in 2011. Offering a simple causality, this claim has attracted substantial political support within the region, as well as among ex-colonial states prone to suspicion of Western military actions. Some researchers have adopted a similar line, that foreign military interventions produce deleterious effects on human rights in the target states.[50]

Russia contrasts such Western interventions for regime change or "spurious" humanitarian objectives with Russia's supposed mission of countering Islamist terrorism in Syria, specifically IS, but also affiliated groups such as Jabhat al-Nusra (despite its disavowal of allegiance to IS) and Hayat Tahrir al-Sham in Idlib province. Moscow seeks to align Russian objectives with the broad international revulsion for the gross human rights violations by IS. However, this obscures the reality, as previously noted, that the great majority of Russian air strikes have been against other Syrian opposition groups fighting the Assad regime.

Even so, IHL considerations also apply to the conduct of the Russian strikes targeting IS (which are in the minority), with the outcome in principle being to degrade this object of the US-led coalition. Noncombatant casualties are equally reprehensible in this case as those incurred in the context of Russian strikes against non-IS opponents to the Syrian regime. This raised legal and normative questions for Western states during US-Russia negotiations over a plan for coordinated US and Russian military strikes against IS and al-Nusra in 2016. Is the United States, in essence, legally permitted to coordinate in this way if it is highly likely that Russia will engage in serious violations of the law of armed conflict in carrying out its part of the operations?[51]

Fundamentally, such a coordination could be viewed as the United States breaching its duty not to assist another state in committing serious violations of international law. This derives from the customary law on state responsibility, whereby a state is responsible if it intentionally and/or knowingly gives another state assistance that contributes to intentionally wrongful conduct that the assisting state may not itself commit. This could be as simple as, for example, the United States regularly providing Russia with targeting intelligence, an option which was probably discussed.[52]

The breakdown of the negotiations, conducted between Secretary of State John Kerry and Foreign Minister Sergey Lavrov, left this as a hypothetical dilemma. Still, it highlights Russian legal culpability, arising from its own coordination with Syrian forces, if we accept the claim by the US ambassador to the UN at the time, which is consistent with reports of local NGOs, that "since 2011, the Assad regime has been intentionally striking civilian targets with horrifying, predictable regularity."[53] For Russia, this culpability is not just a legal issue, but also one that has threatened serious reputational damage in the wider international community. Russia has repeatedly blocked Security Council draft resolutions to prosecute war crimes in Syria. Global opinion was reflected in a UN General Assembly vote at the end of 2016, despite strenuous objections from Russia and Syria, to establish a panel to prepare cases involving war crimes and human rights abuses in Syria. The resolution was passed 105 to 12, with 52 abstentions.[54]

Russian-Style Humanitarianism in Syria

As part of its diplomatic response to these charges of violation of IHL, Russian officials have tried to present Russia as advancing humanitarian objectives in Syria. Russia has engaged in a normative effort to co-opt the humanitarian agenda, while shielding the Assad regime, and so helped legitimize the Russian presence in Syria. As discussed later, this forms part of Russia's broader claim to be advancing civilian protection through its own interpretation of Responsibility to Protect (R2P). This is distinguished from the Western variant of R2P, which evokes humanitarian emergencies to justify military interventions. Russia has accused Western states of repeated attempts to gain support for UNSC resolutions on the use of force, in order to enable their politicized interventions to go forth under the guise of bringing a stop to large-scale human rights violations and genocide.[55] Russia (alongside China) has blocked the approval of such language authorizing force in Security Council resolutions. But at the same time, Russia has tried to use UNSC negotiations on humanitarian access in Syria to propagate its own claim to be offering humanitarian assistance, as well as to reinforce the authority of the Syrian government.

Beyond the UNSC, a forum where Russian claims are frequently strongly contested by Western powers, Russia has sought approval for its humanitarian discourse among like-minded authoritarian states, which have a strongly state-centered rather than human-centered understanding of international law and share Russia's expansive definition of its counterterrorist actions in Syria. For example, in May 2019 a joint communiqué of the defense ministers of member states of the Shanghai Cooperation Organization glossed over the destructive human impact of Russian air operations in Syrian towns. Indeed, it praised Russia for its role in destroying terrorist organizations in Syria, and for "providing humanitarian assistance to the people of Syria and helping restore Syrian infrastructure."[56]

Iran offers similar normative claims for its growing ground presence in Syria. However, Russia has been cautious not to overplay this aspect of Russian-Iranian alignment in its diplomatic discourse. Moscow is aware that much of the international community perceives of Iran's motives in Syria as suspect. Additionally, there are risks of association with the sectarian image of a Shi'a axis of Iran, an 'Alawite Syrian leadership, Hezbollah and other Shi'a militias, and Lebanon.[57]

Russia has tried to enshrine the statist legal principle of Syrian government consent in arrangements for humanitarian access to Syria. Moscow used this to reinforce its narrative on its justified presence in Syria, as well as to force other states to deal directly with the

Syrian government in an effort to bolster its standing in the civil war. Therefore, Russia has opposed the delivery of aid across the borders of neighboring states without the approval of Syria's "legitimate authorities," as contrary to international law. Russia has referred to UN General Assembly Resolution 46/182, which enjoins respect for basic norms of international law in planning humanitarian emergency assistance. On this basis, Moscow has claimed that "Russian diplomats managed to uphold the principle of transborder aid deliveries to civilians with international (UN) oversight and respect for the country's sovereignty and territorial integrity."[58] This followed approval of Security Council Resolution 2165 in July 2014, which formed a UN mission to inspect aid convoys delivering aid to Syria across the borders of neighboring states.

However, as the Syrian regime extended its control of contested territory, Russia hardened its position, further impeding humanitarian access to areas controlled by opposition groups. In December 2019, Russia and China vetoed a draft Security Council resolution (supported by the other thirteen members of the Security Council), which would have extended the delivery of cross-border humanitarian aid to Syria for a year. The Russian envoy to the UN claimed that the Syrian government controlled enough checkpoints to deliver humanitarian aid itself, and that much of the aid had been co-opted by what he defined as "terrorist groups." Then he referred to international legal requirements that aid be provided in coordination with the national government.[59]

Despite its military campaign in Syria, Russia has described its humanitarian assistance as being above the political fray of the Syrian conflict. It has deplored the sanctions introduced by the United States, the EU, and the Arab League against the Syrian regime over its humanitarian excesses. In contrast, Russia's own humanitarian assistance, it proclaimed, "has never been predicated on any preconditions or on the political situation of the moment."[60] Russian air forces conducted various ostensible "humanitarian operations," for example, in spring 2016, during which they brought aid to the residents of Deir ez-Zor, a city which had been blockaded by IS militants. Russia also presented itself as a major donor to projects run by UN humanitarian agencies and the ICRC.

Another set of humanitarian claims concern the role of the Russian Orthodox Church (ROC), which is closely tied to the Russian state, in helping the Syrian people. Russian officials pointed to aid from bodies in Russia such as the Imperial Orthodox Palestinian Society and the Russar Foundation, as well as the Orthodox Syrian community in Russia.[61] Patriarch Kirill of the ROC has stressed the close cooperation of the church with nongovernmental organizations and government agencies in delivering and distributing humanitarian aid in Syria.[62] By 2019, this extended to some church reconstruction in Syria. Syria's Christians have been presented as part of a common culture with the Russian Orthodox community.[63]

The Russian leadership has relied on the ROC to legitimize the broader Russian role in Syria, primarily through a narrative aimed at the Russian population. The Russian media depict Russia's presence in Syria as having the blessing of the ROC. Russian military clerics propagate the same message among the Russian armed forces and emphasize Russian protection of Syria's ancient Christian communities. Russian officials translate this guardian role into a rationale for sustaining Assad's rule in order to prevent persecution, or worse, of Christians by Islamist factions. Foreign Minister Lavrov set the tone years before Russia deployed its forces to Syria with the claim that "Assad personifies the guarantor of the security of the minorities, including Christians, who live in Syria and have lived there for centuries."[64] This argument has some resonance in Russia, as part of a broader state-promoted revival of religious and traditional values. It also appeals to conservative Christian movements in the United States and Europe.

However, references to the religious impulses justifying Russian military action since 2015 have risked inspiring "crusader" imagery among Muslim leaders and communities in the Middle East. This would both fuel local sectarianism and complicate Russia's wider engagement with influential states in the region, as well as with organizations such as the Organisation of Islamic Cooperation, the Arab League, and the Gulf Cooperation Council. Nor can ROC rhetoric expedite Russia's effort to obtain the support of Turkey, Iran, and the Gulf states behind the Astana conflict resolution process. It is also relevant to note that, by 2019, the civil war had forced the exodus from Syria of much of its Armenian Orthodox community and many others affiliated with the ROC. There are clear limits, therefore, to overstating the agency of the ROC in Syria.

Russia's various humanitarian activities have supposedly been facilitated by the opening of the Coordination Centre for Reconciliation of Opposing Sides in Syria at Russia's Khmeimim air base in February 2016, which helped ensure the passage of UN aid convoys to parts of the country that were blocked. Russia even claimed that it undertook a large-scale humanitarian operation in Aleppo in July 2016. However, this occurred even as it facilitated military operations that ushered in a crescendo of civilian deaths and destruction at the end of the year, when the Syrian regime wrested back its control of the city. In brief, the normative claim was that it was only through Russia's efforts that aid "eventually reached all besieged population centres in Syria," and that "Russia remains the only state that is committed to resolving the concrete problems related to ensuring humanitarian access" in Syria.[65]

This Russian interpretation of humanitarianism has been accompanied by narratives on Russia's role as the sponsor of conflict resolution and even as a potential provider of "peacekeeping." These claims portray Russia as the stabilizing, state-building power in the region, in keeping with broader Russian statist principles. A Russian specialist described Moscow's agenda for conflict settlement in 2014 as reflecting "Russia's preferred normative approach: direct talks between the sides of the conflict without prior international intervention and regime change."[66] In fact, Russia intervened militarily the next year expressly to preempt regime change. Moscow's conflict resolution efforts subsequently sought to vindicate that intervention, which occurred just as Assad's hold on power was crumbling, and to shore up the beleaguered regime.

These efforts to lead conflict resolution have been channeled through the Astana negotiation process, in uneasy coordination with Iran and Turkey. Moscow characterizes this process as the precondition to any wider humanitarian relief, including the return of refugees, large-scale reconstruction, and so on. Thus, Russia has tied humanitarian alleviation to a form of conflict resolution heavily skewed towards the political preferences of Damascus. Despite claims that it would be ready to meet all parties in the Syrian conflict, Moscow never appeared seriously prepared to sponsor even-handed talks between (non-jihadist) opposition forces in Syria and the incumbent authorities. Russia has tried to give the impression that it seeks to create an environment in which political negotiations towards a political solution for the future of Syria might occur between a "principled" government and a "moderate" opposition, but most states remain very skeptical of Russian impartiality.

To be sure, Russia cannot simply control the positions Syria adopts. Russian officials have claimed that their support for the Syrian state should not be translated as enduring support for the current Syrian president. They seek to distinguish, rather unconvincingly, between supporting Syrian state institutions and supporting the person of Assad. In addition, Moscow has warned the Syrian government not to pursue Assad's declared goal of retaking control of all Syrian territory through a total military victory over all opponents, including the Syrian Kurds. These mild qualifications to Russian alignment with Syria have had little restraining effect on the Assad regime's policies or on events on the ground, except in forestalling to some extent a total offensive in Idlib province.

A misleading strand of Russia's normative narrative on humanitarianism in Syria, linked to the country's stabilization, has been its qualified support for "peacekeeping" operations in some guise. At an early stage in the conflict, a senior Russian parliamentarian claimed that Russia might consider participation in a peacekeeping operation in Syria if the UN authorized it. However, this would be motivated by more than mere altruism: "nothing does more to enhance Russia's positive image abroad than what our peacekeepers are doing in Africa and the Middle East."[67] In other words, peacekeeping for Russia is largely about status enhancement.

This prospect was never likely since Lavrov ruled that sending peacekeepers to Syria not only would be the decision of the Security Council, but would also require the consent of the Syrian government (which would likely be withheld).[68] Reports had circulated that Russian troops might be committed under the aegis of the Russia-led Collective Security Treaty Organization, perhaps as part of a UN- or Western-led peacekeeping deployment. However, the CSTO secretary-general had envisaged "peace enforcement" in Syria involving the CSTO as potentially utilizing heavy weapons to suppress the fighters of the Syrian opposition forces.[69] This had none of the impartiality of UN peacekeeping. Russian interest in reviving the notion of a CSTO deployment in 2018 seemed intended to show wider support for the Russian strategic presence in Syria: for example, if Kazakhstan were present. However, the Kazakh government was explicit that it could not deploy forces in Syria outside a UN mandate.[70]

Russia and the Application of Responsibility to Protect

Responsibility to Protect has failed to act as a constraint on the violence suffered by civilians in Syria, either before or after the Russian intervention in 2015. This is despite R2P's intended purpose, as an evolving international norm, to deter mass atrocities, and despite considerable evidence of such atrocities in what became the world's worst humanitarian emergency in and around Syria. There has been little effort by states even to invoke R2P, although R2P in itself does not create any legal obligation for states to act. It has not added to the corpus of UN procedural laws, and any coercive intervention related to R2P is only possible as a Chapter VII action with a Security Council mandate. There has been even less effort to invoke explicit international legal frameworks for humanitarian intervention—given the controversy attached to this concept ever since the 1999 intervention in Kosovo—in response to the Syrian conflict, or indeed the parallel conflict in Yemen.[71] R2P has remained backstage in the debate and rhetoric around Russian intervention in Syria, and it scarcely featured even during early Russian support for Assad's regime.

Any coercive action by outside states in the name of R2P requires a Security Council mandate. The fact that this has not been done—despite many rancorous debates on the mounting humanitarian crisis in Syria—reflects the inability of the UN Security Council to act. It follows persistent controversy over the invocation of R2P to justify military intervention in Libya in 2011.[72] In retrospect, Resolution 1973, which authorized the use of force in Libya and was framed by R2P discourse in the Security Council in March 2011, was no model for the future, even though it was adopted just as demonstrations mounted in Syria. It was situational: the principle of R2P was applied in Libya because at the time the need to protect lives coincided with the interests of the intervening states. For Russia, both foreign policy considerations and domestic politics (Putin had not yet returned to the presidency in 2011) were involved.[73]

This reality of state interests is important, but R2P also reflects an underlying competition in the international community over which norms assume primacy in interstate conduct, which has only exacerbated since 2011. The possibilities for action based on R2P have fallen victim to this contest. Many Western states have viewed R2P as a normative complement to Chapter 7 of the UN Charter, which in certain acute crises may authorize forceful intervention in the internal affairs of states. In contrast, a significant group of non-Western states, led by Russia and China, has given primacy to the principle of non-intervention in the application of R2P.[74] As a result, R2P has remained an unconsolidated and rather fluid norm.

Consequently, no agreement has been reached in the Security Council on a resolution to authorize, even conditionally, the use of force aimed at saving civilian lives in Syria, with Russia at the forefront of resistance to such discourse.[75] Russia has blocked all language that envisages coercive action to counteract IHL violations, and has tended to avoid even the terminology of R2P around Syria. This is despite Russian knowledge that the prevention of genocide, of war crimes, and of crimes against humanity are international peremptory norms: that is, under customary international law, this prevention is obligatory for all UN members.

Nevertheless, Russia could make a rather weak case that its action in the Syrian crisis conforms to R2P expectations on state action. It could refer especially to discussion in UN documents such as the 2009 report, "Implementing the Responsibility to Protect," which sets out a framework within which R2P is aimed at strengthening rather than undermining sovereignty through various diplomatic and non-military measures.[76] In this UN discussion, three "pillars" are proposed in envisaging the implementation of R2P, with Russia emphasizing the first and second pillar to support the notion of "sovereignty as responsibility." In line with this, under the first pillar it is primarily the enduring responsibility of the state and its authorities to protect its populations from grave crimes, which fits Russian statist normative preferences.[77]

The second pillar refers to the commitment of the international community to support states in fulfilling the demands of the first pillar. This might be interpreted as capacity building, which involves support for the domestic government and the actions it takes to liberate civilians from the atrocities of armed conflict. Moscow might claim this has been expressed through its efforts to bolster the fight against IS and other radical groups responsible for atrocities.[78] However, the fact that Russia has only given partial commitment to this end on the ground since 2015—prioritizing harsh military actions against other opposition groups in localities with large civilian populations—counteracts this claim.

The third pillar of R2P is the responsibility of member states to respond collectively and decisively when a state is manifestly failing to provide the protections in the first pillar.[79] However, this does not just mean taking enforcement measures under Chapter VII of the UN Charter, as undertaken in the controversy over Libya, but also making regional arrangements and ensuring pacific measures. A jurist sympathetic to the Russian case has argued that in Syria, such measures entail "the implementation of post-conflict reconstruction and reconciliation as a means of restoring rule of law and normalcy after the conflict," as manifested in the peace talks mediated by Putin.[80]

Here, the Astana process could be cited to the extent that it seeks a relatively more inclusive Syrian political structure. Russian officials might further claim that various measures analyzed above under "Russian-style humanitarianism" in Syria (deconfliction zones, humanitarian corridors, etc.) represent efforts at reconciliation, in keeping with R2P's third pillar. However, these claims are unpersuasive, given the evidence of Russia's close collaboration with the Syrian government's actions that gravely breach IHL, and of Moscow's direct contribution to those actions. Therefore, focusing on Russia's role in the Astana process as an expression of R2P's normative vision is similar to arguing that the end justifies the means. It diverts attention from the all-important goal of alleviating egregious human rights violations.

Conclusion: Responses to Russian Normative Claims

Russia's intervention in Syria since 2015, which it presents as a counterterrorist operation, is Moscow's first major military action outside the former Soviet region in the post-Cold War era. It has been important for the Russian leadership to try to construct a convincing legal and normative case for this use of force and gain recognition for its justifications by states in the region, by the wider international community, and within Russia itself. The overall bold claim, as expressed by Putin by October 2019, is that "In Syria, Russia and its partners ... managed to do a lot while adhering to and following norms of international law, respecting sovereignty and thinking primarily about the life, safety and interests of the people."[81] This kind of statement should be understood as an expression of the politics of international law and deconstructed on that basis. The justifications for Russia's intervention, as well as claims to its legality and legitimacy, are not just abstract and juridical. They have real political and policy consequences. We indicate this in concluding with further comments on the purposes, audiences, and reception of Russia's claims.

Russia's core claim of intervention by invitation of the Syrian state has been a strong card to play on the international stage. Firstly, it can be contrasted with Western states' (or Israeli) military strikes on Syrian territory, with Moscow looking to take the moral high ground in many forums, including the Security Council, by claiming to be complying with the very restricted UN Charter exceptions to the prohibition of the use of force. Russia has sought to present itself, at least to the non-Western community of states, as a stalwart defender of international law in condemning President Trump's missile strikes on Syria in 2017 and 2018 (in retaliation for chemical weapons attacks),[82] President Biden's air strikes targeting Iranian-backed militias in Syria in February 2021 (in retaliation for rocket attacks on US targets in Iraq), and Israel's numerous strikes in Syria (aimed at stopping arms transfers to Hezbollah). Russia is thus aware that voicing such condemnation can command attention from countries outside of the Middle East, since there is no recognized international legal right of armed reprisal, right to use military force for deterrence, or right to attack Iran on the territory of Syria.[83]

Secondly, Russia's claim to the legality and legitimacy of its intervention in Syria aims to deflect attention from its egregiously illegal annexation of Crimea and military intervention in eastern Ukraine since 2014. This is not just rhetorical shadowboxing in international forums, but an important effort by Russia to preserve its diplomatic capital and access to countries in a period of polarizing Russian-Western relations. It is part of an attempt in particular to maintain its international reputation and status among the many states unwilling to openly align themselves with the Western portrayal of Russia as an aggressor in Ukraine, as shown in the bloc of UN General Assembly abstentions during key votes over Crimea.[84] Many of these abstaining states have also been reluctant to accede to Western efforts to replace the Assad leadership in Syria, given the turmoil that followed the overthrow of regimes in Iraq and Libya. China especially has become Russia's principal source of political and discursive support in the Security Council, reinforcing Russian claims of Assad's continued legitimacy as the Syrian head of state.

Russia has also had to convince its own domestic elites and public of the legitimacy of its Syria operations. After all, Russian leaders have deplored Western military interventions ranging from Kosovo in 1999 to Libya in 2011. Moscow presented its Syria operations in a different light, claiming to be defending Syrian state authority and "constitutional order." This fitted the domestic political needs of President Putin's leadership, especially since his reelection in 2012, as well as Moscow's narrative about the Western orchestration of "color revolutions." Russian leaders had condemned such uprisings as the Rose Revolution in Georgia (2003) and Orange Revolution in Ukraine (2005), which they claimed culminated in 2014 in an "anti-constitutional coup" ousting Ukrainian President Yanukovych (the Maidan Revolution). In the case of Syria, the Russian domestic audience has received the debate over legal claims and counterclaims in a filtered and simple form, delivered by Russian diplomats through centrally controlled media outlets. The broad message of Russian legality and legitimacy in the media and official commentary on Syria reinforces other narratives on practical Russian interests, particularly the need to suppress terrorist threats to Russia emanating from Syria and to defend the Syrian state as a traditional ally.

However, Russian leaders are aware that much of the Russian public has either not forgotten or has learned of the military quagmire that was Soviet intervention in Afghanistan during the 1980s. Many in Russian elite circles also recall that in this humiliating case global opinion beyond the Warsaw Pact states and their few allies was unanimous in its condemnation of the illegality of the Soviet invasion and occupation. The international community was also cynical about Moscow's claim to be acting in response to an invitation from the legitimate Afghan leadership that was threatened by an insurgency. This helps explain Putin's (frustrated) effort in September 2015 to cast Russia as occupying the center of an international counterterrorist coalition, with the normative resonance that might offer.

This is not to say that the Russian leadership has lacked any interest in how their intervention in Syria relates to principles of international order. They have been acutely sensitive to any claims that standards of political legitimacy—whether democratic or otherwise—can be applied either to justify military action against Assad's regime by Western states or to undermine the legal authority of Assad's invitation to Russian forces based on collective defense. Such claims, which question the standing of the inviting authority, strike at the heart of Russian statist focus on sovereignty and traditionalist focus on the letter of the UN Charter principles. They also serve to delegitimize Russian relationships more broadly with a variety of authoritarian leaderships. Russia also associates this line of normative reasoning with previous efforts by Western states—especially the United States—to bypass the Security Council and so devalue Russia's prized veto rights within it.

Russia's effort to cast Western states and Israel as serial violators of international law with regard to Syria has failed to make much headway in international fora, due to the glaring inconsistency of Russia's principled sovereignty-focused case with its continuing support of separatism in eastern Ukraine and its retention of the annexed region of Crimea. As detailed in this chapter, a fierce and compelling critique of the legal standing of Russian operations in Syria has been presented in the field of international humanitarian law. Russia's flat denial of its responsibility for human rights violations has a depressing familiarity, not only with Russian claims over its various actions in

Ukraine since 2014 (where Russia denies it has been a belligerent party), but also with Moscow's responses much earlier to the large-scale killing of civilians in its domestic jurisdiction, during the second war in Chechnya from 1999.

Russia has not only acceded to gross violations against civilians by the Assad regime; it has also contributed to those war crimes through its methods of warfare and use of banned weapons. Moscow has consistently sought to deflect attention from this to the undoubted crimes against humanity, even genocide, perpetrated by IS and its affiliates, while presenting its own actions as focused on an anti-terrorist effort against this scourge. This strategy has had some reso-nance, given the huge offensives by the US-led anti-terrorist cam-paign against IS and the global outrage against their crimes. In a calculated move, Russia has branded Syrian political opposition forces in the civil conflict as terrorists, including groups such as IS, al-Nusra Front, and Hayat Tahrir al-Sham and their affiliates. However, Russia has suffered serious reputational damage among Muslim and many Middle Eastern states due to images of destruction of civilian-populated Syrian towns, and the scale of refugees and dispossessed resulting from Russian-assisted operations. This raises the question of whether Russian leaders calculate that this negative reaction to Russia's role in the Syrian civil war among Middle Eastern leaders and publics can be offset by a rising approval for Russia for other political and geostrategic reasons.

It is significant that the leaders of the highly centralized political systems found in most of the countries of the Middle East are as averse as Russia to lowering the threshold of state sovereignty. They are critical of foreign judgments about the legitimacy of their systems of rule, let alone democratization campaigns. They appreciate Putin's portrayal of Russia as a staunch upholder of the status quo as well as his more reliable and consistent approach to the region than the unpredictable Donald Trump, especially after the latter suddenly withdrew US troops from Syria in October 2019. Local leaders remain uncertain over the Biden administration's focus on the region or the consequences of its greater emphasis on human rights. Therefore, while the Russian presence is highly valued by some (Iran, Syria, Hezbollah) for opposing American foreign policy in the region, it is also viewed as useful to a degree by some traditional American allies (Saudi Arabia, other GCC states, Egypt, Jordan, Turkey, and even Israel) due to fear of a lack of US commitment.[85] Many of these states also appreciate Russia's willingness to sell them weapons with no regard for human rights issues, and so they restrain their criticism of how Russia uses its armed forces and weapon systems in Syria.

Finally, in considering how Middle Eastern leaders react, there is the *realpolitik* motive of local states wishing to balance against regional rivals, of seeking access to Russia to mitigate its support for a regional rival, such as Israel's and Saudi Arabia's hopes that Russia might be induced to restrain Iran's presence in Syria.[86] This hope also influenced the Trump administration's approach to Russian policy in Syria. It raises an awkward question for Russia and the legacy of its military intervention. Is Russia's intervention in Syria legitimized or delegitimized in the eyes of other Middle Eastern states (not to speak of Washington) on the basis of how far it enables unacceptable Iranian behavior and the continuation of Iran's military presence in Syria? Russia might claim that, in legal terms, it engaged in collective defense of the Syrian state against IS with Iran but has no responsibility for Iranian actions. However, few states find this collaboration with Iran acceptable normatively.

In spring 2018, Russian statements specified that Iranian forces should be withdrawn eventually from Syria alongside other foreign forces. This received a sharp rebuttal from Tehran, which stated Iran would remain in Syria as long as the terrorist threat continued and as long as the Syrian government was interested in Iran's presence. Russia apparently sees no justification for a permanent Iranian military presence in Syria and is aware of how controversial this is internationally. Moscow certainly knows that Iran is advancing a strategic agenda in the region, at the expense of Israel and the Gulf states, through its extensive presence in Syria. Russia seeks to avoid being forced into an overt alignment with Iran against these states, but Russian leverage over Iran in Syria is limited. Indeed, there are growing Russian-Iranian tensions and differences of interest,[87] although Iran is the Middle Eastern state that has most fervently supported Russia's intervention in Syria and has aligned itself with Moscow in sustaining Assad's regime and rejecting Western-style interventionism.

All this is complicated by Iran's support for the presence of Hezbollah and other non-state Shi'a militias in Syria. On the one hand, Russia and Iran present a common front in condemning Sunni Islamist groups such as al-Nusra Front and Hayat Tahrir al-Sham as terrorist, and stress that these groups be designated as such by the UN Security Council.[88] On the other hand, Moscow is aware that Hezbollah and the Shi'a militias, despite their support for the Assad regime, pose significant risks for Russian regional interests. As expressed by the former head of the Russian Reconciliation Centre in Syria: "Iranian financing of Shiite groups and attempts to spread Shiism in originally Sunni territories can stoke up tensions with the Sunnis and Kurds inside Syria." Indeed, he argued that "any further large-scale Iranian penetration into Syria will create a number of serious obstacles to … the development of the political process in Syria, and complicate relations with Israel, the United States, Turkey and the Sunni Arab countries."[89] In other words, it would further undermine Russia's case for its own presence in Syria among key partners for its regional diplomacy.

In considering responses by Middle Eastern states to the Russian normative claims discussed, public attitudes should not be ignored. In broad terms, publics in most Middle Eastern states have accepted the need to maintain positive relations with Russia since it committed its forces to Syria; in Russian terminology, it became a regional power "to be reckoned with." One survey confirms the high proportion of those polled in 2016 and 2017—just as Moscow's support for Syria was having a real effect in sustaining the regime—who agreed that it was important for their country to have good relations with Russia. Indeed, there were often sharp increases over that one-year period in the proportion agreeing with this proposition: Egypt 69% to 86%; Lebanon 56% to 70%; Jordan 29% to 65%; UAE 41% to 93%; Iraq 47% to 58%; Turkey 24% to 100%; and Iran 65% to 68%.[90] However, this seemed to reflect an evaluation of Russia's rising general influence in Middle Eastern affairs rather than an endorsement of its Syrian policy. Therefore, when publics were asked in August–September 2017 whether Russia was playing a positive or negative role with regard to the conflict in Syria, opinion swayed heavily against Russia: in Egypt positive 25%, negative 61%; in Lebanon positive 29%, negative 38%; in Jordan positive 9%, negative 58%; in the UAE positive 4%, negative 57%; in Iraq positive 25%, negative 49%; and in Turkey positive 12%, negative 81%. Unsurprisingly, Iran was the exception: positive 51%, negative 23%.[91]

This strongly critical stance, except in Iran, may have moderated somewhat since then, as the emphasis of Russian policy in Syria has shifted from combat operations to diplomatic efforts through the Astana process. However, it suggests that Russia's legal and normative claims as to its role in Syria, including its counterterrorist narrative, have not much convinced Middle Eastern publics of the legitimacy of Russia's involvement in the Syrian conflict, nor have they succeeded in deflecting attention from Russia's human rights violations discussed. Leaders in Middle East and Gulf states may negotiate with Russia for pragmatic political reasons. However, Russia's negative image in the societies of the region impedes its effort to develop a longer-term and deeper engagement on the basis of the presence it has carved out through its post-2015 military commitment to the Syrian government.

5

RUSSIA AND IRAN

STRATEGIC PARTNERS OR
PROVISIONAL COUNTERWEIGHTS?

Ghoncheh Tazmini

Introduction

The nineteenth-century Russian poet-novelist Fyodor Dostoyevsky wrote that Russia was a slave in Europe but a master in Asia.[1] The prevailing view that the Kremlin has historically used Tehran as a counterweight to balance its relations with the United States and Europe suggests that this quote does not belong to a bygone era. Indeed, Moscow's mercurial maneuverings have made it a challenge to decipher the nature of Russian-Iranian relations. While Russia's interactions with Iran have been ambiguous, manifesting in peaks and troughs and wavering between cooperation and contention, this chapter argues that Russian-Iranian alignment is an enduring feature of the Middle Eastern political landscape.

Russian-Iranian relations can be conceptualized as a double helix, with one strand representing points of contention and the other symbolizing converging interests: intertwined, the two strands perpetuate a permanent state of tension. This incongruity leaves the role that Iran plays in Russia's regional calculus widely contested. With Moscow's expanding footprint in the Middle East, uncertainty over the driving forces behind Russian-Iranian ties only adds to the region's troubled search for equilibrium. Despite their geostrategic and geoeconomic pathways regularly colliding, there is a fundamental connective tissue that binds these pivotal states. Russia and Iran share a similar geopolitical worldview that is defined by some enduring parameters, ones shaped by historical experience, geographic realities, cultural-civilizational peculiarities, and a similar discursive genealogy in relation to the West. This *sui generis* historical-cultural genotype informs Russian and Iranian ideological worldviews, which fundamentally clash with Atlanticist normative standards in the international system.[2] Russia, in particular, challenges the universality of the US-led liberal international order, and, in this pursuit, Iran is a critical partner.

This chapter assesses Iran's role on the premise that Russian foreign policy is geared towards gaining adherents from global sympathizers with what is manifestly an "anti-hegemonic agenda."[3] As Trine Flockhart has prognosticated, a complex network of "inter-order" relationships will determine the character of the coming "multi-order world."[4] Flockhart explains that within the coming "multi-order world," the liberal order will continue, and may even be strengthened internally, but its global reach will be a thing of the past. Moreover, the challenge in a multi-order world will be to forge new forms of relationships between composite and diverse actors across complex lines of division and convergence. Iran and Russia are firmly ensconced in this "multi-order." While space does not permit a comprehensive study of these arguments, introduction of these concepts can mitigate the ambiguity of Russian-Iranian relations, and, by extension, shed light on many of the vectors of analysis covered in this volume, under the general rubric of "Russia and the Middle East."

Before the conceptual signposts of this study are demarcated, it is important to first deconstruct the research question, "is Iran a strategic partner or a provisional counterweight?" This question is inscribed with a sense of conditionality in relation to the durability of the partnership. Given the power differential in favor of Russia, there is a second layer to this question: is Iran simply a pawn or bargaining chip used by Russia as leverage against the United States? Does Iran have agency in this partnership or is it dispensable? To broach these underlying questions, this chapter engages in three strands of analysis. The first strand identifies the methodological shortcomings of existing literature, which feeds into the feeling of uncertainty over the nature of the partnership. The second segment outlines sources of tension between Russia and Iran, as well as areas of cooperation and coordination between the two states. The third strand takes a deeper look at patterns of convergence by factoring in Russian and Iranian ideational dynamics, which manifest in a similar narrative of the world order. By connecting these three strands, the chapter examines the enduring principles that underpin Russian and Iranian alignment.

A couple of theoretical caveats should be noted before we delve into our discussion. One of the lacunae in the study of International Relations (IR) is the focus on the universality, or nigh universality, of discourse, concepts, values, climates of opinion, and strategic preferences. While a comprehensive probe of the Western-centric character of IR is beyond the scope of this chapter, it is important to acknowledge that this focus on the West has created analytical blind spots in determining the nature of Russia's interactions with Iran. Amitav Acharya and Barry Buzan explain that "IR has been largely built on the assumption that Western history and Western political theory *are* world history and world political theory."[5] They add that "IR was designed institutionally, theoretically and in terms of its view of history by and for the core [Western] countries."[6]

Such a view has come under sustained scrutiny and critique, with scholars drawing attention to Western-centric historical narratives, theoretical categories, and political preoccupations. Acharya and Buzan have argued for the need not to necessarily displace existing Western-dominated IR knowledge, but rather to "displace its hegemony by placing it into a broader global context."[7] In this spirit, this chapter broaches the research question from a specifically Russian and Iranian perspective in relation to geopolitical preferences, and historical and conceptual legacies. However, the idea is not to essentialize Russia and Iran's civilizational distinctiveness as the uniquely determining factor in multilateral and inter-state relations. Nor are we suggesting the privileging of Russian or Iranian experience over Western legacies, norms, and aspirations. Rather, the goal is to complement existing studies by embedding the analysis of Russian-Iranian relations in the context of specific historic-strategic culture.

Shortcoming of Existing Literature

There is no shortage of literature detailing the areas of cooperation and conflict between Russia and Iran. There is a perpetual production line of articles asking the perennial question about whether Russia and Iran are partners, allies, rivals, or adversaries. The nature of Moscow-Tehran relations has been characterized as everything from a "random partnership," to a "circumstantial alliance," to a "marriage of convenience."[8] The fact that the question at hand is a recurring one suggests that existing studies are inconclusive. Considering the two countries' widely differing historical, political, and ideological backgrounds, this is not surprising. Moscow and Tehran are indeed strange bedfellows. However, what complicates matters even more is the methodological formula of most studies, which is usually limited to a presentation of a balance sheet of converging and conflicting interests. Thereafter is the formulation of some rather speculative conclusions. This is not to suggest that these claims are not valid; in fact, some of these insights help in formulating this hypothesis. However, I underscore the fact that the nature of Moscow-Tehran relations cannot be calibrated by simply relying on evidence such as, for example, Russian delays in the delivery of the S-300 surface to air missile (SAM) defense systems to Iran. Such an approach to a complex question lends itself to speculative assessments rather than a theoretically rich and empirically grounded analysis.

Another issue is that some of the studies compiled in European and North American institutes are often guided by political agendas. These reports typically vilify Russia and Iran, two powers that challenge US interests in the Middle East. Given President Trump's "maximum pressure" campaign against Iran, there was also a tendency to accentuate incompatibilities between Moscow and Tehran. The literature is replete with policy papers that overplay a history of mistrust, with particular reference to the Treaty of Gulistan (1813) and the Treaty of Turkemenchai (1828), which resulted in the cession of Persian territories in the South Caucasus; the spread of Soviet-inspired communism in Iran; and, above all, the Soviet Union's support of Saddam Hussein in the eight-year Iran-Iraq War (1981–88).[9]

There is also an emphasis on Russia's alleged lack of credibility within Iranian civil society, with reports reminding us of Iranian protesters chanting "*marg bar Rusieh*" (down with Russia) during the widespread demonstrations in Iran in 2009, disputing the presidential election results. Russia was one of the first countries to congratulate Mahmoud Ahmadinejad on his controversial reelection as president.[10] The Kremlin's growing courtship of rivaling Arab monarchies with lucrative multibillion-dollar energy and defense contracts is also cited as evidence that the Russian-Iranian marriage of convenience is on the rocks.[11] This chapter redresses this imbalance by establishing an interpretative framework that explains why diverging interests do not necessarily translate into a strategic rift between Moscow and Tehran. This framework also explains why Russia will not turn its back on Iran, given the international pressures Iran has been under.

One frequently recycled argument is that Iran is being used as leverage by Russia, a self-perceived superpower that views itself on par with the United States and not with Iran. The premise of the argument is that the degree of expansion or contraction in Russian-Iranian cooperation depends on whether relations between the US and Russia are amicable or hostile at the time.[12] The apparent correlation between Russian-US proximity and Russian accommodation of Iranian interests must be acknowledged; however, as we shall discuss in the third segment, there is a fundamental disjuncture between Russian and American perceptions of the post-Cold War world order. A more substantive pivot towards the United States would require a fundamental reconstitution of US foreign policy towards Russia based on the delivery of major concessions according to traditional Russian priorities and preoccupations. It would entail, to begin with, Washington permanently shelving NATO's eastward expansion and turning a blind eye to Russia's geopolitical aspirations in the former

Soviet space.[13] This is a highly unlikely scenario, especially if we consider the deterioration of relations between Washington and Moscow since Russia's annexation of the Crimea.[14]

As we shall investigate in the third segment, Russia and Iran share a comparable dialectic with the West, which informs their foreign policy choices. The aim of this chapter is therefore to provide an overview of this common dialectic, which binds Russia and Iran despite a complicated history and policy disagreements. The hypothesis is that the Russian-Iranian alignment is steady and substantially underestimated, not least because of deeper ideational and discursive points of convergence. Conceptually, there are two separate levels that define Moscow-Tehran relations: on the top plane are both common and disparate *realpolitik* interests that are held down by a gravitational pull onto a foundational level comprised of common principles and perceptions of the international system. Before discussing the crucial foundational level, the first task is to survey the scope of cooperation and contention between the Kremlin and Tehran.

Better Late Than Never

One commonly cited case in support of the argument that Russia's approach to Iran is opportunistic are the delays in the construction of the Bushehr power plant. In early 1995, Russia's state contractor Atomstroyexport signed a contract with Iran's Atomic Energy Organization to construct a 1,000-megawatt light-water reactor in the southern port city of Bushehr, scheduled to be operational in 2001. With Washington sparing no diplomatic effort in persuading foreign subcontractors to walk away from the Bushehr project, Moscow delayed the project.[15] The commissioning started a decade later in September 2011, with the plant becoming operational in the autumn of September 2013.

There had long been indications that Russia was justifying the delays by arguing that Iran was behind with payments, while Iranian officials denied any payment holdup. Asgar Jalalian, Iranian lawmaker and member of a special parliamentary committee for the Bushehr nuclear plant, openly blamed Russia for the delay. Speaking to the reformist daily *Aftab*, Jalalian stated very directly: "We believe the

Russians are not being honest ... about the plant."[16] He added that Iran had already paid at least twice more than the planned construction costs of the project, and that the Russians were demanding additional funds.[17] Anton Khlopkov, a member of the advisory board for the Russian Security Council, justified the delay in more practical terms. He explained that Russian specialists working on the project, facing a host of technical, financial, and political challenges, could not meet the "unrealistic schedule" imposed by the Iranians on the Russian general contractor.[18] Khlopkov argued that the Bushehr project was the Russian nuclear engineering industry's first foreign contract to build a nuclear plant since the collapse of the Soviet Union. At that time, the Bushehr project was one of only four contracts that Russia had for nuclear power plants abroad.[19] The drawn-out process generated both tension and suspicion on the Iranian side, and the narrative that Iran was being played by Russia only gained more traction with the delay in the delivery of the Russian S-300 SAMs.

In 2007, Iran signed an $800 million contract with Moscow. Once again, Russian officials withheld delivery and maintained that the delays were "technical in nature."[20] In 2010, the contract was put on hold by Russian President Dmitry Medvedev, who flagged up the three sets of international sanctions (Resolutions 1696, 1737, and 1747) to justify postponement of the delivery. At the time, United Nations sanctions against Iran over its nuclear dossier did not include the sales or the transfer of conventional defensive weapons. Iranians' ire was thus raised when Russia referred to UN sanctions as the basis for their withholding the sale of conventional defense weapons, as such weapons were not explicitly proscribed.

This decision coincided with the signing of the new Strategic Arms Reduction Treaty (START) between then US President Barack Obama and President Medvedev in 2010, and the cancellation of the Pentagon's plan to deploy elements of the United States' anti-ballistic missile shield in Poland and the Czech Republic, a project that had long soured relations with Russia. These concessions stood in contrast to the rupture between Washington and Moscow resulting from the military conflict in Georgia in 2008 over South Ossetia and Abkhazia. Moscow's apparent *volte face* led Tehran to seek legal action against Russia to gain compensation for what it deemed an illegal breach of contract.[21] Compensation was never paid, but the contract was restored following President Putin's return to the presidency in 2012. In April 2015, President Putin repealed the ban, and Russian foreign minister Sergey Lavrov underlined that Moscow's voluntary embargo on S-300 deliveries was no longer necessary due to the progress in talks on Iran's nuclear program.[22] In April 2016, Russia began delivery of the S-300 system to Iran, with both parties confirming fulfillment of the contract in October 2016. However, no further details were given regarding the variant Iran had acquired or the weapons system's capabilities. There is speculation that what was delivered to Iran could well have had capabilities that are comparable to the more advanced S-400.[23] What was notable about the delivery in 2016 was that Iran received a heavily customized variant of the missile system with unknown capabilities. This detail is significant if we consider the timing of the delivery and the fulfillment of the contract: it is highly unlikely that an upgraded version of the missile system would have been delivered during Medvedev's presidency when Russia was hoping for a "reset" in relations with the US.

Indeed, everything about the nature of the SAM transaction suggested that the Kremlin was using Iran as a counterweight vis-à-vis the United States. When US-Russian relations were promising, Moscow held back from supplying the S-300s and other weapons to Iran, but, during periods of tension, Russian announcements or press reports regarding plans to supply the S-300 resurfaced. When Moscow sensed that the United States was infringing on Russia's strategic interests, Iran drew closer into the Russian orbit.[24] What made Russia's position even more ambiguous was the fact that while Moscow was acting as Tehran's main purveyor of nuclear and conventional equipment, it voted in favor of the six resolutions passed at the United Nations Security Council (UNSC) from July 2006 to June 2010.[25] The Iranian side was not oblivious to this pattern of bargaining. However, what was important was that although Russia did not deliver on time, it did deliver in the end.

"Run with the Hare and Hunt with the Hounds"

Russia has been said to fish in troubled waters, with the goal of identifying vulnerabilities that its policymakers can exploit.[26] Iranian analyst Mohammad Ali Hozhabri supports this view, arguing that Russia's approach is predatorial and that it routinely capitalizes on Iran's political and economic misfortunes. Hozhabri contends that Moscow's behavior has always been, and always will be, a combination of cooperation and non-cooperation. He explains that Russia follows a "zigzag policy," and a "run with the hare and hunt with the hounds" approach to Iran.[27]

Oil diplomacy between Russia and Iran's traditional rival, Saudi Arabia, appears to support this claim. In June 2019, Russian and Saudi Arabian leaders met on the sidelines of the Group of 20 (G-20) meeting in Osaka, Japan, where they reached an agreement over extension of crude output cuts for nine months. Since 2017, the Organization of the Petroleum Exporting Countries (OPEC) and its allies reduced oil output to prevent prices from falling amid soaring production from the United States, a non-member that became a top producer in 2019 ahead of Russia and Saudi Arabia. Iran was OPEC's third-largest oil producer before US withdrawal from the nuclear deal. The subsequent reimposition of US sanctions resulted in a reduction of about 1.5 million barrels a day in Iranian oil exports compared to the previous year.

Iran's oil minister, Hamid Zanganeh, explained that he did not take issue with the extension of the production cuts, but that he opposed the "unilateralism" of the decision, pre-announced by President Putin in Osaka. Zanganeh found it problematic that the agreement was reached at the G-20 summit in Osaka—Iran is not party to the G-20—rather than in Vienna, Austria, where OPEC members were due to meet.[28] At the OPEC meeting that followed in Vienna, Moscow and Riyadh formalized "OPEC+"—a new group of twenty-two OPEC and non-OPEC nations working to buoy falling oil prices by signing a new charter of cooperation. Saudi oil minister Khalid al-Falih hailed the meeting as "historic" and as "one of history's strongest producer partnerships, spanning the entire world from East to West," with OPEC Secretary General Mohammed Barkindo comparing the partnership to an "eternal Catholic marriage."[29]

Iran was more skeptical, with Zanganeh maintaining that the charter would have "no impact on OPEC and its mechanism or decision taking."[30] Zanganeh warned that "OPEC might die," and that the future of OPEC was in jeopardy over the growing dominance of Saudi Arabia and Russia in the cartel's affairs.[31] He cautioned that the producers' group was in the balance, as the Saudi-Russia alliance was increasingly sidelining traditional members.[32] While Russia's initiative can be explained by practical concerns such as plunging oil prices and rapid growth in US shale oil production, combined with worries about slowing demand growth, Iran's concern was Russia's fraternization with its regional archrival, Saudi Arabia. Hozhabri maintains that Putin's oil diplomacy with Saudi Arabia is further evidence that Russia resorts to the "Iranian card" when it suits its interests.[33]

In September 2019, Russia's energy minister, Alexander Novak, announced that Russia and Saudi Arabia were preparing to sign a package of documents that would include a host of new joint projects. Novak announced that, in the near future, Saudi Arabia could start investing in Russian projects in the field of petrochemicals, the production of liquefied natural gas, and the creation of joint research centers. According to Novak, trade turnover between the two states surged, with figures doubling to $420.4 million in the first quarter of 2019 compared to the same quarter in 2018. Saudi-Russian collaboration has also developed in the field of agriculture, with trade reaching $500 million at the end of 2018.[34] In a sign of growing ties, in October 2019, Putin visited Saudi Arabia: his first trip to the Kingdom since 2007. The meeting between Putin and King Salman bin al-Saud signified strengthening relations between the two countries, with the signing of several memoranda of understanding in the fields of energy, petrochemicals, transport, and artificial intelligence.[35] New investments are essential for the embattled Russian economy, which continues to suffer under sanctions related to the country's military engagement in the Ukraine and the low price of Russian oil, a key export.

However, the two states have treaded lightly around the issue of Iran. Riyadh is well aware of Russia's deep and growing ties with Iran, the latest demonstration of which being Putin's statement that there was no evidence that Iran was responsible for an attack on Saudi oil facilities, Abqaiq and Khurais, in September 2019.[36] The Houthi movement in Yemen claimed responsibility for the attacks, which briefly reduced Saudi Arabia's oil output by half, causing a spike in oil prices. Putin condemned the attack but defended Iran by saying there was no proof that Tehran was behind the attack, as had been suggested by the United States and Saudi Arabia. While Iran remains a point of contention, Moscow and Riyadh have concentrated on cultivating deeper economic relations. When President Trump refused to retaliate against Iran for its alleged involvement in the oil refinery attacks, the Saudis began to hedge their bets by not only relying on the US but also fostering ties with Russia. According to the *New York Times*, Saudi Arabia and Iran have taken steps towards indirect talks to defuse tensions in the Middle East, with Riyadh asking Iraq and Pakistan to speak with the Iranian leadership about de-escalation.[37]

The Regional Landscape

While Russia has been supportive of Iran in the region, there are points of contention in various regional theaters. Tensions have brewed over reconstruction and investment opportunities in the Syrian arena. One source of controversy has been the Syrian government's contracting process. In January 2017, the Syrian and Iranian governments signed several memoranda of understanding that included the rights to mine phosphate in the Sharqiyeh field near Palmyra. However, a few months later, the Syrian government awarded a Russian private company an exclusive contract to extract annually and sell 2.2 million tons of phosphate for a period of fifty years from the same mine, with 30 percent of the revenues reserved for the Syrian state. While this may be strictly business for Moscow, from the Iranian side it does appear in line with the view that Russia preys on Iran's political misfortunes. With Iran impaired by tough sanctions, there is a growing tendency for Iranian and Syrian agreements to fail to materialize into binding contracts. According to Sinan Hatahet, this is also the result of the Syrian regime's attempts to play Iran and Russia against one another.[38]

The delineation of spheres of influence in Syria is also a potential source of conflict between Russia and Iran. Both states aim to elect candidates sympathetic to their interests to key positions in the Syrian military and security forces in order to shore up influence in the decision-making process of Bashar al-Assad's regime. Moscow and

127

Tehran have also assumed different roles in their interactions with the regime, the state, and local communities. Russia seeks to institutionalize its influence by supporting a friendly and centralized autocratic regime that exercises a monopoly over governance, the military and security apparatus, and public service provisions.

On the other hand, Iran prioritizes new local partners—Syrian nationals sympathetic to Iran's objectives—while seeking to maintain its influence over Assad. Iran aims to incorporate its Syrian local allies into state functions, including those that manage security, governance, and the economy. Engaged in a regional competition with the littoral Arab monarchies and with Turkey, Iran seeks to establish influence beyond traditional state-level actors. Tehran's relations with influential local communities in Iraq, Lebanon, and Yemen have allowed it to challenge its rivals, and Syria could play a significant part in this equation. Ensuring the relevance and status of local partners, either on their own or within state institutions, constitutes a guarantee for Iran's future interests in Syria and in the region.[39]

Despite these differences, both Moscow and Tehran expect to benefit from their interventions in Syria. However, Russia is set to gain more dividends than Iran, considering the mammoth budget Iran has allocated to Syria since 2015. The cost of Russia's intervention in Syria has been considerably lower than Iran's investment in Assad's survival. Moreover, Tehran's engagement goes deeper than that of Moscow, which has mainly provided logistical and air support. Iran has equipped and financed tens of thousands of fighters in Syria, sent ammunition, provided refined oil products, and lost soldiers on the battlefield. Hence, the Iranian leadership expects trade concessions in the energy and telecommunications sectors, although, to date, few of the Syrian regime's promises have materialized. Moscow has obtained privileges and concessions from Damascus with relative ease, while Tehran has been held back by Syrian state corruption, bureaucratic obstacles, competition with regional actors and Russia, and the reimposition of US sanctions.[40]

Iraq is another arena where the scope of Russia-Iran relations can be assessed. Iran has used its long, porous border with Iraq; longstanding ties with key Iraqi politicians, parties, and armed groups; and its soft power in the economic, religious, and informational domains to expand its influence and establish itself as the key external power broker in Iraq. With deep religious, cultural, and economic ties—and the major role of Iranian-backed paramilitaries in Iraq's defeat of the Islamic State—the Islamic Republic's influence in Iraq is entrenched. Leaders of both countries have embraced strengthening ties: in March 2019, President Rouhani returned from his first trip to Iraq with a plethora of agreements for expanded trade, cross-border infrastructure, and pledges of greater cooperation with Baghdad.[41]

Both Tehran and Moscow seek stability and security in Syria, a country riddled with sectarianism and terrorism, so there is a mutual interest in managing inter-state and intra-state conflict. As Samuel Ramani argues in his chapter in this volume, Moscow's approach has been to establish diplomatic relations with as many sides as possible in each regional theater. Putin's approach to the Middle East involves a combination of cooperating with all existing governments and supporting the largely authoritarian status quo, while avoiding taking sides in their various disputes, such as Israel versus Iran; Saudi Arabia and the UAE versus Iran; and Saudi Arabia and the UAE versus Qatar. In states where there is ongoing internal conflict, and where the central government is weak, Moscow also strives to maintain a balanced stance.

With Russia's resurgence in the Middle East, the Kremlin has expanded its diplomatic reach, asserting itself as the mediator of all Middle Eastern crises. However, Moscow has not demonstrated any intention to challenge or subvert Iran's projection of power into Iraq: Moscow appears to operate on the premise that this arena is Iran's backyard. While this principle is least apparent in Syria—where Moscow has firmly supported the Assad regime against its Arab opponents—Moscow has balanced itself between other antagonists in Syria's many ongoing conflicts, including between the Assad regime and Syrian Kurdish forces, between Turkey and the Syrian Kurds, and between Israel and Iran/Hezbollah. In Libya, Moscow recognizes the UN-sponsored government in Tripoli, but also supports its opponent, General Khalifa Haftar. In Yemen, Moscow has good relations with the Saudi-backed Hadi government, but also with the Iranian-backed Houthis and the UAE-backed southern separatists. In Iraq, Moscow maintains good relations with both the Baghdad government and the

Kurdish Regional Government.[42] In September 2019, in a meeting between Iraq's prime minister, Adel Abdul Mahdi, and Russia's deputy foreign minister, Mikhail Bogdanov, the former praised Russia's role in balancing relations and boosting security and stability in the wider region.[43]

Russia-Iraq relations are largely "transactional" and directed towards trade and investment. In this domain, Russian and Iranian interests in Iraq are likely to overlap, particularly under the strain of US sanctions.[44] Although Iraq does not import oil from Iran, it does rely heavily on the latter for gas imports for Iraqi power plants and for direct electricity imports. Iraq has US waivers to import Iranian gas, but Washington has been pressing Baghdad to phase them out.[45] Russian investments in the Iraqi oil and gas sector are estimated at more than $10 billion, with Russian companies like Lukoil and Gazprom keen on expanding their investment volume, according to Maksim Maksimov, Russian ambassador to Iraq.[46] Iraq's economy relies heavily on crude oil exports, which account for more than 90 percent of the country's revenues. Amid US efforts to drive Iranian oil exports to zero in the world market, the share of Iraqi oil is on the rise. Given the fact that Russian oil companies, among others, have become major players in Iraq, it is conceivable that, in the short term, Washington's strategy to weaken Iranian influence benefits Moscow and its economic ties with Baghdad.[47]

"Russia is not a Fire Brigade"

All of this complicates the task of determining the parameters of Moscow-Tehran relations, particularly in areas where Iran's limitations seem to work to Russia's advantage. President Putin's comments concerning the abrogation of the nuclear deal are emblematic of the complexity of this relationship, which, as the Russian president underscored, has clear boundaries. Following the announcement that Tehran would cease abiding by some of the provisions of the Joint Comprehensive Plan of Action (JCPOA) in response to increased US sanctions, President Putin urged Iran to continue to comply. In Iran's defense, he warned that "as soon as Iran takes its first reciprocal steps and says that it is leaving, everyone will forget by tomorrow that the

US was the initiator of this collapse. Iran will be held responsible, and the global public opinion will be intentionally changed in this direction."[48] At the same time, the Russian president aired his frustration with expectations from Moscow to save the landmark agreement, saying, "Russia was not 'a fire brigade' to 'rescue everything.'" He added that Russia had played its part and "that Europe could do 'nothing' to salvage the deal without the US."[49]

As indicated above, Putin has demonstrated that he is keen to present Russia as an advocate of diplomacy and mediation. In line with this role, Putin criticized the United States for withdrawing from the multi-party nuclear deal. This, of course, was also a projection of his own objection to US unilateralism. In this capacity, Iran is a useful partner as it mirrors some of Russia's deeper vulnerabilities vis-à-vis the United States and Europe. On June 10, 2019, the Russian deputy foreign minister, Sergei Ryabkov, asserted that the "main challenges preventing an efficient implementation of the JCPOA are systemic violations and subversive actions from the US."[50] At the same time, Vladimir Chizhov, Russian Permanent Representative to the European Union, announced that Russia would ignore US sanctions against Iran, and that it would continue trade with the country without creating any special mechanisms, referencing INSTEX, the special payment vehicle envisaged by the European Union.[51]

Thus, despite inconsistencies, Russia has spoken in Iran's defense, even if doing so has been a projection of its own insecurities. That Russia has shielded Tehran despite international acrimony is an act of support that Iran greatly appreciates. At the Valdai Group discussion in June 2019, Iran's ambassador to Russia, Mehdi Sanai, emphasized in the opening session that, contrary to the prevailing narrative, Russia and Iran's relations are short-term or "tactical"; he believes unequivocally that the two follow a distinctly strategic path based on mutual interests.[52] Indeed, Russia has acted as a bulwark against Iran's political and economic isolation. In being willing to work with Iran, Russia acts as an important purveyor of much-needed technology and military equipment, and with no strings attached. That is, Russia exerts no pressure on Iran regarding human rights issues, nor does it attempt to influence Iran's political behavior. With Iran denied spare aircraft parts and aviation technology, Russia has agreed to supply

Superjet aircrafts to Iran's beleaguered aerospace industry, although the purchase was placed on hold due to sanctions. Russia has been willing to navigate Iran's economy when other Europeans were pulling out, and it has welcomed Iran to the Shanghai Cooperation Organization (SCO) and the Eurasian Economic Union (EEU). In July 2019, it was reported that Russian Railways had begun the €1.2 billion electrification of the Garmsar-Ince Burun railway line in Iran, which stretches to Turkmenistan and Kazakhstan, linking Central Asia to the Persian Gulf and beyond. Iran's minister of roads and urban development, Abbas Akhoundi, asserted, "This is the biggest sign that the JCPOA is firmly and strongly in force. Despite all pressures and threats by [US President Donald] Trump, a 1.2 billion-euro project was launched today."[53]

The Russian leadership has also supported the Iranian regime by calling for noninterference in Iranian domestic affairs. While Iran faced international opprobrium, Russia regarded the widespread protests in 2009, and the reelection of hardline incumbent president Mahmoud Ahmadinejad, as an internal matter. In January 2018, Russia criticized the United States in the Security Council for denouncing Iran's crackdown on street protests sparked by price hikes and unemployment. And, in February 2018, Russia vetoed a resolution proposed by the UK, and backed by the US, charging Tehran with violating an arms embargo on Yemen. As indicated above, Russia has been instrumental in deflecting punitive action against Iran, even if it does so in fits and spurts, and even if it is to maintain regional stability in a country that lies on the periphery of the former Soviet space.

Iranians have also been forthcoming: during both Chechen wars in the mid-1990s and early 2000s, Tehran helped mute criticism in the Islamic world towards what was perceived as excessive use of force by Russia against Muslims. Despite the criticism, and with Iranian assistance, Russia was granted observer status to the Organization of the Islamic Conference (OIC). In the mid-1990s, Tehran helped to end a bloody civil war in Tajikistan—the newly independent Central Asian state with close religious and linguistic affinity to Iran—by playing a key role, along with Russia, in negotiating peace among the warring factions. Around the turn of the century, Russia and Iran cooperated closely in supporting the Northern Alliance in Afghanistan against the Taliban, well before they became the major opponent of the US-led coalition in the country.

Growing Collaboration

In 2016, Russia's use of an Iranian air base to bomb targets across Syria marked a striking new development in the history of Russian-Iranian relations. Iran authorized the Russian Air Force to fly from the Shahid Nozhe Air Base in central Iran to conduct bombing operations in Syrian territories that were said to be controlled by terrorists. The decision to allow the Russian military to operate from Iranian territory reflected deepening political and military ties between the two countries, with their collaboration in Syria being the most significant military engagement Iran has had with any foreign country since 1979.

The two countries also have common security and commercial interests in developing hydrocarbon projects in the Caspian Sea.[54] The landlocked Caspian Sea is bordered by Iran, Russia, and three states that were established following the dissolution of the Soviet Union: namely Azerbaijan, Kazakhstan, and Turkmenistan. On August 12, 2018 in Aktau, after twenty-two years of negotiations, Iran and Russia—along with Kazakhstan, Azerbaijan, and Turkmenistan—signed the "Convention on the Legal Status of the Caspian Sea." The preamble of the Convention stipulates, among other things, that the Convention, made up of twenty-four articles, was agreed on by the five states based on principles and norms of the Charter of the United Nations and international law.[55] While the Convention paves the way for the development of key pipelines and infrastructure, the landmark agreement does not provide answers to all legal questions pertaining to the exploitation of natural resources and delineation of the seabed. All the same, the treaty still represents an important step for regional security and economic development.

One of the key principles adopted at the Aktau Summit was that the Caspian Sea should be free of foreign military ships, a point that Iran and Russia had emphasized at every meeting over the past two decades. Iran's security concerns over the use of the Caspian Sea as a regional base by third-country states were largely eliminated by the ratification of the legal convention. Crucially, the Convention prevents any country, besides the five littoral states, from having a military presence in the Caspian Sea. According to the agreement, no single Caspian state can use its territory for military action against a neighboring country. That way, in case of a possible conflict—especially in terms of US-Iran tension—there should be no threats to Iran from the Caspian Sea dimension. Greater regional cooperation also offers hope for the local environment. Pollution caused by sewage from Iran and damage caused by oil and gas extraction pose a threat to the Caspian Sea's wildlife, especially its sturgeon population. While the agreement may result in further exploitation of the sea's oil and gas reserves, it also provides a framework for the five member states to work collaboratively on cleaning or mitigating further environmental degradation.[56]

Russian and Iranian collaborative efforts were extended even further in June 2019, at the 15th meeting of the Joint Commission for Economic and Trade Cooperation in Isfahan.[57] The convention was attended by Russian and Iranian ministers, governors, and investors who signed a plethora of agreements covering energy, railway, agriculture, pharmaceuticals, and tourism. Iranian energy minister Reza Ardekanian commented on the success of the meeting, reaffirming the two countries' determination to reinforce ties in the face of US sanctions. On the Russian side, President Putin declared that "both Iran and Russia are affected by illegal sanctions. It is hoped that the sanctions can be used as an opportunity to expand ties and increase cooperation."[58] The Russian president reiterated that Russia was prepared to continue its oil investment in Iran to the tune of $50 billion in the face of US sanctions on the Iranian oil and gas sector. Iranian officials confirmed that a dozen projects in the petroleum sector had been presented to Russia's Gazprom, Rosneft, Gazprom Neft, Zarubezhneft, Taftneft, and Lukoil.[59]

During the talks, Iran spoke of its interest in working with Russian gas giant Gazprom to develop oil fields, liquefied natural gas (LNG) projects, and energy swap deals. Iran and Russia have yet to implement the oil-for-goods scheme signed in 2014, and extended for an additional five years, which calls for Iranian crude exports of up to

500,000 barrels per day in return for Russian goods. The scheme includes Iran's use of Russian machinery, equipment, and installations in the development of Iran's petroleum, mining, construction, and transportation sectors. One of the more significant deals signed included the revamping of the Ramin thermal power station in Ahvaz and the construction of four 1,400-megawatt thermal power plants in the southern Hormuzgan province, all with Russian support. The Iranians also weighed in on the need to fulfill earlier agreements on implementing the second and third units of the Bushehr nuclear power plant.[60]

Another sign of growing regional and economic collaboration is the free trade agreement (FTA) between Iran and the Eurasian Economic Union (EAEU).[61] The interim agreement enabling formation of a free trade area between Iran and the EAEU was signed on May 17, 2018, and officially came into force on October 27, 2019. The FTA creates conditions for preferential trade between Iran and the EEAU members: Armenia, Belarus, Kazakhstan, Kyrgyzstan, and Russia. The FTA provides Iran with access to a single market comprised of 183 million people and with an aggregate GDP of $4 trillion. Reza Rahmani, Iran's industry minister, explained that the FTA was important in counteracting Iran's isolation in the face of US sanctions. Economist Mohammadreza Jahanbiglari predicted that if properly implemented, the FTA could see Iran's trade turnover with EAEU member states quadruple to reach $10 billion within one year. The Islamic Parliament Research Center, the research arm of the country's legislative assembly, presented a more conservative estimate, noting a minor impact from the FTA on the country's economy, while underscoring that the FTA could help the country develop non-oil exports.[62]

Russia has been forthcoming in helping Tehran establish alternative ways for Iranian banks to interact with the global financial system. As part of its sanctions regime, Washington polices international transactions via the Belgium-based SWIFT banking network.[63] In 2018, after Trump abandoned the nuclear deal, SWIFT cut off Iranian banks from its messaging system. With Iran joining Russia's EAEU, it will have access to an alternative to SWIFT: the Russian variant known as the "System for Transfer of Financial Messages" (Russian acronym

"SPFS").[64] This will be a blow to US sanctions, as Tehran will be equipped to engage in transactions with banks and companies using the SPFS, free from Washington's oversight. Russia began development of SPFS in 2014 amid Washington's threats to disconnect Iran from SWIFT. The first transaction on the SPFS network involving a non-bank enterprise was made in December 2017. Around 500 participants, including major Russian financial institutions and companies, have already joined the payment channel, while some foreign banks have shown interest in joining. In September 2019, Iran's domestically developed financial telecommunications system, known as "SEPAM," replaced SWIFT and connected to Russia's SPFS.[65]

Russian-Iranian Alignment

After disentangling areas of both divergence and convergence between Moscow and Tehran, the context for interrogating the foundation of this complex partnership is more clearly established. To begin with, it is important to have the correct periodization or phasing in assessing Russian-Iranian relations. Interactions between the two states have evolved since the breakup of the Soviet Union in 1991, after which Iran's foreign policy became more pragmatic and less ideological in orientation as the country emerged from the Iran-Iraq War in 1988. Since 1991, there has been greater depth and longitude in inter-state relations. Therefore, the history of mistrust between the two countries before this date cannot be conflated with doubts over the nature of their relationship today. It is important to adequately convey the evolution of trust levels between the two states. That is, historical mistrust needs to be contextualized properly. In the past three decades, growing cooperation and converging geopolitical interests have seemingly fostered a more symbiotic relationship, thus outweighing both sides' mutual suspicion. For example, it is unthinkable that Russia would seek to annex Iranian territory as it did in the nineteenth century.

Since 1991, Russia and Iran have developed a comparable dialectic with the West, which informs foreign policy choices and, by extension, bilateral relations. It is in this light that the strategic dimension of their cooperation finds meaning. However, the argument in this study transcends crude national stereotypes and tropes, including that Russian and Iranian leadership are united in their quest simply to challenge US primacy. The premise of this argument is typically as such: in the case of Russia, the source of anti-Americanism is a desire to regain former superpower status and influence, and, in the case of Iran, the source of the "death to America" narrative is Iran's revolutionary ideology and Islamic episteme.

It is an oversimplification to assume that Russia is guided by revanchist foreign policy goals, with Iran as a pawn in its regional calculus. There is a longstanding failure to appreciate the multiple influences on Russian and Iranian foreign policy, and how they play out in different political theaters. The post-Cold War world order, which saw American hegemonic posturing, has rendered a "strategic alignment" between Moscow and Tehran somewhat inevitable. Russia and Iran are fundamentally aligned—if not allied—in the sense that they are both anti-hegemonic, opposing the idea that a single state or constellation of states (order) is able to impose particular normative values and power structures as universal.

As indicated above, 1991 was chosen as the point of departure for the assessment of Russian-Iranian relations as it symbolized the year that Russia and the West ended the Cold War. However, they then entered an era of "Cold Peace" characterized by the failure of Western security organizations to transcend Cold War institutions and habits at a time when Russia had demonstrated openness to adapt to Western norms and institutions. Instead, Russia was shut out of negotiations over the creation of a Cold War security order in Europe; NATO and the EU saw matters in terms of enlargement of their own existing structures, not as the creation of something new in dialogue with Russia.

Encirclement of Russia with military bases, the relentless expansion of NATO, the positioning of missile defense systems on Russia's doorstep in the former Soviet space, the sale of weapons to Georgia and Ukraine during their conflict with Russia, and the subsequent imposition of sanctions are all red lines that polarize Russia and the US and Western Europe.[66] From the perspective of Western powers and Russia's neighboring states, it was Russia that was unwilling to jettison its imperial mindset and become a modern nation-state capable of interacting more effectively with both its neighbors and the wider world.[67]

A Troubled Dialectic with the West

From the Russian perspective, the EU and NATO represented the "Historical West"—the victors of the Cold War, with the United States as the linchpin for the European continent—as opposed to what Russia had hoped would be a "Greater West," or the "Common European Home." In the years between 1985 and 1991, there was substantial debate and discussion in the Soviet Union, Western Europe, and the United States on the prospects of this concept, which had originally been advanced as a key foreign policy goal by Mikhail Gorbachev, the last Soviet leader. Following the ending of the Cold War, more immediate and parochial security concerns moved center stage, with the "Common Home" concept falling out of fashion.[68]

The Historical West's willingness to expand but not to transform generated frustration, disillusionment, and resistance on the part of an excluded Russia, which sought instead to create a Greater Eurasia through the creation of the Eurasian Economic Union. The argument is that the West sought continuously to limit Russia's freedom, sphere of influence, and markets, while expanding its own, thus giving rise to "Cold Peace" geopolitics. The goal, in Russia's view, should have been to develop a strategic concept that could manage their differences within an emerging multipolar world. Russian neorevisionism emerged as an expected backlash against the expansionist logic of Euro-Atlantic liberal hegemony.

Here we can discern a fundamental commonality between Russia and Iran. Since its establishment as an Islamic republic in 1979, Iran has been ostracized and put under sanctions and embargoes by the United States. As a fulcrum in a turbulent region and the recipient of some of the most inconsistent treatment meted out during and after the Cold War, Iran has been both one of the United States' closest allies as well as a "rogue" state on an "axis of evil," targeted by covert action and contained by sanctions, diplomatic isolation, and the threat of overt action. Since the attacks of September 11, 2001, Iran has played a significant role in the War on Terror, while also incurring US wrath for its links to international resistance groups and for its alleged pursuit of nuclear weapons.[69]

Defying easy characterization as a hybrid theocracy-democracy, the Islamic Republic does not fit neatly within the rubric of existing political categories. The standoff in the summer of 2019, bringing the United States and Iran to the brink of war, is yet another installment in a forty-year effort to invalidate the regime and its political system. While Russia was spared the label of pariah, the December 2018 US National Security Strategy Document ranked it alongside the "rogue powers of Iran and North Korea" and "transnational threat organizations, particularly Jihadist groups."[70] The previous edition under Obama listed Russia as a threat alongside the Ebola virus and IS.[71] Thus, both Russia and Iran are "outsiders," unaccommodated in the existing world order.

This is the common thread that binds these two countries and gives their partnership longevity despite areas of occasional conflict. The Moscow-Tehran axis is not an ad hoc alliance: rather, it is based on careful calibration of strategic, geopolitical, and economic priorities that are informed by similar perceptions of a Western-dominated political order. Both states place a premium on state sovereignty, denouncing Western interventionism, color revolutions, and democracy-promotion campaigns as normative processes and procedures by which the Atlantic ideological and power system advances the self-interest, influence, and security of Western states. Like their Kremlin counterparts, Iran's revolutionary elite strongly believe that prevailing international law and norms are based on hypocrisy, designed to perpetuate the hegemony of Western powers. This socialist, Third-Worldist, and revolutionary zeitgeist, or foreign policy culture, informs Iran's strategic preferences. It entails pro-Palestinian sentiments, anti-Zionism, anti-imperialism, and Islamic communitarianism: distinct preferences and priorities that challenge some deeply entrenched Western political axioms.

Conclusion

This study has argued for the need to consider the interplay of cultural-ideational dynamics and strategic preferences in post-Soviet Russia and post-1979 Iran. It has shifted attention to the role of ideas, perceptions, culture, and identity in defining the parameters of Russian-Iranian relations. While these two states may clash on issues relating to national interest, both countries share a similar worldview, which is defined by some lasting features, including geographic realities, civilizational peculiarities, historical experiences, normative values, and cultural orientations. As noted in this study, the theoretical inclination of most research is grounded in realism and *realpolitik*, with its emphasis on national interest and great-power politics, without factoring in the role of ideas and identities, and how they manifest in foreign policy choices. A deeper analysis of the aforementioned "foundational level" explains why, despite colliding geostrategic and *realpolitik* interests, Russian and Iranian relations are enduring.

We are now better equipped to address the research question: is Iran simply used as a bargaining chip or as leverage by Russia against the United States? Iran is a strategic partner that is occasionally leveraged as a counterweight vis-à-vis the United States and Europe, with the aim of fulfilling Moscow's broader mission of fostering anti-hegemonic alignments and alliance patterns that challenge the liberal international order. The idea is not to uproot the international order, but rather to make room for states like Russia and Iran that do not fit neatly within the existing constellation. As such, Moscow and Tehran are united in their goal of advancing Flockhart's "multi-order" in which different orders of sovereign states are nested within an overall international system. The connective tissue that binds Russia and Iran is embedded within this broader assemblage of shared principles, priorities, and preoccupations.

6

THE DRIVERS OF RUSSIA-GCC RELATIONS

Nikolay Kozhanov

Introduction

Since 2015, Russian relations with the Gulf Cooperation Council (GCC) have demonstrated a strong tendency for positive development. After the serious cooling down of GCC relations with Moscow in 2012–14—caused by the Gulf monarchies' negative reaction to Russia's support of the Assad regime—this rapprochement was determined by a complex mixture of factors, including the growing intensity of Moscow's presence in the region; changing dynamics of US relations with Russia, the GCC, and the Middle Eastern powers; evolution of energy markets; existing tensions between Middle Eastern countries; and the transformation of GCC foreign policy visions. This chapter will look into the influence these factors have on the current development of Russia's relations with the GCC. It will assess the prospects for dialogue between the GCC states and Moscow, including the ability of each side to bring relations to a new qualitative level.

Key Drivers of Russia's Relations with the GCC

All in all, Russia's current approach to the region is determined by the Kremlin's intentions to use the Middle Eastern agenda as leverage in its relations with the West, secure its economic interests, and ensure domestic security.

First and foremost, the Russian leadership is keen to maintain Russia's position as an influential external player in the Middle East, including in the Gulf region. However, Moscow is not confident of Russia's ability to respond effectively if forced into a reactive mode by other players in the region. The Kremlin therefore seeks to retain initiative and thus shape the regional agenda according to its own needs and resources. This makes prediction of Moscow's next moves in the region a challenging, but not impossible, task.[1]

Moscow's involvement in the conflicts in Syria and Libya, its close contacts with the Palestinian authorities and Israel, and its attempts to maintain good ties with the warring sides in Yemen all help to demonstrate Russia's importance as a global player to both the regional players of the Middle East as well as the West, thus compelling the Gulf countries and their Western partners to take Russia's worldview into account while keeping communication channels with Moscow open. In other words, Russia's presence in the Middle East advertises its capacity to project power and helps Moscow avoid international isolation. Russia can play troublemaker when necessary to show that ignoring its interests might be dangerous. In this respect, Russia considers its relations with the region as just another (albeit important) bargaining chip in its relations with the United States and the European Union.[2]

Conversely, Russia's economic agenda drives its decision-makers to treat the Middle East (and the Gulf per se) as important in and of itself, ensuring that the Russian government does not view the region solely through the prism of relations with the West. Russia's economic goals in the region are twofold: first, it considers the GCC to be an important source of investments and a market for some of its industries: above all, arms manufacturing; agriculture; the nuclear sector; and oil, gas, and petrochemicals. Second, the state budget's dependence on hydrocarbon exports and the Kremlin's concerns about oil prices potentially falling below $40 per barrel—which would mean Moscow would be unable to put money into its reserve funds and sustain all budget needs—compel Russia to actively cooperate with the Organization of the Petroleum Exporting Countries (OPEC) and its informal leader Saudi Arabia. Russia's hydrocarbon producers and service companies have also intensified their attempts to acquire stakes in energy projects in the GCC.[3]

Thus, in 2019, Russia and Saudi Arabia finalized a deal on Saudi Aramco's investments in Russian oil service company Novomet.[4] Another Russian petrochemical company, Sibur, was invited together with Sinopec to join the project on the construction of Al Jubail petrochemical factory currently conducted by Saudi Aramco and Total.[5] Also in 2019, Saudi Aramco's negotiations with Rosneft and Lukoil regarding the creation of joint ventures in the petrochemical sector entered an active phase.[6] In addition, these companies are studying options for exchanging oil to meet the demands of their refineries around the globe. According to these plans, the companies might agree that Saudi Aramco can provide Lukoil or Rosneft with the volume of oil necessary to satisfy their clients' needs in exchange for the same volume of oil provided in return.[7]

Such a strategy could speed up product delivery to clients, decrease logistics costs, and increase companies' access to different (usually distant) markets. During his contacts with Russia in 2018, then Saudi minister of oil Khalid al-Falih argued that Riyadh is determined to increase the production capacities of its refineries. Yet, according to al-Falih, Riyadh does not have enough oil to satisfy the growing needs of its petrochemical sector. Consequently, Saudi Arabia hopes that Rosneft can help Riyadh compensate for its lack of resources. In exchange, Saudi Aramco is ready to invest in Rosneft and Lukoil's efforts to buy/build refineries in other countries. Al-Falih argued that there is vast potential for cooperation between Saudi Aramco and Rosneft in the petrochemical sector and oil trading.[8]

Russia also needs GCC money to finance its economic projects abroad. In 2014–15, Moscow substantially intensified its relations with Egypt. It has ambitious plans regarding the development of economic cooperation with Cairo in such fields as nuclear energy; the arms trade; and the hi-tech, automobile, and space industries. The

Egyptian authorities are unable to invest significant sums of money in the majority of these joint projects without external sponsors. Russia also does not have enough funds for these projects. As a result, the Kremlin has negotiated with the UAE and Saudi Arabia as to possibilities for creating a joint trilateral fund (with Egypt) to invest in infrastructural projects in Egypt. So far, the negotiation process has moved slowly. Yet, according to some analysts, Saudi Arabia and the UAE have stated their intention to help Cairo finance some of these Russian-Egyptian projects and have even encouraged their private companies to look into possible investment opportunities.[9]

Further, after decades of negligence, Russia has declared its intention to develop closer relations with OPEC. This decision was driven largely by domestic political considerations. Since fluctuations in oil prices immediately affect key Russian macroeconomic figures, it is important for the Kremlin to demonstrate that Putin is able to deliver on his promises of economic growth. Consequently, 2016 was marked by the intensification of the dialogue between Russia, Saudi Arabia, and the UAE regarding joint efforts to stabilize prices in the global oil market, with all countries seriously motivated to work out joint market policy in light of the 2014–16 oil price fall. They managed to adopt and, later on, extend the so-called OPEC+ deal, a 2016 agreement signed between OPEC and non-OPEC members, including Russia, committed to decreasing their oil production in order to encourage the growth of oil prices on the international market.[10]

Since then, Moscow and Riyadh have several times supported the extension of the oil deal. They have also exercised many efforts to coordinate the prolongation of the agreement fulfillment with the other members of the deal. At present, Russia estimates the current cooperation with Riyadh within the framework of the OPEC+ agreement as being successful. Moreover, the Kremlin is convinced that, even after the end of the OPEC+ agreement, the two countries will continue to cooperate and exercise joint efforts to stabilize the international oil market.[11]

Finally, the Kremlin's Middle East policy is also driven by concerns over radical Islamic movements in Russia and post-Soviet Central Asia. Between 2014 and 2016, these concerns centered on Russian-speaking jihadists with combat experience in the Middle East returning to the post-Soviet space. Since that period, the Russian government has been trying to establish stable channels of information exchange between Moscow and Riyadh on the security situation in the Middle East. Thus, on January 23, 2019, the head of SVR (Russian intelligence service) Sergey Naryshkin visited Riyadh to meet Mohammed bin Salman and the head of Saudi General Intelligence Directorate (GID) Khalid al-Humaidan. Among other issues, they discussed cooperation between the two security services.[12]

Now, however, Russia is more concerned about Middle Eastern elites potentially providing ideological and financial support to radical Islamists in Russia and the post-Soviet republics of Central Asia, a region which Moscow has traditionally viewed as within the sphere of its direct national interests. This has led to Moscow increasing its communication with religious figures and political elites in the GCC, in an attempt to persuade them to support "moderate" (also called "traditional") Islam in Russia and avoid excessive contact with radical groups associated by the Russian leadership with Wahhabi and Salafi Islam. The Kremlin was also interested in preventing the provision of any financial and ideological support to the Muslim Brotherhood and Tahrir al-Islam movements traditionally labeled as terrorist organizations in Russia.

The Kremlin has allowed more active contact between the government-supported leaders of Russia's Muslim community—including the religious leaders and local governments of the majority Muslim-populated republics of the Russian Federation, such as Chechnya, Tatarstan, Bashkortostan, Dagestan, and Ingushetia—with the religious circles and political establishments of Egypt, the UAE, Qatar, and Saudi Arabia. By convincing GCC elites that the rights of Muslims are not being abused in Russia, Moscow intends to leverage these contacts to strengthen its relations with Muslim countries in general and attract investments from the GCC states in particular.[13]

Over the past several years, these efforts have borne substantial results. Russian muftis have been welcomed to Mecca as esteemed guests, and Saudi officials have refrained from criticizing Moscow for the real or imagined abuses of Muslim rights in Russia. Moreover, on January 21, 2019, Saudi Minister of Islamic Affairs Sheikh Abdullatif al-Sheikh took part in the 29th International Islamic Conference in

Cairo, where he met with the deputy head of the Russian muftis' council, Rushan Abbyasov, to discuss the rights of Russia's Muslim community. After this meeting, al-Sheikh gave an official interview where he praised Russian authorities for their just and fair policies towards Russia's Muslim community since the fall of the USSR. His statements marked a drastic change in Saudi rhetoric regarding Russia's treatment of its Muslim community post-1991.[14] Previously (at least, until 2016), Moscow was often criticized for suppressing Islam in the Caucasus and Volga region, and was even occasionally positioned as one of Islam's enemies.[15]

More broadly, Russia's domestic situation increasingly determines its approach to the Middle East in two ways in particular: first, the Kremlin uses Russia's presence in the Middle East for its propaganda needs, including attempts to shore up support for Vladimir Putin among Russian society. Russia's success in Syria and its mission of saving the pro-Kremlin regime there is portrayed as an achievement in the country's diplomacy. Trips by Russian officials to the region are often offered as proof that Russia is an influential international player.[16] Second, growing domestic unrest and the potential problem of Putin's succession is making Russia more cautious when taking decisions on the Middle East.[17] As the possible transition of power from Putin to a successor in 2024 nears, the Kremlin is avoiding unnecessary problems and complications in foreign policy.

New drivers for Russia's approach to the GCC have been emerging since 2018. First, Russian policymakers are concerned with forecasts about the decline of Russia's influence in the GCC region. Russia's leadership believes that its ability to exercise influence there is determined by "pragmatically" balancing between key regional players. Moreover, Russia's military presence in Syria, and the GCC countries' perception of Russia as an "influential third power" able to broker deals in the region, makes the Kremlin an important dialogue partner for regional and non-regional players. Since 2018–19, however, it began to look as though these foundations of Russia's presence in the Middle East might become shaky.

With the gradual end of the "hot" phase of the war in Syria, Moscow's military involvement could potentially be losing its importance to the political track of the conflict. This is not good for Russia, as it is already expending a good deal of effort dominating the political track in Syria where—in contrast to the military theater—regional powers such as Iran, Turkey, and even the Gulf states are able to effectively challenge the Kremlin's ambition. This could negatively affect the Middle East's perception of Russia as a dominant power, downgrading it from its status as the second-most influential non-regional player after the United States. Another successful military adventure in the Middle East could potentially help Moscow maintain this image in the region, but it is not prepared for such a move and, as noted above, would prefer to avoid any risky steps.[18]

Meanwhile, Russia's ability to play the role of regional broker is being questioned. Its political efforts in Syria are facing growing challenges from regional players, including Iran, as well as "silent resistance" from the regime in Damascus, which does not want to implement even the minimal political changes suggested by the Kremlin. Thus, Turkey and Iran are now questioning Russia's "right" to determine political developments in Syria.[19] In Libya, Russia is reported to have refused to substantially increase its arms supplies to Libyan National Army leader Khalifa Haftar, which has caused disappointment in the Tobruk-based government.[20] In Yemen, Russia's influence on the Houthis is limited in spite of its attempts to position itself as a potential mediator. Truth be told, Moscow does not play an important role in international attempts to settle this conflict.[21]

Any weakening of Russia's ability to exercise power in the Gulf would not necessarily imply the immediate diminishing of its physical presence there. Nevertheless, these difficulties signal to the Kremlin that it will need to do more to secure its positions in the region, and Moscow is more worried about doing so than about actually expanding its presence. However, even such a holding strategy implies active policies by Russia. To demonstrate its importance, Russia is trying to get more involved in regional diplomatic initiatives that do not require much material investment, as well as be more active in forming and developing regional alliances. For instance, 2019–20 was marked by numerous multilevel visits by Russian officials to the Middle East and the Gulf, which were intended to demonstrate Moscow's leading role in the international arena.[22]

One "stand-out" attempt at Russian diplomacy was the release of Russia's "Concept of collective security in the Persian Gulf" by the

Ministry of Foreign Affairs in July 2019. The Kremlin believes that it will be able to use this document not only in the Gulf, but further afield too, again to show that Russia plays an important international role. Russia's diplomats believe that current tensions in the Gulf mean that the international community will be ready to support its initiative. The Ministry of Foreign Affairs also argues that the publication of the "concept" is a response to attempts by Western actors to impose a "Western solution" on the region. The Kremlin believes that the emergence of a new security system in the Gulf is inevitable. Yet, given Russia's ambitions to play a larger role in the region, it does not want this new system to be established without Russia's participation. There are no illusions in Moscow that the concept will be adopted by others as it is. However, it is intended to secure Russia's position at the table in any discussion on the future structure of international relations of the Gulf.[23]

One new factor that could alter Russia's approach to the GCC is the emergence of domestic actors who could affect the policymaking process with regard to the region or the individual countries there. Russian energy companies have a growing influence on policy decisions. The interests of hydrocarbon producers play a part in motivating the Kremlin to balance between key forces in the Gulf so as to ensure that Russia is not putting all its eggs into one basket. After Russia began its "return" to the Middle East in 2012, it had to deal with numerous non-state and quasi-state structures. To develop ties in the region, it was forced to use "parallel diplomacy" with formal and informal Russian structures that have no relations to the Russian Ministry of Foreign Affairs. For example, to be able to speak with different actors in Libya, Russia relied not only on the ministry but also on Russian individuals not openly associated with the official agencies that dealt with foreign matters. Such individuals' personal views inevitably affect policy as they also try to push their own agenda.[24]

The head of the Chechen republic, Ramzan Kadyrov, and his team form part of Russia's "parallel diplomacy." In the past, using connections in the Chechen community abroad, Kadyrov established ties with the Misrata forces in Libya. Kadyrov also played a role in improving Russia's relations with Saudi Arabia and the United Arab Emirates—both investors in Chechnya—where he had often been a guest in recent years. The Kremlin uses Kadyrov to carry messages to Riyadh and Abu Dhabi when it does not want to draw attention to the matters discussed. Kadyrov's visits to the two countries usually precede important decisions taken at the official level. For example, in August 2018, Kadyrov was invited to Saudi Crown Prince Mohammad bin Salman's palace to celebrate Eid al-Adha. It is reported that during this visit matters discussed included the export of S-400 missile systems to Saudi Arabia, the potential training of Saudi special forces in Chechnya, the future of Syria, and Putin's visit to Riyadh, which eventually took place in October 2019. Only when Kadyrov relayed the message from the Saudi leadership to Moscow that King Salman was willing to host the Russian president in Riyadh did the Kremlin make an official declaration about the trip.[25]

Finally, Middle Eastern countries, above all the Arab monarchies of the Persian Gulf, are forming their own lobbies inside Russia at regional and federal levels. According to some Russian analysts, the influential pro-Saudi lobby in Moscow includes Minister of Energy Alexander Novak and the head of the Russian Direct Investment Fund, Kirill Dmitriev. Some Russian high-ranking diplomats working on the Middle Eastern vector of Russian foreign policy are also believed to have strong pro-Saudi sympathies. Finally, Russia's mufti, Albir Krganov, and his deputy, Rushan Abbyasov, are frequent guests to the Gulf states.[26] These people are quite influential and capable of countering negative political influence on the development of the Russian-Saudi dialogue.

Russian and Middle Eastern Perception of the United States' Role in the Gulf

The United States is also a factor in the development of Russian relations with the GCC. Under Barack Obama (2009–17), Washington gradually became less inclined to involve itself in Middle Eastern affairs. Instead, the United States adopted the strategy of "restrained power," which implied active interference in regional affairs—including the use of force and coercion—only when and where it was really needed.[27] These concerns were first demonstrated in 2011 by America's reluctance to save its loyal ally, President Hosni Mubarak, from the revolutionary uprising in Egypt; ultimately, US authorities did nothing to help Mubarak stay in power. Moscow saw this as treachery, and considered it a blow to America's image.[28]

Later on, Iran's readiness under President Hassan Rouhani to discuss the issue of the nuclear program with the international community made the American leadership less interested in putting pressure on Iran regarding Tehran's foreign policy in the Middle East so that they could achieve results on the nuclear negotiation track. These results were important for the White House, as they allowed President Obama to justify the Nobel Peace Prize he was awarded in 2009 for helping to solve the problem of Iran's nuclear research.[29] In the GCC, however, this was perceived as the United States trying to improve its relations with Tehran at the expense of the Gulf monarchies (especially, Saudi Arabia), who had always believed that the US presence in the region was a guarantor against Iran's excessive expansion.[30] This inevitably led to further speculation in the Middle East that, given its growing energy self-sufficiency, the United States might be even less interested in protecting the flow of oil through the Strait of Hormuz.[31] Finally, in 2013, Washington's decision to refrain from using force against Bashar al-Assad clearly signaled to the Middle Eastern and Gulf countries that they should not be solely reliant on US presence in the region. Instead, they should diversify their external contacts in order to use them to achieve existing foreign policy goals.

Donald Trump's victory in the 2016 US presidential elections did not change this situation much. While his pompous trip to Saudi Arabia in May 2017 certainly improved US relations with Riyadh, other actions such as his proposition of the so-called "deal of the century" to tackle the Israeli-Palestinian question, on the contrary, created new points of contention between the American leadership and the GCC. Then, Trump's initial attempt to support Riyadh's blockade of Qatar in 2017 pushed Doha further in its attempt to diversify its foreign policy partners, although the US president was quick to change his mind and declare neutrality on the GCC crisis. Moreover, Trump's periodic statements that his foreign policy would be predetermined by US domestic needs fueled the region's concerns that the White House would stick to the policy of noninterference and neutrality in the Middle East.[32]

After 2013, Russia, on the contrary, seemed to acquire greater interest in the region and readiness to become involved. Instead of considering the Middle East a region of secondary importance for Russian foreign policy—like it had been under the two other Russian presidents, Boris Yeltsin (1991–99) and Dmitry Medvedev (2008–12)—with Putin's return to the presidential seat in 2012, Moscow began to pay significant attention to it. As opposed to his predecessor, Putin appeared to be less pro-Western and more pragmatic. He was seriously disappointed by the failure of the attempted reset in relations between Moscow and Washington under Medvedev and, consequently, more determined to develop relations with non-Western countries.

In 2013, Moscow was also concerned about losing its standing in the Middle East as a result of the fall of friendly regimes in the region during the Arab Spring. Kremlin strategists sought to use Russian presence in the region as a way to reestablish Russia as an important player on the international arena.[33] Consequently, Russian foreign policy towards the region became tougher in defending its red lines and, at the same time, more astute. This, in turn, reminded regional players, including Qatar and Saudi Arabia, about the role of a political alternative to the United States that Moscow had played in the region during Soviet times. Nowadays, Russia certainly could not match the economic and political capacities of the USSR. It was also unwilling and incapable of confronting the Americans on every matter. Still, it was clearly successful in exploiting the interest of the GCC members towards the diversification of Russia's own foreign policy relations.

It is important that Russia avoids using ideological rhetoric in its official dialogue with the Gulf countries. Unlike its approach to the post-Soviet space, in this region Moscow tries to avoid imposing its views either by force or by economic coercion except in cases of extreme necessity. In dialogue with the Gulf countries, Russia tries to focus on their commonalities rather than differences and contradictions. In most cases, Russia also remains extremely pragmatic. The Russian authorities' opportunism and loose adherence to moral values in their foreign policy approaches certainly helped Moscow to find friends in the Gulf region. Thus, on October 26, 2018, a day after the phone call between Putin and King Salman, the Kremlin's spokesman Dmitry Peskov stated that Russia trusts Riyadh's claims that the Saudi ruling family was not involved in the killing of journalist Jamal Khashoggi, a Saudi dissident who was brutally murdered at the Saudi consulate in Istanbul in 2018.[34] This statement was unprecedented for the Kremlin, and for Putin, who usually prefers to keep silent on such scandals that occur within the Gulf region and/or are perpetrated by Gulf state authorities. This political gesture was well received in Riyadh and strengthened bilateral ties between the two countries, enhancing the relations between Putin, King Salman, and Crown Prince Mohammed bin Salman to the level of personal friendship.

For now, Russia maintains its support of the Saudi side in Khashoggi's case, even if there is clear and indisputable evidence confirming Mohammad bin Salman's involvement in the murder of the Saudi dissident. Apart from the obvious benefit of new economic contracts with Saudi Arabia that the two countries' friendliness could engender, the Russian leadership hopes that the scandal around Khashoggi's assassination will create a split between the KSA and the West (particularly the United States), thus further pushing Riyadh towards Moscow. Russian businesses have the same hopes. While large Western businesses distanced themselves from the Saudi economic forum (the so-called "Davos in the desert") that started in Riyadh on October 23, 2018, Russian companies and investment bodies—including the Russian Direct Investments Fund (RDIF)—clearly announced they would be participating in the event irrespective of the ongoing political situation. Moreover, the size of the Russian delegation participating in the forum was deliberately increased.[35]

Meanwhile, despite its current tactic of balancing between key players of the Middle East and the Gulf, Russia is fully prepared to struggle for its interests. Russia is open to dialogue with many regional groups, but it also defends certain red lines (such as not accepting the regime fall in Syria) whose crossing could elicit retaliatory measures from the Russian government. This was another contributing factor to GCC countries improving ties with Moscow. Under these circumstances, two events—the failure of the United States to conduct a military operation in Syria in 2013 and the beginning of Russia's military deployment in Syria after 2015—were integral in strengthening the GCC's perception of Moscow as an influential player in the region.

Moreover, Russian military deployment in Syria in September 2015 not only became the symbol of its decisiveness when it came to protecting its allies but clearly showed that Russia could be a game changer. Its military operation ensured the survival of the Assad regime and demonstrated that the Western monopoly on the use of force in the Middle East, which had emerged after the fall of the USSR, was over. The GCC, in turn, interpreted this as a sign that Russia should no longer be considered a weak player. Consequently, when Moscow decided to provide support to the forces of Khalifa Haftar in Libya, it did this in coalition with Egypt, the UAE, and Saudi Arabia.[36]

For a long period, Russian support for Bashar al-Assad remained one of the main deterrents for the development of the Russian-Saudi relationship. Since the beginning of the Syrian civil war, Riyadh has heavily criticized the Kremlin for its stance on the conflict. However, in order to shape the situation in Syria towards its interests, Russia also needs to cooperate with Saudi Arabia. To achieve this, Moscow has used a stick-and-carrot strategy. On the one hand, since the deployment of its military forces in Syria in 2015, Moscow has been persistently weakening those military groups supported by Saudi Arabia. By 2017, the Kingdom was put in a situation in which it had to cooperate with Russia, or else its remaining assets on the ground in Syria could have been taken out of the game. On the other hand, Russia has offered a number of incentives for Saudi Arabia to intensify the political dialogue on Syria. First, in mid-2017, Russia supported Saudi efforts to assemble a united opposition group to take part in Geneva talks. Second, the Kremlin demonstrated to Riyadh that there are other topics of mutual interest (including the situation in the international oil market) that could be discussed once the disagreements on Syria are either put aside or overcome.[37]

Finally, the Kremlin also demonstrated its readiness to give certain concessions to Saudi Arabia in exchange for reciprocal moves from Riyadh. Thus, by mid-2017, Russia had agreed not to voice any objections against Saudi actions in Yemen in exchange for Saudi Arabia's flexible position on Syria.[38] Moreover, on January 21–23, 2018,

Russia hosted a visit by Abulmalik al-Mekhlafi, the foreign minister of the Saudi-supported Yemeni government of Abdrabbuh Hadi. Previously, Moscow had supported Hadi's opponents from Abdullah Saleh's team. As a gesture of support from the Russian side, Moscow acceded to a formal request by Hadi's government to send fifty tons of grain to Yemen.[39] In addition, Russia is capitalizing on its role as a regional broker. Given Russia's ability to maintain good relations with different players of the Middle East, it offered Riyadh several times to mediate for issues between Saudi Arabia and Iran, as well as between Saudi Arabia and Qatar.

The rationale behind Russia's transactions with the Saudi side is simple. The Kremlin clearly understands that the Assad regime's final victory in the Syrian civil war should be legitimized through a formal political agreement between belligerents. Consequently, Moscow is trying to prepare the ground for a dialogue between the Assad regime and its opponents where the opposition is, de facto, expected to recognize its political and military defeat in exchange for some limited concessions from the Saudi regime. In addition, Russia assumes that Saudi connections with certain groups in the Syrian opposition might prove useful. As a result, according to some experts, Moscow is discussing options to ensure Saudi support in bringing the Syrian opposition to the negotiating table. In exchange, Russia is ready to secure Saudi presence in post-conflict Syria.[40] Moscow is also talking with Riyadh on the issue of Syrian reconstruction as well as the reestablishment of Damascus connections with the Arab countries and regional organizations such as the League of Arab States (LAS).

The quid pro quo approach achieved necessary results: Saudi Arabia helped Moscow launch a dialogue with the part of the Syrian opposition supported by Riyadh. In 2018, Saudi Arabia gave its silent consent to Bahrain and the UAE reopening their embassies in Damascus. In addition, on April 19, 2019, the deputy head of the Russian Ministry of Foreign Affairs, Sergey Vershinin, and Russian special president envoy on Syria, Aleksandr Lavrentyev, visited Riyadh and Damascus. In Riyadh they met with Mohammed bin Salman. Subsequently, they allegedly delivered to Assad the consent of the Saudi regime to discuss the restoration of ties between Riyadh and Damascus.[41] If this discussion goes well, it will be an important political achievement for the Kremlin. Russia is also gradually persuading Riyadh to support Syria's return to the LAS, and there is reportedly some progress in the discussion on Saudi Arabia lending assistance to the reconstruction of Syria.[42]

It is necessary to admit that these transactional relations benefit both sides. By 2017, Saudi Arabia became interested in receiving international support for its efforts in Yemen; further confrontation with Moscow in Syria would only deprive the Saudis of having a substantial role in the post-conflict future of Syria.[43] Saudi efforts led to a situation in which, on January 22, 2019, Russian special envoy to the Middle East Mikhail Bogdanov met with the Yemeni and UAE ambassadors to Russia and the deputy head of the Saudi embassy to discuss Yemen. This was a regular working meeting where the sides discussed the situation around the al-Hudayda port. However, some Russian experts began to argue that Moscow is gradually leaning towards the pro-Saudi side in the Yemeni conflict.[44]

Challenges for the Russian Dialogue with the GCC and the Future of Moscow's Relations with the Gulf Monarchies

Moscow's capacities to develop relations with the GCC have their natural limits. Firstly, Russia's success in developing these ties is more often than not determined by the policy mistakes made by the EU and the United States. This suggests that "corrections" in Western approaches to regional issues would limit Russia's capacity for maneuver. Despite certain problems in the GCC members' relations with the United States, they see Washington as their main foreign partner. Consequently, any steps the GCC states take to develop relations with Russia are always considered within the framework of their relations with Washington. Under these circumstances, the GCC countries are sometimes ready to cross certain red lines that would potentially irritate the Americans.[45]

Moscow's relations with Tehran and its ties with the Syrian regime are also factors deterring the development of Russia's relations with the Arab monarchies. Thus, any improvement in Russian-Saudi relations would have little noticeable impact on Russia's sometimes prickly but nevertheless longstanding strategic alliance with Iran. On the one hand, in spite of the periodic Saudi attempts to involve Moscow in the anti-Iranian camp, Russia's strategy of balancing between key regional players precludes any alliances aimed against any third side in the region. Moreover, Russia sees Tehran as an important player in the Middle East, Central Asia, and the Caucasus, and one whose neutral attitude towards—if not out-right support for—Russia's regional initiatives is important to ensuring their success. In Syria, Russia and Iran also remain mutu-ally dependent on each other. Under these circumstances, Moscow cannot afford to take any steps that would be openly antagonistic towards Tehran. Moscow sees Iran as an occasional partner in its efforts to counterbalance US plans in the region, while somewhat mistrusting Saudi Arabia. As a result, Moscow is often reluctant to put pressure on Iran—for instance, to decrease Tehran's presence in Syria—which displeases Riyadh.[46]

In Syria, Riyadh ties its assistance to the transformation of the Assad regime and the decreased presence of Iran in the country. However, Moscow has had little progress, or even interest, in acced-ing to these prerequisites, which further irritates the Saudi authori-ties. Qatar, in turn, occupies an even more critical position in relation to Russian attempts to save the Damascus regime. Doha continuously rejects any Russian initiatives related to the reconstruction of Syria or its reincorporation in the international community as well as in regional organizations such as the LAS.[47]

Russia's economic potential is also limited. It is often the Russian government, not business, that drives the country's economic pene-tration of the Gulf. Although there exist certain advantages provided by state protection of businesses and semi-government corporations, state patronage also has substantial disadvantages. Firstly, it limits the initiative of Russian corporations, which often act on the direct orders of Moscow. Secondly, the existing government support is selective and is provided only to businesses connected with the political elite of Russia. As a result, medium and small businesses, as well as private corporations without close connections to the state, usually face dif-ficulties in dealing with the Gulf states. The lack of government sup-port in certain areas, in turn, weakens the Russian position in various fields and creates serious problems for the development of Russian-GCC economic ties.[48]

Russia's problems in developing economic ties with the Gulf are also related to the specifics of the economy of the Russian Federation. In spite of the Russian authorities' proclaimed attempts to accelerate economic growth, Russia is still heavily dependent on the export of raw materials such as minerals, hydrocarbons, and wood. Moscow's declared policy of diversification and modernization has been implemented at a slow pace and has failed to reach the initial projected goals. Russia is demonstrating aspects of a country with a rentier economy, and its technological conservatism when compared to the West in certain fields makes these aspects more obvious.

Consequently, Moscow has a very limited range of products and technologies to offer the Gulf. For instance, Saudi Aramco expressed interest in buying a share in the Arctic LNG–2 project in Russia.[49] One of Saudi Arabia's key reasons for investing in the Liquefied Natural Gas (LNG) industry is to get access to LNG technologies so that Riyadh might become an important player in the LNG market. However, Russia is only just developing its own technologies in natural gas liquefaction, so Riyadh would need to invest in Russia's development of LNG technologies first, hoping that it would not be hindered by sanctions. Meanwhile, participation in, for example, US LNG projects could grant access to more developed technologies. As a result, Saudi Arabia decided to invest in the US LNG industry instead of Russia's project, openly pointing out to Novatek that there are other more interesting and profitable projects that pose less risk. Riyadh also demanded Russia revise its financial demands with regard to the purchase of project shares.[50]

The Fall and Rise of OPEC+

This serious negative impact on Russian-Saudi relations has led to Moscow's decision to leave OPEC+. In spite of official statements on the benefits of Russia's participation in this framework, Energy Minister Alexander Novak said on March 6, 2020 that Russia would withdraw from the Vienna Agreement after April 1, 2020. Moscow's decision to limit its engagement with OPEC+ was a result of the organization's declining ability to influence the global oil market. Russia finally accepted that the era of high oil prices was gone and nothing would make it return. The mood regarding the future of oil prices was clearly reflected in state budget planning that was built around the assumption of prices floating in the corridor of $50–60 per barrel (likely closer to the lower end) until 2036. Moreover, Moscow prepared for a long-term (up to four years) drop in oil prices to below $50pb, expecting them to return to $50–60pb after this period of time. Russia's leadership was also well aware of the growing influence of entities other than OPEC+ members on oil prices, as well as of forthcoming structural changes in market fundamentals that neither Russia nor OPEC+ can control.[51]

In addition, Russia is nearing a psychological threshold in 2023–24 when its oil output is expected to start its fall from 11 mbpd to 9.4 mbpd (or, according to other estimates, 6.3) mbpd in 2036. Moscow wants to do its best to prepare for this, but these plans implied the development of new oil-production projects, which was hardly possible under current production limitations. Businesses and politicians called upon the Kremlin to further support oil exports, so, in early 2020, Russia adopted an "all to the market" strategy to maximize exports and increase income while its oil output was still high. In January 2020, the export tariff on oil was lowered by 15 percent, with the ultimate goal being the gradual abolition of the oil export tariff. It was expected that an increase in output would be the result. As of January–February 2020, some experts dubbed 2020 "Sechin's year," referring to the fact that Igor Sechin, head of Rosneft, had always been strongly against Russia's participation in OPEC+ and his calls for Russia to leave this structure had finally been heard by the Kremlin.[52]

However, Moscow seemed to have underestimated the consequences of its withdrawal from OPEC+. The Kremlin expected that its move would scare other participants, making them accept Russia's demands not to cut production, or Moscow possibly assumed that the negative impact of the OPEC+ fall would not be that dramatic. According to some market analysts, Russia's initial expectations were based on the assumption that the 2020 annual oil price would stay in the corridor of $40–45pb, with the possibility of a temporary fall below $40pb. Moscow believed that prices would return to the $50–55 corridor in 2021 as oil demand in China resumed after the end of the COVID-19 pandemic. Instead, Putin found himself facing a full-fledged oil war from the Saudi and Emirati sides. With the COVID-19 pandemic progressing and the Gulf countries intending to increase their production capacities far beyond March 2020 levels, oil prices falling below the $30pb threshold in the long term seemed to be feasible. This scared the Kremlin. Less than a week after Moscow's decision to pull back from OPEC+, Russia started calling upon OPEC+ members to keep their oil output within the limits that had existed in January–February 2020. In early April 2020, Russia agreed to participate in another OPEC meeting that resulted in the signing of a new agreement that implied unprecedented production cuts by its participants. Nevertheless, Russia's decision to walk away from the OPEC+ deal left a bitter taste in Riyadh's mouth that will likely last for a long time.[53]

In addition, Moscow's withdrawal from OPEC+ could potentially trigger a domino effect, leading to economic and political instability. This move soured the Kremlin's relations with Saudi Arabia and the UAE, making them skeptical of cooperating with Russia in future investment projects as well as encouraging the Gulf crude producers to continue squeezing Russia out from European and Asian oil markets even after the OPEC+ production cuts were reinstalled.[54]

The overall situation clearly showed that—in spite of the deep interest Russia demonstrated over the past four years in developing cooperation with Gulf hydrocarbon producers—these alliances are fragile and unstable. Moreover, Russia and Saudi Arabia have periodically competed for oil markets in Asia and Europe even during the good years of their relations. In 2015–19, in spite of domestic production cuts, both countries increased their supplies to China in a competition for the spare share of the Chinese market that had been created by growing domestic demand, a decrease in Iran's oil exports to China, and Beijing's attempts to diversify its sources of hydrocarbon imports.

Saudi Arabia and Russia have also been competitors in other regions. The Kingdom's decision in July 2019 to further discount its oil sold to Europe was a cause for concern in Russia. These concerns were renewed when, following Russia's March 2020 decision to leave OPEC+, Saudi Arabia declared its intention to provide

European consumers with discounts on its oil for April 2020. Moscow also never missed an opportunity to exploit the misfortunes of its Arab "partners": in September 2019, an attack by Iranian proxies on Saudi oil-refining infrastructure in Abqaiq and Khurais led to Riyadh being temporarily unable to fulfill its export obligations to Asian countries. Russia immediately seized this opportunity to position itself as a more reliable supplier to India in order to increase its share of the country's market.[55]

Russia's investment cooperation with the GCC countries—and, especially, Saudi Arabia—was negatively affected by Moscow's decision to remove itself from OPEC+. Thus, as reported by the Russian media, by mid-March 2020, Saudi Aramco's purchase of Novomet's share was suspended. According to some market sources, it was the Saudi side that decided making investments in Russia was inappropriate at a time when the two countries were engaged in what was tantamount to an economic war. Other experts argue that suspension of the deal was initiated by the Russian side under pressure from the head of Rosneft, Igor Sechin, who is against cooperating with Riyadh and attempting to create as much damage as possible to the bilateral dialogue between the two countries.[56]

Conclusion

All in all, existing limits obviously prevent Russia and the GCC countries from strengthening their relations. In March 2019, this was clearly demonstrated by the outcomes of Lavrov's visits to Qatar, Saudi Arabia, the UAE, and Kuwait. This trip was supposed to demonstrate to the GCC countries and other local players that the Kremlin retains great interest in Middle Eastern affairs and an ability to influence them. Consequently, the Kremlin deliberately decided that Lavrov's trip to the Gulf countries should be a tour. On the one hand, it was a tribute to the traditional principle of Russian diplomacy in the Middle East to balance between key players of the region. Immediately after negotiations with the Qatari authorities, the Russian foreign minister visited Saudi Arabia (a leader and initiator of Qatar's 2017 blockade) as a way to demonstrate the equal distance Moscow maintains between the two antagonizing camps and its readiness to talk to both sides. Moreover, Lavrov's tour to the Gulf countries was reflective of US official visits to the region in that it included a broad agenda addressed to several members of the GCC. By adopting US GCC touring strategy, Moscow demonstrated that it has no less ambition than Washington.[57]

Russia periodically needs to confirm its status as a leading regional power. Theoretically, this can be done economically, militarily, or politically. The economic means are obviously not an option, as Russia is disadvantaged due to the deterioration of its own economy. Over the past several years, the Kremlin tried to attract the Gulf monarchies towards a number of ambitious investment projects in Russia, but these attempts were either unsuccessful or have not yet achieved results. The exchange of business delegations between Russia and the GCC is very active and accompanied by official statements from both sides regarding plans to invest billions of dollars in the Russian economy. However, it is not political statements but market principles that will ultimately determine GCC business investments in Russia. Russia's overall business environment is not the safest or the most appealing, and there are much more profitable alternatives elsewhere. Consequently, it was no surprise that Lavrov's GCC trip to boost economic cooperation with Saudi Arabia and Qatar was unsuccessful.[58]

In the absence of strong economic leverage, Moscow has had to capitalize on two other methods of influence: its military presence in Syria and the existing perception (or myth) of Russia as a capable broker for handling problems in the Middle Eastern region. With those in mind, between 2019 and 2021, Lavrov traveled to the region several times with a number of initiatives. Believing in Russia's capacity to shape the future of post-conflict Syria, but in need of financial and diplomatic support for launching the process of political reconciliation and economic reconstruction, Moscow expected that Lavrov would persuade the Gulf monarchies to agree that Damascus would resume its participation in the LAS. This was a necessary move to further legitimize the Assad regime and allocate economic support to it. Moscow's calculations were simple: in exchange for Russia guaranteeing them a future presence in Syria, the Gulf states would provide economic assistance in the reconstruction of the war-torn country.

These calculations, however, proved flawed. Saudi Arabia and Qatar gave a predominantly negative response to the question of Damascus's return to the LAS. Russia had overestimated the capability of its military investments in Syria to affect international relations of the Middle East. The Syrian war had entered a new stage in which military leverage was less important than the political process. Moscow has managed to ensure through military force the survival of Assad's regime. However, it will now need a political process to legitimize these "achievements." In other words, the Kremlin needs to launch a political dialogue between the Syrian regime and the remnants of the opposition in order to make the latter recognize defeat. While Russian dominance on the battlefield is largely unquestioned, its influence on the process of the political reconciliation and reconstruction of Syria is challenged by regional players. Additionally, there is no guarantee that Russia can indeed ensure the Gulf states a future presence in Syria. Consequently, the GCC states are not in a hurry to agree to Moscow's proposals.[59]

Between 2018 and 2020, Moscow also tried to reaffirm its importance as a regional broker by discussing the Gulf crisis with the Arab monarchies. Moscow's initiative to reconcile Qatar with the so-called "blockade countries" spanned around the suggestion to resume the ministerial consultations of the Russia-GCC forum—whose meetings were put on hold when the Qatar diplomatic crisis broke in 2017—in Moscow. According to insights received from Arab diplomats, in 2019, Lavrov proposed a list of concessions each side could offer the other.[60] However, there was almost no reaction to it. The Gulf region was overwhelmed by mediators from the United States, the EU, and the Middle East itself. Russia was only one additional voice in the choir persuading the GCC states to reunite, but was weaker in terms of its influence. The GCC rift was too deep and too personal for its participants to handle by simply appealing to the opposing camps. A mediator must have had sufficient power to guarantee that a proposed truce would will be adhered to, and this is something Moscow lacks. As it was argued by a diplomat from the Gulf, "Russia has to have cards to play the mediation game and it does not."[61]

As a result, it was not surprising that Lavrov's GCC tours were fruitless. This lack of results can potentially have two alternative impacts on Russian policies in the Gulf. Moscow will either understand its current limits and try to overcome them or, as has previously been the case, it might decide that the region is unreceptive to Russia's foreign policies and so will put a hold on its efforts with the GCC. The first option is not very likely to occur, as it will require efforts and resources that Russia does not currently possess. The second option is far more plausible: Russian economists are already signaling a "Middle Eastern fatigue" among Russian businesses and their disappointment at the lack of GCC investments.[62] This, in turn, might affect the political side of the Russian relations with the Gulf as well.

7

RUSSIA AND THE YEMENI CIVIL WAR

Samuel Ramani

Introduction

On September 21, 2014, Houthi militias seized control of Yemen's capital Sanaa after instigating a month of protests against spiraling fuel prices and participating in numerous armed clashes with forces loyal to Yemeni President Abd Rabbuh Mansur Hadi. The Houthi coup d'etat surprised much of the international community, which had been apprehensively monitoring Hadi's inability to mitigate Yemen's socioeconomic cleavages. Everyone had failed to anticipate the speed with which Hadi would withdraw from Sanaa or how former Yemeni president Ali Abdullah Saleh would align with the Houthis. In order to forestall a potential deterioration in its relationships with Saudi Arabia and Iran, Russia has consistently embraced a policy of strategic nonalignment in Yemen.

This approach to the Yemen war does not mean that Russia has remained completely neutral in the conflict. Rather, Russia has framed itself as a defender of international law and legitimate political institutions in Yemen but has refused to provide material support to any Yemeni faction or explicitly endorse military interventions by external powers. In keeping with this strategy, Russia has repeatedly stressed its support for Yemen's UN-recognized government and abstained from UNSC Resolution 2216 in April 2015, which condemned the Houthi coup, but it has also presented itself as a consistent critic of the Saudi-led military intervention in Yemen. Although the ambiguities inherent in Russia's response to the Yemeni civil war have set it apart from its great power counterparts, as the conflict passes its five-year mark strategic nonalignment still remains Moscow's guiding principle in dealing with the Yemen war.

After briefly outlining the evolution of Russia's post-1991 policy towards Yemen, this chapter will examine the motivations for and manifestations of Russia's strategic nonalignment policy in Yemen. As Russia possesses few material interests in Yemen and is not compelled to support any particular faction, Moscow has used its distinct approach to the Yemeni civil war as a lever to strengthen its regional influence. The inextricable links between Russia's Yemen policy and its broader geopolitical aspirations will undergird this study, as these connections have received comparatively little attention in extant literature on Russian policy towards the Middle East. Subsequently, this chapter will assess the implications of Russia's approach to Yemen and its relationships with Iran, Saudi Arabia, and the United Arab Emirates (UAE). After laying out the regional-level impact of Russia's strategic nonalignment policy in Yemen, the chapter will examine Russia's vision for an inclusive peace settlement in Yemen, which includes a policy of constructive engagement with the Houthis. The chapter concludes with an overall evaluation of Russia's policy of strategic nonalignment in Yemen and its effectiveness in advancing Moscow's geopolitical interests.

The Evolution of Russia's Post-1991 Foreign Policy towards Yemen

After it achieved independence from British colonial rule in 1967, the People's Democratic Republic of Yemen (PDRY), which was commonly referred to as South Yemen, became the Soviet Union's strongest ally in the Middle East. The PDRY regime's Marxist ideology was the driving force behind its alignment with the Soviet Union, and Norman Cigar noted in 1985 that "as South Yemen's domestic system became more radical, links with Moscow have become closer."[1] The Soviet Union's suspension of financial aid to the PDRY contributed to the reunification of Yemen in 1990. In keeping with Russia's broader retrenchment on Middle East affairs, Moscow maintained peripheral relations with the new Yemeni state, which was led by President Saleh. Russia briefly departed from this trend of disengagement during the 1994 Yemeni civil war, when Moscow attempted to mediate between Saleh's legitimate Yemeni government and the Democratic Republic of Yemen (DRY), a self-declared south Yemeni state, but this arbitration gambit failed.

Although, during his first term in office, Russian President Vladimir Putin met with Saleh twice in Moscow, Russia distanced itself from Saleh's struggles to quell Houthi and Southern Movement insurgencies in the final years of his tenure. Prominent members of the Russian analytical community were concerned about the potential for Yemen's political divisions to result in more acute instability or political violence within Yemen's borders. While recounting his 2005 trip to Yemen, former Russian prime minister Yevgeny Primakov described hardened divisions between secularists and Islamists that had developed during the 1980s, and he noted how anti-Marxist factions in southern Yemen viewed the unification of Yemen in 1990 as the "real revolution," to the chagrin of the ideologues.[2]

Russian officials welcomed the UN-brokered leadership transition from Saleh to Hadi in 2012, even though Moscow was generally critical of the Arab Spring. After this transition, Russia participated in the National Dialogue Conference (NDC), which oversaw the stabilization of Yemen after this turnover of power. Nevertheless, Russia continued to adhere to self-imposed limits on intervention in Yemen's internal affairs. In April 2013, Hadi told Putin in a press conference that the proliferation of weapons in Yemen and the tribalistic nature of Yemeni society could potentially instigate a new civil war, but Russia did not provide Yemen with security assistance in response to this ominous warning.[3]

Russia's willingness to hedge its alignments during Yemen's numerous episodes of instability helped it respond in a flexible manner to the outbreak of civil war in 2014. Russia maintained diplomatic representation in both Aden, the new seat of Hadi's UN-recognized government, and Houthi-occupied Sanaa to avoid siding with a potential losing faction in a rapidly burgeoning civil war. After the Saudi Arabia-led coalition intervened militarily on Hadi's behalf in March 2015, Russia called for an immediate ceasefire in Yemen and abstained from UN Resolution 2216, which held the Houthis responsible for the outbreak of the civil war. Although Russia has not definitively taken sides in Yemen, it is important not to conflate Moscow's caution with the role of a detached spectator.

Since 2016, Russia has engaged in parallel-track informal negotiations with representatives of both Hadi's government and the Houthis. Since the Southern Transitional Council (STC) was established in November 2017, Russia has also revived its historic interest in southern Yemen. Russian Deputy Foreign Minister Mikhail Bogdanov welcomed STC leader Aidarus al-Zubaidi to Moscow in March 2019,[4] and he discussed the STC's declaration of self-rule in southern Yemen with al-Zubaidi in April 2020.[5] These diplomatic initiatives have allowed Russia's presence in Yemen to remain impervious to shifts in the balance of power. Russia has also used its permanent seat on the UNSC to highlight the humanitarian costs of the Saudi-led military intervention, and in February 2018 it vetoed a UNSC resolution which claimed that Iran was complicit in illegal arms transfers to the Houthis.[6] Now that the evolution of Russia's involvement in Yemen has been introduced, the next two sections of this chapter will articulate the geopolitical interests and status aspirations that undergird Russia's policy of strategic nonalignment.

The Geopolitical Interests That Undergird Russia's Position on the Yemeni Civil War

Despite the long history of their bilateral relationship, Russia's economic stakes in Yemen are limited. The only significant transactional links between Russia and Yemen existed in the defense sector, as Yemen purchased 83 percent of its arms from Russia after the collapse of the Soviet Union, and by 2010 it possessed up to $2.5 billion in extant deals with Moscow.[7] Yemen's most notable procurement of arms from Russia was its purchase of $300 million worth of MiG-29 jets in June 2002, which caused an international controversy, as US officials feared that Saleh would resell them to Iraq. The proliferation of defense contracts with Yemen slowed after Saleh's fall, and by 2016 Yemen received only 1.2 percent of Moscow's post-2000 global arms sales, lagging behind countries like Egypt, Iraq, Syria, Iran, and Algeria.[8] Overall trade between Russia and Yemen also remained stubbornly low, and Russian President Dmitry Medvedev confessed to Saleh in a February 2009 press conference that Russia-Yemen commercial relations were "probably not growing as fast as we would like."[9]

In spite of these limited material stakes, Russia is leveraging its policy of strategic nonalignment in Yemen to expand its influence on the Persian Gulf and, prospectively, the Red Sea.[10] This strategy is loosely modeled after the Soviet Union's efforts to balance a strategic alliance with South Yemen and diplomatic relations with North Yemen during the Cold War, albeit with a less intensive deployment of resources. During the 1980s, the Soviet Union encouraged South Yemen to be more accommodating towards its neighbors,[11] in part due to its desire to normalize relations with the GCC (Gulf Cooperation Council) countries. Russia's consistent support for a peace settlement and efforts to facilitate dialogue in Yemen, at a time when Moscow's disagreements with the Gulf countries regarding Syria were at an all-time high, could be viewed as a similar de-escalation measure. Once Russia devised a mechanism to work around its differences with the Gulf monarchies and established positive diplomatic relations with every country in the Persian Gulf region, Moscow used its multi-vector engagement strategy in Yemen to shore up its nascent regional partnerships. Russia's regular diplomatic relations with the Houthis have facilitated its engagements with Iran on conflict resolution in Yemen; its support for Hadi's legitimacy has reassured Saudi Arabia; and its urging the international community to pay attention to southern Yemen's concerns has appealed to the UAE. Although Russia's involvement in Yemen is a secondary driver of its regional balancing strategy, it reinforces Moscow's post-2015 efforts to court GCC investments and present itself as a constructive voice on collective security issues in the Persian Gulf.

Looking ahead, Russia hopes to convert its positive relations with all major factions in Yemen into a sphere of influence in the Red Sea and bordering regions of eastern Africa. The Soviet Union viewed its naval base in Aden as a foundation for geopolitical influence in the Horn of Africa, and its ambitions for hegemony over the Red Sea contributed to its $400 million in annual patronage to South Yemen's economy. Russia hopes that its policy of strategic nonalignment will allow it to establish a geopolitical foothold in Yemen that is capable of surviving shifts in the balance of power and will potentially help Russia to belatedly enter the geopolitical competition for influence in the Horn of Africa.

In an August 2017 interview, the former Commander in Chief of the Russian Navy, Feliks Gromov, argued that Russia should establish a military base in southern Yemen to protect oil tankers transiting from the Gulf of Aden to the Suez Canal, and join the international scramble for Red Sea facilities that began with China's arrival in Djibouti.[12] The financial costs of establishing an installation in Aden might render this proposal impractical, and the Russian Defense Ministry has not formally adopted Gromov's recommendations. Due to these restraining forces, Russia announced plans to establish a lower-cost naval logistics base in Port Sudan in November 2020,[13] but the long-term strategic value of Aden should not be entirely over-looked. As Russia's efforts to expand its influence in the Persian Gulf and Red Sea are linked to its aspirations for great power recognition, status aspirations profoundly shape Russia's Yemen policy and will be discussed in the next section.

The Role of Status Aspirations and Soft Power in Shaping Russia's Policy towards the Yemeni Civil War

Russia's strategic nonalignment policy in Yemen aims to bolster international perceptions of its great power status and is inextricably linked to the legacy of Moscow's pro-Assad campaign in Syria. Russia wants to demonstrate that the regional status acquired from its successful pro-Assad intervention extends to other conflict zones, and it also hopes to partially ameliorate the reputational damage that Moscow incurred by attempting to whitewash Assad's war crimes. In order to burnish its international image, depict itself as a norm entrepreneur, and further its soft power aspirations, Russia has advanced three major narratives and policy proposals towards the Yemeni civil war.

First, Russia has presented itself as the international community's foremost protector of the sanctity of international law in Yemen. This approach has caused Russia to combine support for internationally recognized Yemeni institutions with criticisms of Saudi Arabia's involvement in a unilateral military intervention in Yemen. After Hadi's resignation, Russian Foreign Minister Sergey Lavrov unfavorably compared the Houthi coup in Yemen to the Euro-Maidan revolution in Ukraine, in which the president of a UN-recognized government, Viktor Yanukovych, had also been overthrown.[14] Lavrov's statement called upon Riyadh to embrace a "national reconciliation" in Yemen instead of using military force.[15] Konstantin Kosachev, head of the Russian Federation Council's Foreign Affairs Committee, embraced a similar position by claiming that the Houthi takeover of Yemen "cannot be qualified as anything other than a coup," and noted that Saudi Arabia's "direct military intervention in the conflict [had occurred] without the UN sanction."[16]

As hopes for a rapid ceasefire faded and the prospect of a protracted civil war in Yemen loomed, criticisms of the conflicting parties sharpened. In an interview with *Izvestiya* on April 13, 2015, the Secretary of the Security Council of Russia, Nikolay Patrushev, condemned Saudi Arabia's refusal to seek UNSC approval for its intervention in Yemen. Patrushev warned that Riyadh's unilateralism would exacerbate Sunni-Shi'a tensions in the Middle East, contribute to the proliferation of terrorism on the Arabian peninsula, and create a Somalia-style failed state scenario in Yemen.[17] This statement reflected Russia's frustrations with Saudi Arabia's decision to answer Hadi's call for international assistance with force, after Russia and China had blocked three similar requests in the UNSC over concerns that a war in Yemen would spread to the entire Gulf region.[18]

The enactment of UN Resolution 2216 did not satisfy Moscow's concerns, as Russian policymakers believed a resolution drafted by stakeholders with vested interests, like Jordan and the Gulf monarchies, would prevent the adoption of a genuine multilateral solution.[19] These criticisms aligned with Russian Foreign Minister Sergey Lavrov's April 2, 2015 statement that an impartial Security Council resolution was the most potent deterrent to Saudi Arabia's refusal to seek UNSC consent.[20] Ultimately, Russia's actual efforts to stop the

Saudi-led military intervention paled in comparison to its strident rhetoric. On April 4, Russia drafted a UN resolution calling for humanitarian pauses in Yemen that did not include specified times for the suspension of Saudi air strikes, and abstained, instead of vetoing, from approving UNSC Resolution 2216 on April 14.

In spite of Russia's decision not to deviate from the international consensus on UNSC Resolution 2216, Moscow began to present itself as a stakeholder that could negotiate effectively with all major factions and realign their conduct with accepted international legal principles. During the first month of the Saudi-led military intervention, Russia's Deputy Foreign Minister Mikhail Bogdanov repeatedly called for a national dialogue between key political forces in Yemen and claimed that opposing Yemeni factions had appealed to Moscow for diplomatic assistance. Russia's decision to maintain close ties with all major Yemeni factions, as the civil war progressed, was inextricably linked to its desire to be perceived as an in-demand dialogue facilitator in Yemen. Russian analysts, such as Oleg Filimonov, argued that fostering cross-sectarian dialogue would cause Saudi Arabia to take Russia's diplomatic proposals in Syria seriously and dispel perceptions of a Russia-Shi'a alliance in Sunni Arab countries.[21] Highlighting Moscow's impartiality could also counter residual negative perceptions of Russia in Yemen. According to former US ambassador to Yemen Barbara Bodine, who spoke with the author in a July 2019 interview, Russia was reduced to the status of a "non-player" in Yemen during the late 1990s and struggled to revive its historic influence in part due to negative memories of the Soviet Union as a "failed patron" of South Yemen.[22]

Russia's strategy achieved a notable symbolic success in October 2018, after the Hadi government and the Houthis turned to Russia for mediation assistance following the breakdown of prospective peace talks in Geneva. On October 5, Yemen's ambassador to the United States, Ahmed Awad bin Mubarak, called for additional diplomatic assistance from Russia,[23] and on October 26 the head of the visiting Houthi delegation to Moscow, Mohammed Abdulsalam, asked Russia to expand its mediation role in Yemen. In January 2019, UN Special Envoy to Yemen Martin Griffiths praised Russia's "unique place" in the peace process and highlighted Russia's retention of an embassy in Sanaa until December 2017 as proof that it was "listened to by all parties."[24]

While these requests for diplomatic assistance have not translated into Russia supplementing the UN peace process in Yemen with an independent initiative, they do bolster Moscow's credibility as a crisis arbiter in the Middle East amongst both domestic and regional audiences. In the long run, fostering perceptions of Russia as an effective dialogue facilitator in Yemen could result in US-Russia cooperation on ending the civil war, which has been pinpointed by Oleg Ozerov, Deputy Director of the Africa Department at the Russian Ministry of Foreign Affairs, as a conceivable scenario.[25]

Second among the narratives Russia is attempting to advance, in order to deflect negative attention that its conduct in Syria has received, Russia has repeatedly sounded the alarm to the international community about the humanitarian costs of the Saudi-led military intervention. The first evidence of Russia's concern for the humanitarian dimension of the Yemeni civil war was Moscow's active involvement in the evacuation of Russian and other foreign civilians in April 2015. On April 5, 2015, the Russian Foreign Ministry reported that it had evacuated 67 Russians and 245 foreign nationals from Yemen by directly cooperating with the governments of Saudi Arabia and Egypt.[26] These evacuations were heralded as a major success in Russia, as Saudi Arabia had blocked the entry of Russian planes into Yemeni air spaces prior to March 31. Russia attributed Riyadh's more cooperative attitude to its draft UN resolution, which called upon Saudi Arabia to restrict air strikes on humanitarian grounds. US Secretary of State John Kerry and the British Foreign and Commonwealth Office expressed their gratitude to Russia for its successful evacuations of Western nationals. These efforts gained widespread positive coverage in the Russian state media, as they revealed Moscow's ability to favorably impact a humanitarian crisis outside of its traditional sphere of influence.[27] The successful rescue of Russian civilians also had powerful domestic resonance, as the Kremlin consistently viewed the protection of Russian nationals and ethnic Russians abroad as a cardinal goal of its foreign policy.

These successful evacuations of foreign nationals emboldened Moscow to vocally signal its concern about Yemen's deteriorating humanitarian situation, at a time when the United States was guarded in its statements on this crisis. Russian policymakers have been especially vocal in opposing the disruption of food supplies and humanitarian aid entering Hodeidah, which was exacerbated by the Saudi-led coalition's blockade and alleged Houthi misappropriations of international assistance. In April 2017, the Russian Foreign Ministry claimed thousands of Hodeidah residents were participating in a bread march to urge the international community to prevent an offensive from Hadi's government against the city.[28] Russia's statement coincided with a major UN donor conference in Geneva, which called for the dispersal of $2.1 billion of food and medical aid to Yemen, and was widely viewed as the most emphatic endorsement of these aid provisions in the UNSC.[29]

To add credibility to its position as a humanitarian signaler on the world stage, Russia distributed humanitarian aid through well-publicized convoy deliveries to Sanaa in July 2015, and in both Houthi and Hadi government-held areas in July 2017.[30] In June 2020, Russia allocated $4 million in food aid to Yemen via the World Food Programme, which reflected its commitment to helping Yemen mitigate the combined impact of war and the COVID-19 pandemic.[31] These policies are linked with Russia's broader efforts to showcase itself as a humanitarian vanguard that takes action on issues the West sidesteps, like encouraging international donors to contribute to Syria's reconstruction efforts or upholding commitments of citizenship to the families of former IS fighters. Focusing on these issues strengthens Russia's soft power-building efforts on the world stage.

Third of these narratives, Russia's opposition to the Saudi-led military intervention in Yemen and sympathetic attitude towards its humanitarian costs reflect its broader ambitions of enhancing its soft power in the Arab world at the expense of the United States. This approach aligns closely with Yulia Kiseleva's theory on the role of soft power in Russian foreign policy, which contends that Russia has paid increased attention to soft power in order to bolster its international status, but also frequently measures soft power in terms of "opposition to the West and its hegemonic discourse."[32] Russian government officials and pro-Kremlin media outlets have delegitimized US involvement in Yemen to varying degrees. During the early stages of the civil war, Russian diplomats linked events in Yemen to other controversial decisions where the United States was significantly involved, like the 2000 overthrow of President Slobodan Milošević in Yugoslavia, and the 2003 Iraq War.[33] In November 2018, the Russian Foreign Ministry released a particularly pointed criticism of US policy in Yemen, stating that "everything indicates that the US side is not planning to change its policy in Yemen," in spite of Washington's pro-peace rhetoric.[34]

In order to delegitimize US involvement in Yemen, Kremlin-aligned media outlets regularly challenged the argument that US support for the Saudi-led military intervention was linked to legitimate security rationales, and instead argued that US policymakers were afraid of the challenge posed by the Houthis to the regional status quo.[35] The Russian media also promoted the argument that US policymakers were supporting the Saudi-led intervention in Yemen to help the Saudi monarchy mask its internal vulnerabilities, and that proposed negotiations were insincere efforts to appease anti-war members of the Saudi royal family.[36] These theories have been supplemented by unflattering coverage of US involvement in Yemen on broadcast media outlets, like RT Arabic and Channel One Rossiya, which include frequent graphic depictions of civilian casualties in Yemen resulting from Saudi air strikes and frame the US as a willing abettor of Saudi war crimes.

Although quantitative data on the resonance of these narratives in the Arab world is limited in scope, circumstantial evidence points to the growing effectiveness of Russia's anti-US media campaign on Yemen. Due to its effective use of social media dissemination, the RT Arabic website is now the fortieth most viewed online webpage in Yemen ahead of Al-Arabiya and Al Jazeera, and it also captures a larger audience than both of its regional media rivals in Syria, Libya, Iraq, Jordan, Tunisia, Kuwait, Egypt, and Algeria.[37] *Sputnik Arabic* reinforces these messages and often highlights local voices, such as Adel al-Shujaa from the General People's Congress, that support the expansion of the Russian diplomatic role in Yemen.[38] As the audience share of Russian state media outlets continues to grow, especially among Arabs under the age of thirty, it is unsurprising that young Arabs ranked Russia as their must trusted regional partner, ahead of the United States, in the Wilson Center's 2017 and 2018 Arab Youth Surveys. The apparent success of the Kremlin's soft power campaign in the Arab world has hinged on its ability to synthesize the image of Russia as a loyal ally. This has been the hallmark of Russia's policy in Syria, with opposition to US-backed unilateralism, as well as the focus of its policy in Yemen. While the durability of Russia's soft power in the Middle East hinges on its continued involvement in the region— once it eventually draws down from Syria—and on the success of its numerous dialogue facilitation initiatives, it is essential to place its soft power promotion efforts in Yemen into a broader strategic context.

The Impact of Russia's Involvement in the Yemeni Civil War on its Regional Partnerships

In light of this chapter's examination of the strategic interests, status aspirations, and soft power building initiatives that are directly linked to Russia's position towards the Yemeni civil war, it is important for a more complete context to expand the scope of analysis into an exploration of how Moscow's Yemen policy has influenced its regional power projection efforts. As Russia has engaged in frequent dialogue with the Iran-aligned Houthi movement,[39] the Saudi-backed Hadi government, and the UAE-sponsored STC, the impact of Moscow's policy of strategic nonalignment and dialogue facilitation initiatives on its relationships with these three regional powers will constitute the focus of this chapter's regional-level analysis.

Russia's Response to the Yemeni Civil War and Partnership-Building with Iran

As Iran emerged as a vital military partner for Russia in Syria just months after the start of the Yemeni civil war, the implications of Russia's handling of the Yemen conflict as it affects the Moscow-Tehran relationship are worthy of deeper exploration. During the initial stages of the Yemeni civil war, Russia, expecting Iran would keep its involvement limited, did not subscribe to the "sectarian proxy war narrative" that gained immediate support in the United States,[40] nor did it make direct comparisons to the Egypt-Saudi Arabia rivalry in North Yemen during the 1962–70 civil war. Reflecting on these assumptions, Grigory Kosach, a professor at the Russian State Institute of the Humanities and expert on the politics of the Arab world, argued in April 2015 that Iran would restrict its involvement in Yemen. This was largely due to the detachment of the Houthis' Zaidi brand of Shi'ism from the sect's mainstream community and Tehran's unwillingness to risk derailing a potential deal on its nuclear weapons program with the United States.[41]

Iran's alleged provisions of substantive material support to the Houthis challenged this logic and sharpened divergences between Russia's and Iran's perspectives on the Yemeni civil war. The differences between Russia's and Iran's perspectives on Yemen were especially pronounced in March 2015, when Putin unsuccessfully urged Iranian President Hassan Rouhani to refrain from deeper involvement in Yemen and subsequently consulted with Israeli Prime Minister Benjamin Netanyahu, who raised the issue of Iran's interference in Yemen.[42] As Russia-Iran relations have improved in recent years, Moscow has refrained from overtly pressuring Iran on its conduct in Yemen. In contrast to the US government's periodic linkage of Iran's support for regional proxies with the progress of nuclear program-related negotiations, Russia has consistently argued that Tehran's conduct in Yemen should be decoupled from the nuclear issue.

Nevertheless, differences between the Russian and Iranian approaches to the conflict have persisted. Hamidreza Azizi, a former assistant professor at Shahid Beheshti University in Tehran and fellow at the German Institute for International and Security Affairs, notes that Iran is primarily focused on changing the balance of power in Yemen and forcing Saudi Arabia to legitimize the Houthis, while Russia is chiefly preoccupied with preserving the existing balance of power in Yemen.[43] In Azizi's view, these disparate points of focus meant Iran did not share Russia's alarm at the death of Saleh, as the ex-Yemeni president had broken with the Houthis and limited Russia-Iran cooperation in Yemen to tactical collaboration.[44]

In spite of their different perspectives on the Yemeni civil war, Russia and Iran have continued to regularly consult on the conflict. These consultations encompass a wide variety of issues, which include the establishment of intra-Yemeni dialogue and the de-escalation of tensions in Hodeidah.[45] The foundations for Russia-Iran dialogue on Yemen were established by alignments in both countries' perspectives on international norms surrounding Saudi Arabia's military intervention in Yemen. For example, on April 30, 2015, Iran's Deputy Foreign Minister Hossein Amir-Abdollahian openly described Saudi Arabia's de facto implementation of a no-fly zone in Yemen as a violation of international law.[46] This statement was a much more strident articulation of concerns expressed by Lavrov and Kosachev about Saudi Arabia's willingness to unilaterally intervene without UN Security Council approval, which were noted earlier in the chapter. The US government's support for Saudi Arabia's military operations also strengthened Russia's solidarity with Iran: both countries had previously opposed US-led military interventions, including the 1999 Kosovo War, the 2003 Iraq War, and the 2011 NATO intervention in Libya, and they now regarded Yemen as a new theater of pernicious US power projection.

Although Russia and Iran disagree on Hadi's legitimacy, both countries share some common ideas on the mechanisms that could undergird an effective peace process in Yemen. Iranian Foreign Minister Mohammad Javad Zarif's four-point peace plan called for resumption of broad national dialogue, and the establishment of a constructive unity government as the immediate replacement for Saudi-led military activities.[47] This position directly aligns with Russian official statements on the need for an internally driven reconciliation between Yemeni factions. This area of common ground echoes similarities in Russia and Iran's official positions on peace in Afghanistan, as Iran has actively participated in the Moscow-format talks between the Taliban and Afghan subnational actors. As Russia and Iran seek to extend their diplomatic cooperation beyond the Syrian context, strengthened normative bonds in Yemen could contribute to a more complete upgrade of their bilateral diplomatic partnership.

In addition to facilitating the consolidation of Russia and Iran's normative partnership, Moscow's defense of Iran at the UN against allegations of arming the Houthis in public (February 2018) and private (December 2018) settings reinforced the Kremlin's self-projected image as a loyal partner to allies in crisis. According to Fyodor Lukyanov, the editor in chief of *Russia in Global Affairs* magazine,

Tehran did not share this perception of Russia. Many Iranian officials view Russia as a country that would express solidarity with its opposition to US policies in general terms, but then pull back from colliding with Western policies in order to avoid a deeper US-Russia schism.[48] As Russia viewed Iran as an increasingly important regional partner, it was keen to change this perception of itself. Iranian officials viewed Russia's delivery of the S-300 air defense system to Iran in 2015 as a show of solidarity with Tehran against a possible spillover of the Yemen war into a broader Iran-Saudi Arabia conflict.[49] However, Russia's most notable defense of Iran occurred in February 2018, when Moscow vetoed a British-drafted UN resolution that blamed Tehran for violating the international arms embargo against the Houthis. To justify its veto, Russia's Permanent Representative to the UN, Vasily Nebenzia, described the conclusions of the UN Panel of Experts as "selective and contentious" and warned that punishing Iran over unconfirmed allegations would escalate sectarian tensions.[50] US Deputy Representative to the UN, Kelley Eckels Currie, harshly criticized Nebenzia's comments and accused Russia of "protect[ing] Iran's efforts to destabilize the region and spreading its malign influence."[51]

In spite of US frustrations, Russia held firm and blocked another British draft resolution condemning the Iran-Houthi alliance in December 2018. Russia's defense of Iran against allegations of arming the Houthis was a notable display of solidarity with Tehran. In January 2018, Yemen's Foreign Minister Abulmalik al-Mekhlafi had asked Russia to urge Iran to stop interfering in Yemen's internal affairs, but Moscow ignored Yemen's pleas.[52] Iran's Tasnim News Agency praised Russia's decision, as it vindicated Tehran's insistence that the Houthis had strengthened their military capabilities independently.[53] Hamidreza Azizi stated that Iranian policymakers viewed Russia's veto as symbolically significant. It demonstrated that Moscow's displeasure with the Houthis launching strikes on Saudi Arabia's territory would not translate into acquiescing to diminished Iranian influence in the Middle East.[54] Russia's veto also paved the way for the Russia-Iran partnership's crystallization ahead of the Trump administration's May 2018 withdrawal from the Joint Comprehensive Plan of Action (JCPOA).

How Moscow's Handling of the Yemeni Civil War Influenced Russia's Partnerships with Saudi Arabia and the UAE

Due to the central role Saudi Arabia played in the escalation of the Yemeni civil war, Russian policymakers were cognizant of the potentially significant impact their approach to the conflict would have on the Russia-Saudi Arabia bilateral relationship. Russia's relationship with Saudi Arabia has fluctuated greatly since March 2015. Russia's coordination with Iran in Syria, which began in September 2015, resulted in acute strains in Moscow's relationship with Riyadh. King Salman's visit to Russia in October 2017 and Saudi Arabia's corresponding reduction of support for Syrian rebel groups ameliorated these tensions. Although these changes impacted Russia's engagements with Yemeni internal factions, intriguingly, they did not moderate Russia's criticisms of the Saudi-led military coalition's activities, nor did they result in a drastic reevaluation of the drivers of Saudi conduct in Yemen. The reasons for Russia's static attitude towards Saudi Arabia's involvement in Yemen, during a period of profoundly changing diplomatic relations, and the implications of Moscow's handling of the Yemeni civil war on the Russia-Saudi Arabia relationship will dominate this section's analysis.

In addition to the aforementioned statements by Lavrov, Kosachev, and Patrushev, which raised doubts about the appropriateness of Saudi Arabia's decision to intervene in Yemen without UN Security Council approval, some members of the Russian analytical community challenged Saudi Arabia's official justifications for intervention in Yemen. In interviews with *Vedomosti* in March 2015, Leonid Issaev, an associate professor at the Higher School of Economics in St. Petersburg, contended that Saudi Arabia's efforts to link the Houthis to al-Qaeda were detached from empirical realities.[55] Nikita Smagin, an expert on Iran at the Russian International Affairs Council, argued that the "Iranian threat overrode the threat of radical Islam" in the eyes of Saudi policymakers.[56] Sergey Serebrov, a senior researcher at Moscow's Institute of Oriental Studies, challenged the Saudi narrative that the Yemen war was purely a struggle between Iran-backed Houthi coup plotters and the Hadi government by highlighting the role of long-standing intra-clan rivalries, which boiled over in 2015 and caused the war.[57]

Another prevailing hypothesis in Russia was that Saudi Arabia intervened in Yemen for expansionist reasons, as Riyadh wanted to secure access to Yemen's strategically significant locations. One commonly voiced narrative within the Russian foreign policy establishment was the hypothesis that Saudi Arabia wanted to seize Aden from the Houthis to completely dominate the Bab el-Mandeb Strait and its accompanying oil tanker passage routes.[58] However, Russian policymakers believed that Saudi Arabia's aspirations were based on gross overestimations of Riyadh's ability to succeed militarily in Yemen. Within the Russian Ministry of Defense, it was widely believed that Saudi Arabia would fail to achieve a military solution in Yemen, as Riyadh was unable to quell Houthi unrest with force in 2009 and was unlikely to deploy large numbers of ground troops to Yemen. If the conflict in Yemen escalated into a broader war between Saudi Arabia and Iran, the prognosis, from Russia's standpoint, was similarly grim for Riyadh. Yevgeny Satanovsky, the president of Moscow's Institute of the Middle East, stated that Iran would triumph over Saudi Arabia as easily as a "Caucasian shepherd dog would overpower a cocker spaniel," and argued that unless international oil prices were severely impacted, the war would be between local actors.[59]

In spite of the skepticism amongst prominent Russian experts about Saudi Arabia's intentions and capacity to succeed militarily in Yemen, Russia still viewed its policy of strategic nonalignment and dialogue facilitation efforts in Yemen as potential catalysts for an eventual de-escalation of tensions with Saudi Arabia. These aspirations for normalization have been facilitated by consistent dialogue between Russia and Saudi Arabia on Yemen. This pattern of engagement began in the immediate aftermath of Russia's abstention from UN Resolution 2216, as Saudi Crown Prince Mohammed bin Salman urged Russia to align more closely with Riyadh's position on Yemen during his visit to St. Petersburg on June 19, 2015.[60] Even though Russia did accede to Mohammed bin Salman's request, its desire to avoid "violating the status quo on the Arabian Peninsula" and strengthen its relationship with Saudi Arabia caused Moscow to disapprove of "Iran's war games" in Yemen.[61] During King Salman's October 2017 visit to Moscow, peace in Yemen was also discussed,[62] as it was Saudi Arabia's highest-priority foreign policy issue. Although

Assad's growing strength in Syria and Saudi Arabia's continued air strikes in Yemen caused periodic bilateral frictions, Riyadh valued Russia's restrained approach to the Yemen conflict and its refusal to interfere in what Saudi Arabia viewed to be a domestic problem.

The stagnant progress of Saudi Arabia's military intervention in Yemen could also allow Russia to present itself as a potential back-channel facilitator of diplomacy between Saudi Arabia and the Houthis. Kirill Semenov, a Russian defense analyst specializing in Libya and Yemen, notes that Russia wanted to pursue this role due to the stagnation of Saudi Arabia's military intervention after the autumn of 2015, growing disagreements between Saudi Arabia and the UAE on Hadi's viability, and the ineffectiveness of Kuwait's prior mediation initiatives.[63] Peter Salisbury, the International Crisis Group's senior analyst for Yemen, concurs with Semenov's perspective by stating that Russia could establish itself as an informal diplomatic backchannel during periods of stagnation in UN peace talks.[64] The collaboration between Russian medics and Saudi officials on providing treatment to Saleh in October 2017 also underscored the potential for Russia and Saudi Arabia to cooperate in Yemen, if the interests of both countries coincide. To increase its credibility as a dialogue facilitator in the eyes of Saudi policymakers, Mark Katz, a leading US-based expert on Russian policy in the Middle East and professor at George Mason University, contends that Russian Ambassador to Yemen, Vladimir Dedushkin, actively supported Ahmed Salem al-Wahishi's nomination as Yemen's ambassador in July 2017.[65] The revival of the UN peace process in Yemen under the supervision of Martin Griffiths ensured that Russia's dialogue facilitation offer was a contingency, rather than a developed policy, but implementation difficulties with the December 2018 Stockholm Agreement could change this calculus.

In the meantime, the primary area where Russian involvement in Yemen could strengthen the Russia-Saudi Arabia relationship lies in the sphere of energy security. Ambassador Ahmed Salem al-Wahishi praised Russia's private expressions of solidarity with Hadi's government after the July 2018 Houthi strikes against Saudi oil tankers temporarily disrupted Saudi Arabia's oil shipments through the Bab el-Mandeb Strait.[66] Notwithstanding this solidarity, Russia has actively discouraged Saudi Arabia from emphasizing Iran's culpability in Houthi strikes on Saudi oil facilities, and Moscow views the cessation of hostilities in Yemen as intertwined with the issue of energy security in the Gulf. While Russia has successfully engaged some of Saudi Arabia's GCC counterparts—like Kuwait, which has brokered negotiations to end the Yemeni civil war and periodically endorsed Russia's reticence to blame Iran for Houthi actions, and Oman—Moscow has struggled to promote the merits of its integrated approach to Gulf security to Saudi policymakers.[67] Russia's decision to unveil a Gulf security plan in July 2019 and Putin's successful trip to Saudi Arabia in October 2019 suggest that it wishes to present itself to Riyadh as a voice of moderation, in spite of Saudi Arabia's reluctance to accept Moscow's message.

Russia's policy of strategic nonalignment in the Yemeni civil war has also impacted its strengthening relationship with the UAE, which was upgraded to a strategic partnership in June 2018. Much like their Saudi counterparts, UAE policymakers have frequently consulted Russia on resolving the Yemeni civil war and pledged to cooperate with Russia on counterterrorism, as Abu Dhabi has emphasized its critical role in combatting al-Qaeda in the Arabian Peninsula (AQAP).[68] Russia and the UAE's regular consultations on Yemen could also be motivated by partial synergies in their approaches to final status issues pertaining to the conflict. Former US Ambassador to the UAE, Marcelle Wahba, notes that UAE policymakers are "not allergic" to a loose federation in Yemen, mirrored after Iraq, if it could help mitigate intraregional divisions, and they believe that Hadi can be replaced by a less polarizing official as leader of this federation without breaching UN Resolution 2216.[69] This position aligns with Russia's calls for an all-inclusive political settlement in Yemen, and prior support for Saleh as a leader who could unite warring factions.

Another emerging area of Russia-UAE cooperation in Yemen is the status of southern Yemen. In addition to the aforementioned discussions between Zubaidi and Bogdanov, Russia arbitrated numerous dialogue facilitation initiatives between rival southern Yemeni factions in 2018. Russian officials, like Vladimir Dedushkin, have also repeatedly emphasized the importance of resolving the southern question for an end to the Yemeni civil war,[70] which could be interpreted as a tacit criticism of the STC's continued exclusion from UN peace talks. Russia's willingness to pay attention to the situation in southern Yemen, while other countries have ignored it, has been cordially welcomed in Abu Dhabi, even though Moscow remains reticent about the UAE's unilateral use of force. These concerns surfaced after the UAE annexed Socotra on April 30, 2018, which prevented Yemen's prime minister, Ahmed Obeid bin Daghr, from leaving the island. After these developments, Russian state media outlet *Sputnik* published a story claiming the UAE intended to convert the island of Socotra into an "eighth emirate" in order to bolster its influence in the Gulf of Aden and complement its growing military presence in Somaliland.[71] An STC official familiar with Russia's strategic objectives in southern Yemen noted that Russia's private frustration with the UAE's assertiveness in Socotra and southern Yemen were linked to its desire to compete with Abu Dhabi for influence in this strategically important region.[72]

The STC's seizure of Aden in August 2019, which escalated tensions between UAE- and Saudi-aligned forces in Yemen to the brink of a proxy war, sharpened the areas of both synergy and discord between Russia and the UAE on southern Yemen. From the inception of the standoff, Russia attempted to strike a balance between the seemingly irreconcilable positions of Saudi Arabia and the UAE. Citing their correspondences with Russian defense experts, *Kommersant* journalists Marianna Belenkaya and Elizaveta Naumova predicted that the Saudi-UAE dispute over southern Yemen would be short-lived, and that both countries had chosen Yemen as a convenient theater in which to air their grievances.[73]

In a noteworthy contrast with public statements released by the United States and the European Union, Russian Deputy Ambassador to the UN Dmitry Polyanskiy refrained from expressing public support for Yemen's unity during an August 10, 2019 statement.[74] Andrei Baklanov, Russia's ambassador to Saudi Arabia from 2000 to 2005, explained the ambiguous nature of Polyanskiy's statement by noting that a united Yemen remained Russia's preferred outcome, but Moscow would be open to the creation of an independent south Yemeni state if intraregional political violence continued.[75] Polyanskiy's comment reflects a broader trend in Russian policy towards southern Yemen. In June 2020, the Yemeni government accused the STC of piracy after it diverted $255 million in Russian-printed banknotes that were en route to Yemen's central bank. The Russian Foreign Ministry acknowledged the incident but did not criticize the STC's conduct.[76]

In order to appease elements within the Saudi foreign policy establishment,[77] which viewed the UAE's actions as a betrayal of the coalition's mandate, Russia publicly revealed its frustrations with the UAE's unilateralism for the first time by expressing concern about Emirati air strikes in Aden on August 31, 2019.[78] The November 5, 2019 Riyadh Agreement, which called for power-sharing between the Hadi government and the STC, caused Russia to reassess its position on Emirati conduct in Yemen, and the Russian Foreign Ministry praised Saudi and UAE mediation efforts the day after this pact was signed.[79] However, aside from its August 31 statement, Russia has refused to criticize Emirati conduct otherwise, despite the fact that the UAE is believed to have encouraged the STC's subsequent violations of the Riyadh Agreement.

Russia's Approach to Conflict Resolution in Yemen and the Sustainability of Moscow's Engagement with the Houthis

To foster a more inclusive political order in Yemen, Russia has called for political settlement negotiations that engage a panoramic array of factions. Nikolay Surkov, an associate professor in the Oriental Studies Department of Moscow State Institute of International Relations (MGIMO), argues that international stakeholders should negotiate consistently with tribes and leaders on the ground to establish clearly identifiable partnerships amongst Yemeni elites, and then proceed to push them towards developing a common position.[80] Mirroring Russia's support for reconstruction investments in Syria during an ongoing civil war, a 2017 report from Moscow's Institute of World Economy and International Relations (IMEMO) called upon China and other international actors to revitalize Yemen's oil industry, as providing Yemen with an independent revenue stream would increase its capacity to resist Saudi air strikes.[81] To restrict international actors' willingness to inflame the Yemeni civil war, Russia has argued that conflict resolution negotiations in Yemen should be accompanied by parallel-track negotiations aimed at achieving a Saudi Arabia-Iran rapprochement. This position is in stark contrast to US efforts to combine peace in Yemen with a confrontational foreign policy towards Iran, reflecting the popular view in Moscow that the existing system of collective security in the Middle East is dysfunctional.

In addition to spelling out strategies for advancing intra-Yemeni dialogue and a peace settlement in Yemen, Russia has facilitated the implementation of a political solution to the Yemeni civil war through active engagement with the Houthis. While the economic reconstruction and collective security dimensions of Russia's conflict resolution strategy in the Yemeni civil war remain aspirational objectives, the credibility of Russia's professed aim to create an inclusive settlement in Yemen has been enhanced by Moscow's constructive engagement policy towards the Houthis. As the civil war intensified and prospects for a Saudi-orchestrated military solution dwindled, Russia cautiously engaged the Houthis. Russia engaged with Houthi representatives and Houthi-aligned General People's Congress (GPC) officials on a semi-regular basis, and in December 2016 a Houthi delegation visiting Moscow claimed that it "highly assessed" Russia's approach to Yemen.[82]

In spite of Moscow's thaw with Sanaa and growing tensions with Saudi Arabia, Russia refrained from directly aligning with the Houthis because it wished to leverage its multi-vector approach to Yemen and possessed reservations about Houthi belligerence. The Kremlin's exercise of caution towards the Houthis was exemplified when Oleg Dremov, Russian *charge d'affaires* to Sanaa, swiftly recanted a statement endorsing the Houthi-Saleh coalition in August 2016, and further by Putin's non-response to Houthi calls for military assistance in July 2018. The assassination of Saleh in December 2017 caused Russia to briefly reassess its relationship with the Houthis; Russian diplomats in Sanaa fled to Riyadh in the wake of concerns about whether the Houthis would foment instability in Yemen. Sergey Serebrov noted, however, that concerns about the safety of Russian diplomats were in the event that Ahmed Ali Abdullah Saleh, the ex-president's eldest son, rallied GPC militias against the Houthis, arguing that Russia's withdrawal from Sanaa would not result in Russia abandoning its policy of engaging with all factions in Yemen.[83]

While the exact scope of Russia's dialogue with the Houthis is unclear, interviews with Sanaa-based experts conducted for this chapter and the aforementioned contextual examination of Russia's plan for peace in Yemen provide clues on Moscow's area of focus. Russia's first priority when it comes to engaging with the Houthis is to encourage members of the rebel group to participate in multilateral peace talks. The arrivals of Houthi delegations to Moscow in December 2016 and October 2018 occurred in the aftermath of aborted peace processes in Kuwait and Geneva, respectively, and Russia undoubtedly wanted to highlight its potential to help restore the Houthis' confidence in peace talks. According to Yemeni analyst Mareb Alward, the Houthi delegations in Moscow consisted of less extreme figures within the movement, like Mohammed Abdulsalam, who had participated in Oman-sponsored dialogue facilitation initiatives.[84]

The Houthi leadership has also expressed divided opinions on Russia. In May 2020, Mohammed al-Bukhaiti, the head of the Shura Council of the Houthi government in Sanaa, warned Russia against militarily involving itself in Yemen or becoming a foreign occupation force.[85] By contrast, the Houthi movement's leader Mohammed al-Houthi told *Sputnik Arabic* in March 2021 that he would welcome Moscow-hosted talks between "the Republic of Yemen and the countries of aggression."[86] The notion that militant Islamist groups should not be viewed as unitary categories, but should instead be subdivided into moderate and extreme elements, has defined Russia's engagement with the Taliban. Due to the numerous fault lines among the Houthis, this policy of dividing militant groups also influences Russia's efforts to bring the Houthis to the bargaining table.

The second objective is to act as a liaison between the Hadi government and the Houthis, as Russia wants to demonstrate that it is the only great power that can engage with the two predominant warring parties. Abdulsalam Mohammed, the chairman of Sanaa's Abaad Studies and Research Center, stated that there is a widespread consensus in the Yemeni analytical community that Bogdanov, during his October 2018 meeting with Mohammed Abdulsalam, put pressure on the Houthis to cease using political prisoners as bargaining chips and tried to convince them of the potential benefits of withdrawing from Hodeidah.[87] The salience of these concerns for Hadi's government contributed to their possible presence as agenda items in Russia's most recent summit with the Houthis.

Although Russia's engagement with the Houthis bolsters its prestige as a contributor to a diplomatic resolution of the Yemeni civil war, there are substantial normative obstacles to Russia's acceptance of a federal solution in Yemen that grants the Houthis de facto hegemony over large areas of northern Yemen. Russia has historically viewed with apprehension grassroots Islamist movements and militant groups that overthrow secular authoritarian leaders through extralegal means, and it has sought to thwart their campaigns to gain international recognition. This view of Islamist non-state actors explains why Russia has designated the Muslim Brotherhood as a terrorist organization since 2003 and collectively described moderate Syrian opposition forces as Islamic extremists throughout the civil war. Nonetheless, Russia's rapprochement with Egypt under Muslim Brotherhood President Mohammed Morsi in 2012, its dialogue with Hamas on Israeli-Palestinian peace, and its outreach to the Taliban at the 2018 Moscow-format talks on Afghanistan demonstrate that Russia can pragmatically negotiate with Islamist groups. Russia's engagement with the Houthis fits both of the criteria that have historically exempted Islamist groups from being categorized as terrorists.

The first exemption applies to Islamist militant groups primarily focused on combatting an external adversary that has intervened militarily with questionable legal grounding. Former Soviet diplomat Viacheslav Matuzov argues that Russia does not designate Hezbollah and Hamas as terrorist groups because they developed in response to Israel's occupations of southern Lebanon and the Palestinian territories, and they engaged in combat with Israel to "liberate" these regions.[88] While Russian officials did not explicitly describe Saudi Arabia as an occupying force in Yemen, the Kremlin's efforts to delegitimize the Saudi-led coalition's conduct during the early stages of the war suggests that, in Russia's viewpoint, this exemption applies to the Houthis.

The second exemption that Russia has cited to justify diplomacy with militant Islamist groups is based on assessments of their ability to command popular legitimacy in the areas they occupy. Russia's de facto recognition of the Taliban's indispensability in Afghanistan, as well as its dialogue with Hamas shortly after the 2006 Gaza elections, provides evidence for Moscow's willingness to engage with Islamist groups that command substantial popular loyalty. Accordingly, supporters of Russia's engagement with the Houthis have emphasized their enduring popular support as a factor that necessitates the movement's inclusion in a Yemeni peace settlement. Grigory Lukyanov, a senior lecturer at the Higher School of Economics (HSE), argues that the indispensability of the Houthis was illustrated by the movement's preservation of internal cohesion and strong popular support, even after Saleh's murder in 2017 and allegations that the Houthis were involved in exacerbating Yemen's humanitarian catastrophe.[89] While Russia's desire to strengthen its partnerships with Saudi Arabia and the UAE will prevent it from unilaterally pushing for the recognition of Houthi sovereignty in northern Yemen, the above mentioned areas of exemption will likely deter Moscow from blocking a peace settlement that calls for this outcome.

Concluding Thoughts

Although Russia has cautiously refrained from embroiling itself deeply in a protracted conflict that shows few signs of abating, Moscow has subtly taken steps to bolster its influence over the resolution of the Yemen war. Russia's policy of strategic nonalignment has allowed it to maintain positive relations with all major warring factions in the Yemeni civil war, leaving it well placed to carve out a dialogue facilitation role, if it so chooses. Russia's strategic nonalignment policy has also allowed it to emphasize different elements of its position on the Yemeni civil war to regional powers intertwined in the conflict, thus simultaneously strengthening its partnerships with Iran, the UAE, and Saudi Arabia. While these achievements and potential openings for greater influence in Yemen are noteworthy, the narrative of Russian involvement in the Yemeni civil war is not one of unquestioned success, as Moscow still faces obstacles to implementing its vision.

The sustainability of Russia's regional balancing act, which is the cornerstone of Russia's Middle East strategy—viewed in Moscow as Putin's crowning diplomatic achievement on the world stage—has been periodically obstructed by Russia's normative challenges to the

Saudi-led military intervention as well as frustrations with Houthi belligerence. Russia's rhetorical focus on the humanitarian costs of the Saudi-led military coalition's air strikes and food security in Yemen rings hollow in the West and much of the Arab world due to Moscow's role as an abettor of war crimes in Syria. Yet, Russia can point to its ability to strengthen its relations with Saudi Arabia and Qatar—in spite of their deeper disagreements over Syria—and its growing role in highlighting humanitarian issues that the West ignores as proof that these obstacles can be overcome. As the international community coalesces around the need for a political settlement in Yemen, Russia's preservation of good relations with all warring factions in Yemen could give it a surprisingly important role in resolving a seemingly intractable conflict.

8

MAKING UP FOR LOST TIME

RUSSIA AND CENTRAL MAGHREB

Yahia H. Zoubir

Introduction

Academic and journalistic reports have argued that in recent years Russia has been on a serious offensive in the Middle East in general and North Africa in particular. Some argue that, "with the world's attention focused on the question of Russian influence in the United States and the European Union, the Kremlin is quietly making inroads in another region critical to both the United States and Europe: the five North African states of the southern Mediterranean shore."[1] Placing the issue in a broader context, it has been suggested that, "from Morocco to Egypt, Moscow has been expanding influence through arms and energy deals, tourism promotion, and diplomatic overtures to warm relations and slowly dislodge US influence in North Africa."[2] Most of the recent articles on Russia suggest that the country's moves in the region represent a threat to US and European interests. As one author put it, "while U.S. attention is focused on fires already raging in the Middle East, Russia is quietly expanding its presence in North Africa, to the detriment of U.S. interests."[3] In sum, most see Russia's strategy in the region as posing an existential threat to the West.[4]

Undoubtedly, Russia's activities in the Central Maghreb (Algeria, Morocco, and Tunisia) have been noticeable in recent years. However, unlike those who see Russian policy as part of a far-reaching scheme, this chapter supports the view that Moscow has no grand design for the region. One can only subscribe to Watanabe's proposition that:

> In order to secure its status as a major external powerbroker in the region, Russia is reviving Soviet-era ties with a number of countries in the Middle East and North Africa, as well as forging new ones. Moscow lacks a clear strategy—its approach is pragmatic, engaging a variety of regimes and employing a range of policy instruments. Yet it lacks the economic clout and desire to take on great power responsibilities in the region. Russia is likely to boost its regional profile through economic and military cooperation, as well as through diplomacy, capitalizing on the West's absence or missteps.[5]

While Russia is a relatively important player in the Maghreb, the region itself is not vital for its interests, nor did it represent strategic importance for the Soviet Union during the Cold War.[6] However, although like the United States Russia did not historically view the Maghreb as a strategic regional entity,[7] it has nonetheless succeeded in building good, long-term relations with the Maghreb states, particularly with Algeria.

Like China today,[8] Moscow has sought to revive and consolidate those traditional relations to reassert its great-power status on the world stage, and has expressed more clearly its intent to defend its political, trade, security, and cultural interests. Indubitably, there are many parallels between Russia's approach to the Maghreb and Moscow's style of engagement in the region during the Soviet era, without the ideological overtones that had been characteristic back then.[9] Today, Moscow's policy in the Maghreb is more pragmatic and more appealing to the incumbent Maghreb governments seeking to balance out—or even perhaps distance themselves from—

Western powers perceived as being too intrusive in their domestic affairs (e.g., promotion of human rights) or as unreliable in lending support (e.g., Donald Trump's election to the US presidency left Morocco uncertain as to the United States' position on Western Sahara before Trump's recognition, on December 10, 2020, of Morocco's sovereignty over the illegally occupied Western Sahara in exchange for Morocco's normalization of relations with Israel in the Abraham Accords). Indeed, the Maghreb governments have shown increasing affinity for the Russian and Chinese authoritarian models of governance—Putin's iron-fist rule and "Chinese authoritarian capitalism"—the type that Algeria, Morocco, and Tunisia (until the overthrow of President Ben Ali) have practiced, whatever the particularities of their rule. This is especially true since the so-called Arab Spring, which Moscow, Beijing, and most Arab states have interpreted as an attempt by Western powers to induce regime change in the region.[10]

This chapter will first provide a review of Soviet Russia's relations with the Maghreb states. This will demonstrate the ties that Moscow had established previously and help explain the restoration of these relations. Because of Russia's close partnership with Algeria, the chapter will provide a deeper review of the bilateral ties that Moscow has developed with Algiers. While Moscow does not view the Maghreb as a strategic regional entity, it is nonetheless an integral part of Russia's strategy in the Mediterranean.[11] This chapter will analyze the major areas of cooperation in which Moscow has engaged. Finally, the chapter will discuss the limitations of Russia's policy towards the Maghreb states.

Soviet Objectives in the Maghreb during the Cold War

During the Cold War, Soviet objectives in the Maghreb were consistent with Moscow's global anti-colonialist and anti-imperialist strategy in the Third World within the context of the East/West rivalry.[12] The Maghreb offered a potential geopolitical advantage: the Mediterranean; the Arab-Israeli conflict, whose influence had expanded to the region; and anti-Western sentiments. Although the Maghreb was never vital to the territorial security of the USSR (unlike its direct neighbors, such as Afghanistan, Turkey, and Iran), the Soviets, like the Russians today, were cognizant of the fact that the Maghreb sits at NATO's southern flank. Therefore, Soviet presence in the region, no matter how important, constituted a potential counterweight to NATO's naval forces.

This presence played, in some respects, a deterrent or spoiler role to NATO's military and political strategy, and to possible regional interventionism. States like Algeria wished that the Soviet Union would clarify its role in preventing such potential NATO threats to progressive regimes, should they occur. In particular, they raised the question as to the basic position of the Soviet Union with regards to situations where a progressive country is the victim of aggression by an imperialist country.[13] In the 1960s, the Soviets welcomed the emergence of radical non-communist regimes in the developing world. The general criteria used to describe a non-communist, "national democratic state" were: 1) nonalignment and anti-Western orientation; 2) minimization of Western economic influence; 3) tolerance of local communists; and, 4) development of the state economic sector. The states of the Maghreb fulfilled some of these criteria.

The absence of some conditions in a particular state did not prevent the Soviets from establishing good, pragmatic relations with that country, as was the case with Morocco, for example. Moreover, the Soviets described Algeria as having followed the "non-capitalist path" of "revolutionary democracy."[14] The normalization of state-to-state relations between the Soviet Union and the countries of the Maghreb aimed to reduce Western, mostly American, influence in those regions. Further, assisting such countries in their economic development would help increase the prestige of the Soviet Union and at the same time, from an ideological perspective, create an "anti-imperialist" environment.

Like Russia today, the Soviets used different instruments to strengthen their presence in the Maghreb: economic and military aid, trade agreements, diplomatic support for Arab causes at the United Nations, political support for the Palestinians, and support for its nationalist/socialist partners. On the whole, Soviet objectives in the Maghreb were primarily to be present and to have influence in the region, to develop strong relations with the states and political parties to counterbalance US influence, to exploit the United States and its allies' failures to its own advantage, to prevent intraregional conflicts, and, most importantly, to consolidate its image as a friend of the Arabs while reinforcing the region's perception of the United States as an enemy of the people. Interestingly, some of these objectives are present in Russia's current policy and part of its objectives today. Reviewing Soviet-Algerian relations will undoubtedly demonstrate a continuity in the relations that were revitalized in the late 1990s and have continued to thrive.

Building Soviet-Algerian Relations: The Foundation of Russian-Algerian Ties

Relations between Algeria and the Soviet Union developed painstakingly during the Algerian war of independence (1954–62). Throughout the 1950s, the Algerian National Liberation Front (FLN) maintained friendly relations with the Soviets. During that period, despite certain constraints—chiefly Russia's hope to achieve détente with France—the Soviets nonetheless helped, albeit gradually and cautiously, the Algerian nationalists and even voted in favor of including the "Algerian question" at the United Nations Security Council. Moscow and post-independence Algeria then continued to pursue contrasting interests throughout the Cold War era as well as in the post-Cold War period.[15]

Algeria's post-independence rapprochement with Soviet Russia was partly the consequence of problems between the United States and Algeria that resulted from the role played by the United States during the Moroccan-Algerian conflict—the so-called "Sand War"— in the fall of 1963.[16] That same year, the United States refused to sell Algeria badly needed military equipment for the ill-equipped National Popular Army (ANP).[17] Instead, in November 1963, the Soviets agreed to supply modern military equipment to Algeria.[18] Undoubtedly, the mutual distrust between Algeria and the United States, as well as Algeria and its former colonial power,[19] compelled Algerians to a closer political and military relationship with the Soviet Union, an association which continued well into the late 1980s and has been solidly reestablished since 2001.

In December 1965, the new president, Houari Boumediène—who overthrew his seemingly pro-Soviet predecessor, Ahmed Ben Bella—visited Moscow, where he secured more economic and military aid from the Soviets, marking a strengthening of relations between the two countries. However, the Soviet Union was never an important economic partner to Algeria: Russia made up less than 1 percent of the total volume of Algeria's trade and this remains so to this day, even if new economic deals are currently helping Russia make headway in both the Middle East and the Maghreb. Indeed, Algeria's most significant relation with the Soviet Union remained first and foremost in the military realm, and to a lesser degree in the energy domains. Although Algeria sought to minimize its dependence on Soviet armaments, preferring not to allow the USSR such leverage over it,[20] ultimately it was unable to do so; the cost of Russian weaponry was (and still is) quite competitive, and Russian terms of credit were more favorable than the alternative. Furthermore, for Algerian strategists, the main security threat comes from its neighbor Morocco, which is equipped with Western, mainly US, military hardware. Most of Algeria's weaponry came from the Russians, to whom it owed a relatively high debt, receiving Soviet weapons to the amount of $5.7 billion between 1978 and 1987.[21]

Despite the importance of these ties, nationalistic Algeria refused the Soviet Union's repeated demands for a naval base: more precisely, the sheltered one in Mers-el-Kébir in western Algeria.[22] Soviet-Algerian relations were rather strong in the 1970s, contrary to what they had been in 1965–70, when Algerians had watched Soviet détente with the West with suspicion.[23] However, despite their close ties with Algeria, the Soviets avoided extending support to or diplomatic recognition of the Algerian-backed Sahrawi Arab Democratic Republic (SADR), which was proclaimed in February 1976, a move that would have alienated Morocco and threatened Russia's economic interests with it. Russia preferred to take a neutral position, while pushing for a diplomatic solution and preventing military confrontation between Algeria and Morocco, a position that has endured thus far.[24]

Undeniably, although the USSR did not overtly support the POLISARIO Front,[25] a national liberation movement fighting for independence from Spain and later from Morocco, the supply of Soviet weapons to Algeria is what allowed POLISARIO to wage war successfully against Morocco. This influx of weaponry also allowed Algeria to maintain its military superiority in case of direct confrontation with Morocco. Oil and gas revenues initially enabled Algeria to purchase these weapons, but when the price of oil depreciated, as it did in 1986, Algeria was obliged to purchase weapons on credit, even if by the mid-1980s the Soviets were demanding to be paid in hard currency.[26] In 1987, Algeria purchased $2.5 billion worth of Soviet military equipment. From its independence in 1962 to 1989, Algeria is said to have purchased more than $11 billion worth of Soviet military equipment.[27]

Russia and Algeria in the Post-Soviet Era

The collapse of the Soviet Union and Russia's preoccupation with the transition, as well as internal civil strife in Algeria, resulted in a waning of the two countries' hitherto robust relations. Algeria was faced with a quasi-civil war, while Russia had to deal with its own domestic development.[28] In fact, Russia's presence in Africa declined altogether after the Soviet Union disbanded. Not only was the Russian economy in shambles, but even its traditional military contacts with the southern Mediterranean countries were limited.[29] Indeed, Russia under Boris Yeltsin (1991–99) was absent from the Mediterranean.

In the 1990s, the Russian Federation—which Algeria recognized on December 26, 1996—was virtually absent politically and economically from Algeria. The assassination of a few Russian citizens by Islamist extremists in Algeria forced Russia to leave the country altogether. In addition, there was still tension between the two countries regarding the terms of the reimbursement of the debt Algeria had incurred towards the Soviet Union.[30]

This explains why the Algerians, who could no longer rely solely on the Russians in the 1990s, had to seek additional sources for their military and combat-training equipment.[31] In 1997, the Algerians signed contracts with South African, American, Ukrainian, and Belarusian companies for the acquisition of aircraft, helicopters, and other military equipment. Despite the diversification of its suppliers, in 1996, Algeria made the decision to develop "strategic cooperation" with Russia in order to modernize the ANP's mostly obsolete military equipment.[32] Russia, having concerns about Algeria's ability to pay off its debt incurred under the Soviet Union, was further troubled by Algeria's arms purchases from Russia's competitors, the Ukraine and Belarus, a move Algeria had used as a bargaining chip in the hopes that Russia would reduce prices.[33] Ultimately, Russian arms sales to Algeria declined substantially from what they had been during the Soviet era, falling from an annual average of $580 million in the 1980s to approximately $170 million between 1991 and 2000.[34]

The Soviet Union and Morocco and Tunisia during the Cold War

Unlike Soviet-Algerian relations—which derived their strength from ideological affinities and military cooperation—relations between Morocco and the USSR, whose agriculture relies heavily on phosphates, were based essentially upon economic and cultural interests. The USSR's interest in Morocco began in the 1950s; King Mohamed V (rule 1927–61), the father of the pro-Western Hassan II (rule 1961–99), established diplomatic relations with the Soviet Union in September 1958. After his second trip to Moscow in the fall of 1966—the first was in 1962—King Hassan secured military and economic assistance agreements.[35]

The Soviets recognized that their interests with Morocco were important enough to maintain good relations with the monarchy, despite its pro-Western stance. The seemingly balanced policy that the king pursued, and the Soviets' need to diminish US influence as well as strengthen their own interests in Morocco, provided the necessary justification for Moscow's cooperation with a "reactionary regime," in the Soviet parlance. From a Moroccan perspective, ties with the Soviet Union helped to reduce criticism by radicals and made it difficult at the same time for the Soviets to become too involved with Morocco's leftist opposition, in addition to its wish it offset Algeria's close ties with Moscow.[36]

The two Arab-Israeli wars in 1967 and 1973 offered the opportunity for Moscow to improve its image among the Moroccan population, which was quite attached to the Palestinian cause. This, of course, followed the USSR's strategy of exploiting US policy positions to Moscow's advantage. By 1978, Morocco became the Soviet Union's largest trading partner in Africa.[37] This was the result of the phosphates deal signed by the two countries on March 10, 1978;[38] dubbed by King Hassan the "contract of the century," it was of enormous importance to the Soviet Union. The Soviets had a reasonable production of phosphates, but the necessity of supplying their Council for Mutual Economic Assistance (COMECON) partners was instrumental in persuading them to sign. Under the terms of the multibillion-dollar, thirty-year contract with Morocco,[39] Moscow opened a $2 billion line of credit for the development of a new phosphate mine—discovered by the Soviets themselves—at Meškala.

Soviet-Tunisian relations have never been close, mostly due to Tunisia's identification with the West as well as President Habib Bourguiba's staunch anti-communist stance. Bourguiba made it clear that his political sympathies lay with the West, to whom he turned in an appeal for greater economic assistance. The slow response from the West, primarily from France, subsequently compelled Bourguiba to make overtures to the Eastern bloc. Tunisia subsequently received economic and technical assistance from the Soviets. With the presidency of Zine El Abidine Ben Ali (1987–2011), Soviet-Tunisian relations showed improvement. However, with the collapse of the Soviet empire, relations between Tunisia and the nascent Russian Federation were unimpressive.

Russia and the Maghreb since the 1990s

The modus operandi of the post-communist Russian state was nearly identical to that of the Soviet Union: establish Russia's presence in the area; reaffirm its superpower status; seek new partnerships; develop economic relations with regional states; provide an alternative to Western domination; revive the relations that the Soviet Union had built up; find a market for Russian military hardware; position Russia's role in global security; take advantage of Western mismanagement of the Middle East and North Africa (MENA) region; and counter Western hegemonic ambitions. The rise of "jihadism" has also impelled Russia to hinder its spread to Russian territory. Since the

Maghreb and the contiguous Sahel region boast major jihadi groups, fighting jihadism before it reaches Russia has been a primary imperative in those areas as well.[40]

Undoubtedly, the Maghreb region offers several economic prospects, with energy and armaments providing the greatest benefits. However, there exist other sectors, such as nuclear energy, fishing, railroads, agriculture, and tourism. For Russia, the Maghreb is an extension of the Middle East, which gives it real value. Perhaps more importantly, the Maghreb's Mediterranean location gives it an inestimable geopolitical dimension. There is "a [Russian] vision that integrates the Maghreb countries into the Mediterranean space, a geographical area whose control has been coveted by Russia throughout its history."[41] Whatever Moscow's real objectives, it is certain that in the Maghreb, as in the entire North Africa region, the Russians have been intent on reviving and reinforcing their relations with Algeria, and on creating new opportunities with Morocco and Tunisia. Moscow's involvement in the Libyan crisis illustrates this approach. Indeed, following NATO's intervention in Libya in 2011 and the ensuing regime change, Russia has played a considerable role in Libya post-Gaddafi. Its policy has been opportunistic, supporting one side through the Wagner mercenary group while maintaining relations with both sides in the inter-Libyan conflict.[42]

The Reawakening of Algerian and Russian Foreign Policies

The reawakening of Russian and Algerian foreign policies occurred almost simultaneously around 1999. Under Prime Minister (and later President) Vladimir Putin, Russia sought to regain its role as a great power in order to counter US world hegemony.[43] Putin understood that this could not be done without rebuilding the Russian economy. The Russian leadership decided to prioritize regaining the status it once held in the MENA region due to its considerable geopolitical interests, but also to gain clear advantage by reducing Western influence in the area.[44] Given Russia and Algeria's close political and military relations in the past, it was only natural for Moscow to seek to revitalize those relations. Moreover, Algeria had greater geopolitical significance for the Russians from the late 1990s onwards, given

Russia was eyeing up a return to North Africa. There are other reasons for this interest, notably Algeria's influential role in the region of the Sahel, as an extension of the Maghreb.

Another motive is Russia's interest in developing close ties with oil- and gas-producing countries.[45] Obviously, the energy issue was, and still is, critical for Russia as a policy instrument to exert influence, especially regarding relations with Europe, which is heavily dependent on Russian supplies. Indeed, Russia's fossil fuel industry is one of the means through which Moscow has sought to reaffirm itself as a superpower, especially when the prices of oil increased exponentially (until 2014). Equally significantly, from a Russian perspective, the Maghreb constitutes a potentially lucrative market not only in terms of arms sales—a considerable market for the Russians—but also for big industrial and infrastructural projects. Although the Europeans, Americans, Chinese, Indians, and others are already there, Russia has sought to become a key competing player. Finally, the Russians have been cognizant of the fact that France no longer enjoys the influence it once did in the Maghreb—witness the recurrence of tense Franco-Algerian relations—and the United States has increased its presence in the Maghreb-Sahel region.[46]

Algeria has several reasons for renewing its relations with Russia. First and foremost, this was part of Algeria's all-out diplomacy, whose primary objective was to break the country's decade-long isolation.[47] Since Algeria had enjoyed close ties with the Soviet Union, now that the two countries were both recovered domestically, it was only natural to revamp what had been a mutually advantageous relationship in the past. Given that the Algerian armed forces are equipped predominantly with Russian materiel, it was evident that renewed relations with Russia were necessary to effect the modernization of those forces. Russian military personnel would also be needed to repair the old equipment and eventually train Algerian forces in the use of their new, state-of-the-art weapons. More importantly, Algeria could acquire this modern materiel at a lower cost from Russia than from Western countries and without conditions attached to the sales.

More challenging for Algeria was the fact that, although its financial situation was improving with the gradual rise of the price of oil, it still could not afford to purchase the more expensive Western materiel; and besides, Western powers were reluctant to sell the country sophisticated weaponry. Both the United States and Europe, under France's influence,[48] were not sympathetic to Algeria's regional geopolitical ambitions, afraid it would upset the regional balance of power and weaken Morocco, the West's ally in the region.

Many of Algeria's high military commanders had been trained in the former Soviet Union and thus constituted a lobby in favor of stronger military ties with Russia.[49] The military dimension was not the only reason for Algeria to rekindle relations with Russia; Algerians were also hoping that the Russians would invest in the Algerian market. For Russia, "this renewal has enabled Moscow to regain ground in the Maghreb, to broaden its presence in the Mediterranean area, to become more involved on the economic and political levels in Africa and to initiate a redefinition of its relations with the countries bordering Algeria."[50] Moreover, as was the case during the Cold War, both countries often agree in their analysis of world events.[51] Furthermore, their domestic political and economic systems have significant parallels, with both countries run by authoritarian political systems and both economies dependent on hydrocarbons revenues.

The Rejuvenation of Algerian-Russian Relations

Hardly three weeks before the election of President Abdelaziz Bouteflika on April 15, 1999, A. Y. Zoubakov, the Russian government's chief of administration, led a delegation to Algiers as an important step in rejuvenating bilateral relations. A military agreement had already been signed between the two countries in the previous month, and Algeria was in the process of modernizing and professionalizing the ANP. Subsequently, flurries of reciprocal visits took place; Mohammed Lamari, Algeria's Head of the Chiefs of Staff, traveled to Moscow on several occasions. Foreign Minister of Russia Igor Ivanov's visit to Algiers on October 7, 2000, was the first time a Russian foreign minister had visited Algeria. The various bilateral discussions resulted in Bouteflika's trip to Moscow in April 2001, a watershed moment in Algerian-Russian relations.

During that visit, Bouteflika and Putin signed a "Strategic Partnership Agreement," making Algeria the first Arab and African country and the second state after India to sign such a partnership with Russia. The agreement, described as "a document without precedent in Russia's relations in the Arab World and Africa,"[52] aimed at strengthening political, economic, and military relations between the two countries. The agreement, signed on April 4, 2001, covered a multitude of areas, including economics, culture, tourism, and archives. However, unsurprisingly, its main focus involved the supply of military equipment and expertise to Algeria, to an amount of $2.5 billion.[53] Aware that a strategic partnership between Russia and Algeria, especially given its emphasis on the latter's military dimension, would inevitably provoke fears in Morocco, the EU—primarily France—and NATO, the two countries included in the text of the declaration note that this partnership was not "directed against a third state or a third group of states and does not intend on creating a political-military alliance."[54]

Following his meeting with President Bouteflika in Algiers in May 2001, Russian Vice Prime Minister Ilya Klebanov announced that the two countries had agreed to develop their bilateral relations in all areas, and that Algerian Minister of Energy Chakib Khelil and Russian Deputy Minister of Energy Alexei Miller had decided to set up a working group to coordinate bilateral cooperation in the production of oil, gas, and electricity.[55] In June 2001, after his return to Russia, Klebanov announced the beginning of a ten-year program of military and technical cooperation with Algeria.[56] The Russians had also agreed to sell the ANP twenty-two SU-24 MKs and six IL-78 tanker aircraft for refueling, which had been commissioned the year before for $120 million.[57]

The Military Dimension in Algeria-Russia Relations

The military cooperation between Algeria and Russia developed considerably following the signing of the strategic partnership in 2001. However, Algeria was not the only country with which Russia sought to strengthen its military cooperation; Russia was unfurling a deliberate policy aimed at reconquering the Arab market, this time including the Gulf countries, which were traditionally US and European customers. Russia's more pragmatic, ideologically lenient policy has resulted in arms deals with Kuwait and the UAE. President Putin has toured the Middle East and North Africa, Arab leaders have in turn visited Moscow, and Russian defense organizations have participated in all the international arms exhibitions held in the Middle East. Eventually, the increase in oil and gas prices raised Russia's dependence on arms sales, which was one of its driving exports following the breakup of the Soviet Union. Still, arms sales nonetheless enabled Russia to penetrate new MENA markets—including Bahrain, Qatar, and Saudi Arabia—thus thwarting US and European domination. For Algeria, which needed to modernize the ANP's navy, army, and air force equipment, the increase in hydrocarbons revenues allowed it to purchase a variety of weapons not only from the Russians but also from the United States and other arms suppliers.

From 2001 onward, Algeria and Russia cooperated in all areas and were determined to implement their strategic partnership. In the military arena, the most noteworthy point of cooperation between the two countries was an order the Algerians placed for the purchase of more than forty military transport helicopters. In 2005, Algeria and Russia reiterated the necessity of reinforcing their relations, not only in the military arena but also at the commercial, economic, and technical levels. Intending to broaden relations between the two countries, Putin insisted on the implementation of the strategic partnership and stressed the need to set up a joint-government commission. More importantly, Putin reasserted Russia's commitment to modernizing Algeria's armed forces. He also sought cooperation in the field of energy. Moreover, Putin wanted the two countries to find a formula to settle Algeria's debt.[58] Within months, a joint commission was set up and held its first meeting in Moscow on October 7, 2010.

In March 2006, Putin traveled to Algiers, the first visit of a Russian official of that level since Nikolai Podgorny's in 1969. Although four protocols were signed during the visit,[59] none of them related to military cooperation. Nevertheless, military cooperation was highlighted as a major priority because of Putin's visit, the two countries having signed a major arms agreement that brought the value of total contracts for delivery of Russian military equipment to Algeria to $7.5 billion. The previous year, the two parties had already agreed that Russia would cancel debts Algeria owed to the Soviet Union amounting to $4.7 billion, a sum that represented 29 percent of Algeria's total foreign debt at the time.[60]

Reports indicated that Russia would sell up to 100 of the most modern combat aircraft to Algeria, including MIG-29 SMT fighter planes, together with sophisticated anti-missile air defenses. The deal was that Algeria would benefit from having $1 billion exempted from its debt to the Soviet Union for each $1 billion purchase of Russian equipment. In other words, Algeria's debt would be totally expunged if it purchased equipment in an amount equivalent or superior to the debt. In the agreement between the two sides, Algeria put forth a $7.5 billion order in military hardware. The amount was directed for the most part towards the purchase of new materiel; the rest related to revamping or repairing previously bought equipment. The agreement pertained to the delivery of aircraft, tanks, submarines, air-defense systems, and anti-tank missiles, among other hardware. This was, according to many sources, the largest single contract in military-technical cooperation in Russia's post-Soviet history.

Despite the diversification of its suppliers, Algeria's main arms provider remains Russia by a long shot; in 2011, Algeria represented 13 percent of Russia's arms market. In 2007, it appeared that Algeria might become Russia's main military partner, surpassing India and China, which are traditionally Russia's main customers. Regardless, Algeria remains to this day one of Russia's main clients in the military realm, and between 2000 and 2016, Algeria accounted for over half of Russian arms exports to the MENA region.[61] In March 2007, Algeria submitted a tender to Russia for the purchase of Su-32 fighter-bombers and Mi-28N Night Hunter helicopters, requesting that they additionally supply Su-30 Flanker fighters, MiG-29 Fulcrum fighters, Pantsir S1 short-range missile-gun systems, and T-90S tanks. The contracts were expected to be signed in 2007–08.[62]

Algerian-Russian military cooperation grew stronger since the large contracts of 2006–07. During those years, Russia delivered twenty-four Mig-29SMT fighters to Algeria, to be used by the Russian air force, which it then bought back in 2009.[63] In the summer of 2011, Algeria received two Russian 636 Improved Kilo class submarines, which it had ordered in 2006;[64] the submarines joined the two repaired and modernized ones that Algeria had acquired in the 1980s.

Algeria also ordered two Tiger corvettes for its navy,[65] as well as a Yak130 training aircraft. Hence, from 1991 to 2016, Algeria bought Russian military equipment worth approximately $10 billion, ranking Algeria the third-largest recipient of Russian arms behind India and China.[66] In September 2019, reports suggested that Algeria intended to buy thirty Russian fighter jets—sixteen Su-30MKI(A) and fourteen MiG-29M/M2—together with additional gear and shells for these planes. The purchase represents more than $2 billion.[67]

Because of the security situation prevailing on Algeria's borders, Algerian authorities were compelled to import more specific anti-terrorism equipment—drones, helicopters, self-propelled artillery, amphibious vessels, and armored vehicles—from Russia.[68] However, because of the sustained diversification of its armament, as well as military sales from China and Germany, Algeria imported only 66 percent of its military equipment from Russia during 2014–18, which is still considerable.[69] Algeria continues to receive Russian military supplies of all kinds and seems to be negotiating with Russia regarding the acquisition of S-400 missiles.[70]

While it does not seem that Algeria is interested in those systems, what is certain is that it has continued acquiring state-of-the-art Russian weaponry. In late December 2019, Algeria signed an agreement with Russia for the acquisition of fourteen Su-57 stealth fighters, becoming the first international client to whom the manufacturer Sukhoi will export this flagship of Russian combat aviation. The Algerian air force signed two other contracts for the purchase of fourteen Su-34 bombers and fourteen Su-35 air domination aircraft. An option for two additional squadrons of fourteen aircraft of each type was also signed to counterbalance the eventual withdrawal of aging aircraft from Algeria's air force fleet.[71] These acquisitions were certainly in response to Morocco's purchase from the United States of twenty-five F-16 Vipers in 2019,[72] and Italy's acquisition from the United States of F-35s.[73]

Russia has sold some of the most sophisticated weapons to Algeria, such as air defense radars and systems including the S300 pmu2, Nebo radars, and Rezonans-NE. It has also sold kilo submarines, T-90 tanks, and Su-30 fighters. Moscow has imposed no restrictions on the use of those weapons, and "in some cases some systems, such as the Yak130 and the Pantsir S, entered into service in Algeria before Russia."[74]

In March 2021, it was confirmed that Russia would deliver to Algeria fourteen Sukhoi Su-34 Fullback last-generation attack aircraft. This is an important acquisition for the Algerian Air Force. According to MENADEFENSE,

> the Novosibirsk Aerospace Plant (NAZ) (V.P. Chkalova), began in January [2021] the production of the first batch of six Su 34E for Algeria; this emergency batch will be ready from the end of 2021 and will be used for the training of Algerian trainers. The beginning of the training will take place in Russia from next summer. The rest of the production will be received in 2022 and 2023.[75]

In addition to the purchase of weapons and training of Algerian officers, the Russian Ministry of Defense announced in April 2021 that the ANP would participate in a joint military exercise with the Russian army, to be held in September 2021. The military exercises took place in early October in North Ossetia, at the Tsarskoye military training center, near the Georgian border in southwest Russia. The exercises consisted of "tactical actions for the search, detection and destruction of illegal armed groups."[76]

Energy Cooperation: An Intricate Affair

In 2005 and early 2006—in preparation for Putin's trip to Algiers—during meetings with their Algerian counterparts, Russian officials emphasized cooperation in the energy sector. Several Russian companies have invested in the energy sector in Algeria. Stroytransgaz participated in the construction of the oil pipeline connecting the southern area of Haoud el-Hemra (in Hassi R'Mel) to Arzew in western Algeria. The same company built the gas pipeline linking Sougueur to the central power plant in Hadjret Ennous in the Tipasa wilaya (province), seventy kilometers east of Algiers. Rosneft, for its part, engaged in prospection works in southern Algeria.[77] On the eve of Putin's visit, the Algerian Ministry of Foreign Affairs declared: "It was agreed today that Sonatrach [Algerian national oil company] and Russian companies can coordinate their efforts in the international gas market. They can also be associated in the realization of energy projects in different regions of the globe."[78] A spokesman for the Russian Ministry of Foreign Affairs stated that during Putin's visit, a memorandum of understanding (MoU) would be signed between Sonatrach and the Russian companies Gazprom, Lukoil, and Souyouzgaznef.[79] This corresponded to a period during which the Iranians had floated the idea of a Gas OPEC, and there was talk in Europe that such a plan had been espoused by the Russians and Algerians.

In August 2006, Sonatrach and Lukoil signed an MoU in Moscow agreeing to bilateral cooperation in the hydrocarbons sector, particularly in the exploration and development of oil and gas fields. Gazprom also investigated possibilities for similar rapprochement and visited Algiers in May to discuss cooperating with Sonatrach and sign an MoU in the area of Liquefied Natural Gas (LNG).[80] Given the precedent of the Russian-Ukraine dispute, which had resulted in Russia cutting off supplies to the Ukraine, the European Union looked with considerable misgivings on the signing of the Algerian-Russian MoU and a second one in Algiers in February 2007. The EU is highly dependent on both Russia and Algeria for its gas supplies, as it purchases 25 percent of its supply from Russia, 16 percent from Norway, and 15 percent from Algeria.[81] Initially, the EU worried that Russia and Algeria would coalesce to force an increase in the price of gas, but these fears proved to be unfounded.

One should highlight the fact that Algeria and Russia, despite their cooperation in the energy sector—in particular the gas sector—have differing interests in the long run. Algeria was concerned about the Russian-Ukrainian incident, which it saw as damaging to Algeria's interests as a supplier to Europe. It would not be beneficial to Algeria for Europe to contract with gas suppliers, such as Qatar, Egypt, or Nigeria, other than Algeria. Undoubtedly, Algeria still wishes to maintain its autonomy and can hardly afford to jeopardize its credibility in the international market. The fact that Sonatrach did not respond to Gazprom's repeated calls for joint projects, and its implicit refusal to renew the first MoU of August 2006, demonstrated that Algeria had no intention of colluding with Russia to create a gas cartel. Algeria would hardly wish to jeopardize its position as Europe's preferred supplier, coupled with the networks of gas pipelines it has built, namely Medgaz (Algeria-Spain), Galsi (underwater connection to Italy), and the Trans-Saharan Gas Pipeline (conveying Nigerian gas to be exported through the Algerian network). Energy cooperation with Russia, from an Algerian perspective, only concerns upstream projects and infrastructure; it does not pertain to cooperation in setting prices or quantities in the European market or the expansion of ventures in Europe.

Thus, neither Algeria nor Russia—both of whose main trading partner is the EU, upon which they both depend heavily for foreign investment—can afford to alienate members of their main consumer gas market (97 percent and 75 percent, respectively). For Algeria, gas exports could represent one component of a "strategic partnership" that would govern EU-Algerian relations instead of the Neighborhood Policy that Algeria had snubbed.[82] What is more, despite the initial rhetoric, Algeria has little desire for a gas OPEC, most certainly because it is aware of being more valuable to Europe as an autonomous actor representing an alternative to the Russians whom, because of the Russian-Ukrainian crisis, the EU feared would use gas supplies as political leverage against gas-dependent European consumers. As for Russia, part of its motive for offering a partnership with Sonatrach might have been to secure Algeria's extensive experience in LNG to build a gas liquefaction plant in Russia. Should that scenario materialize, Russia would be able to export its own LNG and compete with Algeria in the European market.[83]

In June 2012, Sonatrach and Gazprom signed an agreement of principle to conduct a swap exchange, a system of regular financial flows enabling each country to optimize its sales in the partner country's key markets. Through this deal, Sonatrach would supply Gazprom's gas to its customers in Europe, while Gazprom would supply Sonatrach's gas to its customers in Asia. In 2014, both companies set up a joint venture in Algeria to allow Gazprom to initiate exploration and development of thirty fields throughout the country.[84] In 2016, Gazprom operationalized nine additional natural gas wells.[85]

In September 2014, the two states announced the signature of an agreement for cooperation in the area of nuclear energy (civilian) and the prospect of building a nuclear plant by 2025, mainly for seawater desalination, prospection and extraction of uranium, and treatment of nuclear wastes.[86] During Prime Minister Dmitry

Medvedev's visit to Algeria in October 2017, the Russian state enterprise Rosatom signed a protocol agreement for energy cooperation,[87] which confirmed its intention to build the nuclear plant by 2025. Contrary to Morocco, which was closer to France and the United States, Algeria's decision to partner with Russia for the acquisition of nuclear energy derives from Russia's willingness to share its technical know-how.

A Wide-Ranging Cooperation

There are many other areas of cooperation between Algeria and Russia besides the energy sector. The two countries often agree on political developments around the world, including the Syrian crisis.[88] The two countries also cooperate in defense matters and counterterrorism, and both share intelligence on jihadist group movements in North Africa.[89] In 2016, a Russian Council article summarized accurately why political ties with Algeria are significant:

> The importance of this country for Russia is determined by a number of factors: Algeria remains one of its most important partners in military-technical cooperation (MTC) and has an independent position in the international arena, including in its approach to the current acute crisis in the Arab world. This is especially true of the situations in Yemen, Libya and Syria. In general, the Algerian position is reduced to the desire to preserve the hitherto existing states of the Greater Middle East region in their former borders and to strengthen the situation, the destabilization of which directly threatens Algeria itself, and in this its actions maximally coincide with the interests of Russia.[90]

Another recent development in Russian-Algerian relations concerns agriculture. While France had been the long-time supplier of wheat to Algeria, Russia has now offered the same quality wheat, beef, and dairy products at more competitive prices. This agreement between Moscow and Algiers will allow Russian companies to export these certified products—by authority of the Algerian Ministry of Agriculture and the Russian Federal Service for Veterinary and Phytosanitary Surveillance, Rosselkhoznadzor—to Algeria, which has a big deficit in this sector.[91] In March 2019, a test batch of twenty-one tons of cereals had been shipped for analysis, but Algeria had declined to move forward with the trade contract at that time due to the failure of the Russian wheat to conform to the specifications drawn up by the Algerian Interprofessional Cereals Office (OAIC).

An Algerian delegation also visited Russia to study not only "the quality of the wheat, but also the conditions of storage, loading and transport, which are determining factors," according to the Ministry of Agriculture, "in order to assess the quality/price ratio."[92] The competition between Russia and France, a major exporter of wheat to Algeria, has not ended. Should Russia eventually win the contract, it would mark an important evolution in relations in the agricultural sector, especially since Algeria is the third-largest importer of wheat in the world (4.4 percent), spending close to $2 billion annually.[93] During his visit to Algeria in January 2019, Sergey Lavrov had discussed the issue of wheat, and he recognized that the "difficulties in trying to establish exports [of Russian wheat] are caused by the inconsistency of Russian standards."[94] It was during that visit that the agreement was reached to send a trial batch of many tons of Russian wheat to Algeria. To France's dismay, Algeria decided to import 28,000 tons of wheat from Russia in June 2021 and 60,000 tons in October the same year.

In the health sector, one major development is the production of the Russian vaccine against COVID-19, Sputnik-V, in Algeria. The vaccine will be manufactured by the state-owned group Saidal in partnership with the Russian laboratory Gamaleya.[95] Algeria opted for Sputnik-V because the vaccine does not require cumbersome logistics for storage and can be kept at very low temperatures. Its relatively low price is appealing to the Algerian government, which has made the vaccine free for its entire population. The possibility that the vaccine would be produced in Algeria was also a major factor in its decision to choose Sputnik-V, as it would include the transfer of technology to Algeria.[96] According to both Algerian and Russian officials, this cooperation in the health sector will extend to other industries.

Russia and the Protest Movement (Hirak)

Since February 2019, there has been a wave of continuous peaceful protests in Algeria, called the Hirak, which led to the military's forcible removal of President Bouteflika, who had ruled the country for twenty years. Throughout the Hirak's weekly marches (which were suspended due to the COVID-19 pandemic before resuming in February 2021), Russia warned the West not to interfere in Algeria's domestic affairs, fearful of a repetition of events that had occurred in Libya and Syria. Russia's official response to the Hirak Movement came almost a month after it began, through a statement from Maria Zakharova, spokesperson for the Russian Ministry of Foreign Affairs:

> We perceive the events in Algeria as a strictly domestic affair in a Russia-friendly country. With that, we hope that the existing problems will continue to be settled in a constructive and responsible manner in the framework of a national dialogue oriented toward stability and further advancement of political and socioeconomic transformations in the interest of the Algerian people.[97]

This position is different from Russia's refusal to support either Tunisia's Ben Ali or Egypt's Hosni Mubarak when the Arab Spring erupted across the region in 2010–11. Kuznetsov is correct in pointing out that:

> Moscow supports a peaceful transition in Algeria and that, "viewed by Russian experts, [Algeria] retains the potential to demonstrate its regionally unique capacity for peaceful internal democratization and refuse to emerge from its roots and refuse to revive previous authoritarian tendencies while also maintaining stability and constitutional order."[98]

Recent events in Algeria, and Russia's rebuke of the regime's misrepresentation of Russia's position in 2019,[99] demonstrate that Moscow watches developments in Algeria closely, prudently aligning itself with the protesters without alienating the state authorities. During the Russia-Africa summit in October 2019, Putin stated that:

> We know that very important political events are taking place in Algeria. We sincerely hope that the Algerian people will overcome the difficulties of the transition period. We are convinced that everything will take place in such a way that the Algerian people will benefit, that they will strengthen their State and their sovereignty.[100]

Clearly, Russia wishes to see stability in Algeria, a major partner in the region. Although reports circulated that Moscow supported the regime against the protesters, Moscow was in fact more interested in seeing a smooth transition that would not jeopardize its interests in the country. Russia denied that its ambassador to Algiers, Igor Beliaev, expressed Moscow's support for the presidential election that Ahmed Gaïd Salah, Algeria's then strongman vice minister of defense and head of the chiefs of staff, had demanded take place "as soon as possible." Moscow repudiated any notion that it was in favor of such an election, and it rejected accusations of foreign interference in Algeria's domestic affairs.[101]

Before Bouteflika was removed from office on April 2, 2019, and in view of uncertain actions of the protest movement unleashed on February 22, 2019, Sergey Lavrov encouraged dialogue between the Algerian government and the opposition.[102] Undoubtedly, Moscow's biggest fear was a scenario like what had happened during the Arab uprisings in Libya and Syria in 2011, which it believed had been concocted in the West. In sum, Moscow was only interested in Algeria's stability and was anxious to see continued strong relations between the two countries, while warning against foreign interference that might wish for regime change.

Following the election of Abdelmadjid Tebboune as president of Algeria, the Russian Ministry of Foreign Affairs declared that "the holding of the presidential election is an important step in the development and progress of Algeria," and that it saw, in these elections, "an opportunity to consolidate and improve relations between the two nations."[103] As if to emphasize Algeria's importance, in February 2020, Putin, who had spoken to Tebboune earlier, declared during the presentation of credentials by Algeria's ambassador to Russia that:

We support the balanced international and regional policy advocated by Algeria, and we believe that there are good prospects for strengthening our economic, military and technical cooperation in order to enhance stability and security in North Africa and the Sahel … The two states have been closely linked by strong and constant friendly relations for many years.[104]

Clearly, both countries are interested in continuing to strengthen and develop their relations. In a *Russia Today* interview in Arabic, Tebboune stated: "We wish to raise our relations with Russia, which is almost a brotherly country and not just a friendly one, to the level of political understanding and similar liberation principles," adding that he wanted to see these ties take a new step "to strengthen economic and cultural relations with this country which we hold in esteem and respect." He insisted that Algeria was honored to be forging close ties with Russia, a country with a historical and cultural legacy, which was commensurate with the political rapprochement and convergence of views between the two countries: "Algeria has and will have no problem with Russia, since we share the same principles."[105] Given the controversy around Tebboune's election and the political system in general, it is evident that the Algerian regime had turned towards an old partner that did not trumpet the necessity of democracy, good governance, or the rule of law.

After the protests resumed in February 2021, Moscow became worried by the potential appropriation of the Hirak Movement by Islamists. The Russian *Gazeta* devoted a thought-provoking article regarding the "Islamization of the movement." A Russian expert, Andrei Chuprygin, argued that the Islamization of the protests was a real threat:

> This is not a new phenomenon for the whole of North Africa, it began with the Arab Spring of 2011 and the victory in the elections in Tunisia of the Islamist "Revival Party" associated with the Muslim Brotherhood (an organization banned in Russia). Algeria is no exception, and during the entire political crisis of 2019 Islamist organizations played a prominent role.[106]

While this view is not necessarily in line with that of Russian officials, it certainly reflects the Kremlin's apprehensions about the rise of Islamism and a potential replication of the destabilization in Algeria following the rise of the Islamic Salvation Front in 1989, which had resulted in decade-long civil strife that almost brought down the state.

Undoubtedly, it is not in the interests of Moscow, which values its "strategic partnership" with Algeria, to allow the destabilization of one of its most reliable partners in the Mediterranean and MENA region. Indeed, Russia and Algeria both wish to preserve and extend their cooperation to all domains. While Moscow has recently developed good relations with Morocco and Tunisia as well, those partnerships are in no way commensurate with Moscow's relations with Algeria.

Russia and Morocco: The Predominance of Pragmatism

Moscow has always been cognizant of Morocco's pro-Western orientation. However, this has not prevented Russia from establishing good relations with the country and even entering a "strategic partnership" in 2002, following King Mohamed VI's visit to Russia, the first official visit by a Moroccan king since Hassan II's trip in 1966. The year 2002 marked a turning point in Moroccan-Russian relations, with the two countries signing a strategic partnership covering economic, political, security, religious, and cultural domains. The two states also expressed their intention of eventually signing a free-trade agreement. Other sectors—such as agriculture, tourism, and commerce—were also added to the agreement the following year.[107]

Trade between the two countries has grown exponentially, from $200 million per year in the 1990s to $2.5 billion in 2015. Since 1998, Russia has been the second-largest customer, after the European Union, of Moroccan agricultural products, mainly citrus fruits and tomatoes. The areas of cooperation between the two countries have expanded considerably in recent years and cover many sectors, including justice, industry, energy, communication technologies, scientific research, civil engineering, logistics, mining, and geological research. Moreover, many Russian companies are present in geological exploration (oil) in Morocco. In 2016, King Mohamed VI visited Russia, his second trip since 2002. He met with President Putin and the two signed a "deep strategic partnership" similar to the Russia-Algeria partnership in 2001. Its objective was to reestablish the free-trade agreement and negotiate the extension of Russian access to Moroccan fisheries on the Atlantic coast.[108] Russia and Morocco had signed a fishing agreement in 2013 in which Russian vessels were allowed to fish in the Moroccan Exclusive Economic Zone. This had not included access to Morocco's illegally occupied Western Saharan waters, but Russian fishing vessels entered Western Saharan waters anyway, despite Russian "positive neutrality" in the conflict.[109]

Russian-Moroccan trade increased rapidly over the years. By 2017, Russia accounted for almost 18 percent of the entire value of Moroccan food exports, and trade between the two countries amounted to over $3 billion.[110] In 2018, Minister of Agriculture,

Fisheries, Rural Development, Water and Forestry Aziz Akhannouch noted that agricultural products represented 77 percent of Moroccan exports to Russia.[111] According to Russian Minister of Agriculture Dmitry Patrushev, "In 2018, total trade turnover exceeded $1.5 billion, and about a third of it falls on agricultural products. Moreover, over the 9 months of this year [2019], trade in agricultural products between our countries increased by 15%."[112] Overall, trade has taken an important dimension in the two countries' bilateral relations.

Tourism has also been an area of interest on both sides. Before the COVID-19 pandemic, the number of Russian tourists in Morocco had grown noticeably,[113] and it is likely to resume growing after the pandemic.

Armaments, Energy, and Security

Although Russia is careful about which types of weapons it supplies to avoid upsetting the balance of power between Algeria and Morocco, it has nonetheless sold weapons—such as armed vehicles and anti-aircraft artillery—to Morocco.[114] Thus, although Morocco is said to have discussed the purchase of S-400s,[115] Russia has apparently refused, as it would be more likely to sell them to Algeria, which has also allegedly entered discussion for such purchase.[116]

Russia and Morocco have also cooperated in the energy sector. Indeed, Morocco signed an agreement with the Russian Rosatom for civilian nuclear energy in 2017.[117] In October 2019, on the sidelines of the Russia-Africa Economic Forum held in Sochi, the two countries signed a $2 billion contract for the Russians to build a petrochemical complex in Nador. This petrochemical complex will apparently have a refining capacity of 100,000 barrels per day, eventually to be increased to 200,000 barrels a day.[118]

Concerned about Islamic radicalization in Russia and in its neighboring states, Moscow signed a memorandum of understanding with Morocco in March 2016 for the training of Russian imams by Moroccans in the hope of inculcating moderate religious beliefs in the Russian Muslim minority.[119] Like the United States, Russia wishes to be seen as a global security player. In this context, an exchange of visits between senior intelligence officials of Russia and Morocco has taken place in recent years.

The Western Sahara Question

With respect to Western Sahara, a non-self-governing territory that Morocco has occupied illegally since 1975,[120] Russia seeks to maintain "positive neutrality," which consists in defending UN resolutions on the region. Although Russia does not recognize the Sahrawi Arab Democratic Republic (SADR), in the United Nations Security Council, Moscow consistently points out that attempts by pro-Moroccan Western powers to modify UN resolutions regarding the conflict would violate international legality. Indeed, Russia has repeatedly prevented such modifications from being adopted. It opposes motions at the Security Council that would undermine the original resolutions regarding the Sahrawis' right to self-determination, a position that Algeria has supported since the inception of the conflict in 1975. For instance, the Russian Federation representative at the UN, Mr. Nebenzia, stated clearly in October 2018 that:

> Our collective efforts should be based on the parameters previously agreed by the Security Council, which, in accordance with relevant Council resolutions, identify the parties to the Western Sahara conflict; are based on the fundamental principle of a mutually acceptable definitive solution; and stipulate the self-determination of the people of Western Sahara in the framework of procedures consistent with the principles and the purposes of the Charter of the United Nations.[121]

Russia was worried that the United States and France were seeking to alter the agreed-upon parameters regarding Western Sahara. Thus, Moscow reiterated "a principled position in support of the existing basis of the settlement."[122] Not only did this allow Russia to maintain a consistent position, but it also meant it could maintain relatively good relations with the POLISARIO Front. Indeed, Sahrawi officials visit Moscow regularly. For instance, in 2015, the Russian Council on Foreign Affairs interviewed at lengthh the late Mhamed Khadad, POLISARIO's coordinator of the UN Referendum Mission in Western Sahara (MINURSO). During his stay in Moscow, Khadad met with representatives of the Russian Foreign Ministry as well as Putin's special envoy.[123] In April 2017, a POLISARIO delegation met with Russian officials from the Ministry of Foreign Affairs. After the meeting, Russian Deputy Foreign Minister Mikhail Bogdanov "reiterated Russia's unchanging position on the need for a mutually acceptable political solution to this long-running problem, based on relevant UN resolutions."[124]

Clearly, Russia seeks to play a mediating role in the conflict if Morocco agrees to it. Thus, in December 2019, after a telephone discussion between Lavrov and his Moroccan counterpart, Nasser Bourita, they issued a statement indicating that "During the conversation, Russia expressed its willingness to deepen the political dialogue with Morocco for settling the Western Sahara question, in addition to discussing other key international and regional issues."[125] Such a seemingly even-handed position leaves the role of mediator open for Russia should it be asked to take it.

In sum, while it is true that "Russia views Morocco as an economic gateway to Africa; [and] it also regards the kingdom as a model to emulate in countering Islamist extremism in its own vicinity,"[126] one should also point out that Morocco, like other North African states, needs Russia—and China, for that matter—to counterbalance its relations with the United States and the EU, and to offset the strong Algerian-Russian relations. Morocco is fully aware that Russia is an important UN Security Council member, and that its neutrality on the question of Western Sahara is beneficial. As one observer put it, "the monarchy has recently attempted to play off the conflicting interests between Washington and Moscow in order to gain greater support from Russia for issues of national importance, including for its claim of sovereignty in the Western Sahara."[127] Still, it is doubtful that Morocco will ever deviate from its pro-Western orientation.

Tunisia and Russia: Growing Mutual Interests

Tunisia, like Morocco, is dependent on the EU, due to history, geographical proximity, and traditional economic ties. However, in 2000, Presidents Ben Ali and Putin met in New York, and were seemingly intent on initiating productive relations between Tunisia and Russia. This triggered several reciprocal visits, such as Foreign Minister Igor Ivanov's visit to Tunis—the first visit to the country by a high-level Russian official—followed in 2001 by Tunisian Minister of Foreign Affairs Habib Ben Yahia's official visit to Russia. This set the stage for the second meeting of the Intergovernmental Commission at the end of 2005, when Minister of Foreign Affairs Sergey Lavrov visited Tunisia.

However, it was ultimately Putin who relaunched Russian-Tunisian relations, albeit on a small scale.[128] These diplomatic developments did not translate into high-level trade relations, which were negligible. The two countries' interest in forming relations accelerated following Tunisia's uprising, the "Jasmine Revolution," which triggered the so-called "Arab Spring." For Russia, the overthrow of Ben Ali and other autocratic leaders in the region represented a threat to regional stability, but it also raised the question as to whether a similar scenario could happen in Russia.[129] At the same time, the upheaval raised concerns regarding the contagious effects of jihadism and Islamic radicalism spreading to former Soviet republics,[130] where Muslim minorities could be affected.

However, the peaceful transition of power in Tunisia, and the willingness of the Islamist party Ennahda to accept the results at the polls during the 2014 election, provided Moscow with a different, encouraging perspective. Moscow invited not only the secular party Nida Tounès but also Ennahda leaders to Russia in 2017 and 2018. Suffering under Western sanctions, Russia was eager to sign a trade agreement with Tunisia to cover agricultural shortfalls. Russia has also sought diplomatic cooperation from Tunisia. In 2019, Russia solicited Tunisia for its support in having Syria reinstated to the Arab League,[131] from which it had been expelled in November 2011. Following his meeting with the late President Beji Caid Essebsi, Lavrov declared: "We have a common view on the need to do everything possible to prevent the erosion of the sovereignty and territorial integrity of the Syrian Arab Republic, to strive for Syria to return to the Arab family and resume its participation in the Arab League."[132]

Given the high terrorist threat that confronted Tunisia, Moscow was quick to join the counterterrorism effort and granted Tunisia a $500 million grant to that effect.[133] Russia's cooperation included sharing satellite imagery of terrorist groups roaming across the region. This was critical, especially in view of the terrorist threat emanating from the chaotic situation in Libya. And, although it is not certain whether any of the hardware was delivered to Tunisia, Moscow also pledged military assistance.[134] In January 2019, the two countries agreed to heighten their cooperation in counterterrorism to prevent the unstable situation in Libya from spilling over into Tunisia.[135]

Energy

Another area where there is significant Russian-Tunisian cooperation is in the field of energy. On June 2, 2015, Tunisia signed an MoU with Rosatom, whose director declared that "for the first time in the history of Russian-Tunisian relations, this document has laid the legal foundation for interaction between Russia and Tunisia in nuclear energy, covering a broad range of topics."[136] In September 2016, the two governments signed an agreement on peaceful uses of atomic energy, on the sidelines of the 60th General Conference of the IAEA in Vienna. The agreement covers several areas of civil nuclear power, such as assistance in development and improvement of Tunisian nuclear infrastructure; design and construction of nuclear power and research reactors, as well as desalination plants and particle accelerators; uranium exploration and mining; research of Tunisia's mineral resources for the purpose of developing its nuclear industry; nuclear fuel cycle services for nuclear power plants and research reactors; radioactive waste management; production of radioisotopes and their application in industry, medicine, and agriculture; nuclear and radiation safety; and the education, training, and retraining of nuclear specialists.[137]

Tourism

The most important development in Tunisian-Russian relations relates to tourism. When Russians could not travel to Turkey and Egypt for political or security reasons, many decided to spend their vacations in Tunisia instead. This was a win-win, as European and American tourists avoided Tunisia. On June 26, 2015, a terrorist gunned down tourists in the resort of Port El Kantaoui, killing thirty British citizens and eight others. For the Russians, Tunisia offered a cheap alternative to more expensive destinations. Hence,

> roughly 600,000 Russian tourists visited Tunisia, a tenfold increase from the previous year and over 10 percent of the country's visitors

that year. Tunisian retail businesses have welcomed Russians' presence, and the government has spoken positively of Russia's assistance in counterterrorism. Officials have also publicly acknowledged Russia's growing regional sway, including in Syria.[138]

The two countries plan on cooperating further in this sector. In February 2018, Tunisian Minister of Tourism and Handicrafts Salma Elloumi Rekik declared that "there is a common desire to bring our relations to the level of strategic partnership in various fields, including economy, trade, culture, security, healthcare and, of course, tourism, where our common interests make us seek and identify opportunities for investment and coordinate efforts to improve bilateral cooperation."[139] In June 2019, the Russian ambassador to Tunisia, Sergey Nikolaev, announced that 800,000 Russian tourists would visit Tunisia,[140] an exceptional number that would help boost the Tunisian economy. Clearly, both Russia and Tunisia are interested in the development of relations. But it is doubtful whether Russia can significantly bolster the slumping Tunisian economy, which remains dependent on the EU.

Conclusion

Since Putin's ascent to power, Russia has established a more prominent presence in the Maghreb region than the Soviet Union had succeeded in doing, in large part because relations with Russia do not come with ideological prerequisites. Vladimir Putin has succeeded in reinforcing old ties (Algeria) and building new ones with states that have traditionally been aligned with the West (Morocco and Tunisia). These relations encompass all domains with the three Sunni Muslim states, and these good ties also help to facilitate Russia's own policies at home towards Muslim minorities. At the political level, Russia's friendly ties with Morocco and with POLISARIO might allow it to play a mediation role, or at least be a valuable honest interlocutor, should the parties (mainly Morocco) choose to take that road.

However, one should not exaggerate the inroads that Russia has made in the region; indeed, Moscow cannot compete with Beijing,[141] which boasts considerably more resources and has an economy that far outweighs that of Russia, a country that suffers the same problems as most rentier states dependent on hydrocarbons. Nor can Russia compete with the EU, the Maghreb countries' main trade partner. Yet, Moscow, through its all-around cooperation with the Maghreb states, has proved capable of sustaining competition with the United States and France in their relations with pro-Western Morocco and Tunisia, as well as independent-minded Algeria. For the Maghreb states, relations with Russia provide a credible counterweight to the West, which often promotes policies that go against these countries' interests.

Moscow has been able to position itself as a credible partner which, like China, does not impose conditions on its partnership. Better yet, from the Maghreb's perspective, Russia has proven its fidelity in supporting the Syrian regime and has demonstrated the sophistication of its weaponry, hence increasing its sales in this domain. In sum, Russia has guaranteed its interests at relatively low cost in the region. The Maghreb states have also appreciated Russia's prudent policy in neighboring Libya, where Western intervention in 2011 caused considerable damage to the entire Maghreb-Sahel region. Russia might be on its way to establishing a compelling presence in the Maghreb,[142] although it is doubtful whether this is an objective in itself or whether Moscow has any grand design for the region. Whatever the case, Moscow has laid the foundations for profitable ties with the Maghreb states, through which it has also secured its return to Africa.

CONCLUSION

Nikolay Kozhanov

Since the beginning of Russia's military deployment in Syria in 2015, the drivers of its policy towards the Middle East have substantially evolved. Its regional policy is driven by a complex mix of traditional factors—such as the ongoing, deadlocked confrontation with the West—as well as new trends. Since 2015, Russia's importance in the eyes of regional and non-regional players has been based on two pillars: its military presence in Syria and its balancing between key regional players. The core set of factors shaping Russia's approach has remained unchanged. It includes the geopolitical ambition to project power, the endless quest for economic profit, and domestic security considerations. Yet, the strength and nature of the impact that these factors have on Russian strategic thinking has changed over the last five years. Moscow is no longer as concerned about the return of "Russian-speaking jihadists" as it was in 2015, while the influence of economic considerations has become much stronger and more obvious. New drivers of policy have also emerged. These include that:

- The growing number of actors inside the political and economic elite—centers of parallel diplomacy, hydrocarbon companies, lobby groups, etc.—have influenced the Kremlin's decision-making process with regard to the Middle East.

223

- The transformation of the global oil and gas markets as a result of the US shale oil revolution and the beginning of the global transition to carbon-free fuels have made it necessary for Russia to strengthen its cooperation with the hydrocarbon-producing countries of the Middle East.

- The complex domestic situation has increased the importance of the Middle Eastern agenda for the survival of President Vladimir Putin's regime.

- The gradual end of the active phase of the military conflict in Syria has increased the importance of a political settlement as a way for Russia to legitimize its battleground achievement. The issue of the political process in Syria is also inevitably connected to the question of postwar reconstruction and its funding.

- Russia's policy has transitioned from its pre-2015 goal to "return" to the Middle East—that is, to regain its role as an important non-regional player—to defending the gains it has made there since 2015.

Russia's leadership always looks at the Middle East through the lens of projecting power globally and confronting the West; its regional priorities play a secondary role. Russia's involvement in the Syrian and Libyan conflicts, its close contacts with the Palestinian National Authority and Israel, and its attempts to maintain good ties with the warring sides in Yemen all help demonstrate to the United States and the EU that Russia is an important global player, thus inviting Western nations to take Russia's worldview into account and keep communication channels open. For example, Moscow can use its involvement in the Syrian and Libyan conflicts to either create common ground for a wider dialogue with the EU, or to put pressure on the EU so that Moscow can make additional gains in both conflict zones or in other issues on the international agenda. Russia is very well aware of the refugee problems experienced by European countries and it periodically blackmails the EU with threats that a slow reconstruction process in Syria may lead to new waves of refugees.

In order to shape international opinion, Russia's leadership does not always play the role of troublemaker or blackmailer. Sometimes, it does the opposite. For example, it backs international initiatives to settle the conflict in Yemen and even provides diplomatic support for their implementation. This is clearly welcomed by Western policy-makers, but it also creates the misperception of Russia as a potential team player and distorts the real picture of the challenge Russia represents for the West. The reason for Russia's cooperative approach in Yemen is simple: it does not have any interests in the country worth fighting over with the West, and challenging Western interests there could spoil relations with Saudi Arabia and the United Arab Emirates. Moscow is not necessarily interested in the final results of the international initiatives it supports in the Middle East, but active participation in their preparation and implementation allows Russia to retain influence and its image as an important player in the absence of any real capacity to become one. Moreover, Russia can still play the troublemaker when necessary to show that ignoring its interests might be dangerous. In this respect, Russia considers its relations with the region as just another (albeit important) bargaining chip in its relations with the United States and the EU.

Security concerns also remain important for Russia's decision-making in the Middle East, although these have evolved considerably since 2015, making security less relevant than political and economic goals. Between 2014 and 2016, Russia's security concerns centered on "Russian-speaking jihadists" with battle experience infiltrating the post-Soviet space from the Middle East. Today, Moscow is more worried about the possibility that Middle Eastern elites might provide ideological and financial support to homegrown radical Islamists in Russia and its "near abroad," especially Tajikistan, Uzbekistan, and Kazakhstan. Moscow has therefore intensified its attempts to persuade Middle Eastern elites to support "official" Islam in Russia instead. The Kremlin has allowed more contacts between the government-supported leaders of Russia's Muslim community and the local governments of its majority-Muslim republics with the religious circles and political establishments of Egypt, the United Arab Emirates, Qatar, and Saudi Arabia. The aim is not only to strengthen relations with these countries and encourage them to invest in Russian regions with which they have religious affinity, but also to convince Middle Eastern elites that the rights of Muslims are not abused in Russia.

For the last several years, these efforts have brought substantial results. Russian muftis have been welcomed in Mecca at the highest level and Saudi officials have stopped criticizing Moscow for the real or imagined abuses of Muslim rights. In January 2019, Saudi Arabia's minister of Islamic affairs, Sheikh Abdullatif al-Sheikh, met with the deputy head of the Russian Council of Muftis, Rushan Abbyasov, at the International Islamic Conference in Cairo. Al-Sheikh has since praised Russian authorities for their policies towards the Muslim community and the rights of Muslims since the fall of the Soviet Union. This marks a drastic change in Saudi rhetoric. Previously, at least until 2016, Moscow was quite often criticized for its suppression of Islam in the Caucasus and Volga region, and even occasionally portrayed as one of Islam's enemies.

The range of problems Russia encounters in the Middle East is also growing and evolving, and Moscow does not have the capacity to address these adequately. At least three trends pose a special risk to its influence in the region: 1) the gradual end of the "hot" phase of the war in Syria; 2) difficulties in balancing regional interests; and 3) growing disappointment across the Middle East over Russia's shortcomings in fulfilling the role of a global power in the region.

With the fighting in Syria becoming less intense, and with military activity more concerned with mopping up the remnants of the resistance, focus is shifting to the political track of the conflict. Russia's dominance in the military theater is unquestioned, but to similarly dominate the political track—in which regional powers such as Iran, Turkey, and even the Gulf states are able to challenge its ambitions— requires more effort and capacity from the Kremlin. The situation with Russian presence in other countries is no less delicate. In Libya, in order to hedge its risks, Russia has had to limit its military assistance to General Haftar, causing dissatisfaction with Moscow from the Tobruk alternative government. In Yemen, Russia's influence on the Houthis is limited, despite Moscow's attempts to position itself as a potential mediator. Further, there has been a lack of progress in getting economic projects with the Gulf Cooperation Council (GCC) countries off the ground. Politically, Russia disagrees with the Gulf states with regard to Syria's future and its re-admittance to the Arab League as well as over how to deal with the Syrian opposition. Russia's recent attempt to launch an oil market price war with Saudi Arabia will definitely leave a scar on the two countries' relations.

Finally, Russia's relations with Israel have faced difficulties, with familiar accusations of Moscow's involvement in the country's domestic affairs. Under these circumstances, Russia's capacity to reach its goals in the Middle East is increasingly limited, meaning it has to punch far above its weight.

Yet, Russia's challenges in the Middle East mostly originate from its domestic realities rather than from the region itself. Moscow is weak economically, which curtails its political leverage and influence in the Middle East. The very nature and evolution of the regime impose limits on the Kremlin's ability to fulfill its plans in the Middle East. Russia's capacity to reach its goals is thus increasingly limited. Nevertheless, the impact of international factors—such as global economic trends, the confrontation with the West, changes in the regional balance of power, and evolution of America's role in the region—on Russia's regional prospects should not be ignored.

In spite of growing problems and limited capacity to respond to emerging challenges, Russia does not intend to withdraw from the Middle East because the region has political and economic value for Moscow's global strategy, which aims to restore its geopolitical standing and ensure the survival of Putin's regime. Russia's presence in the region advertises its capacity to project power and helps it to avoid international isolation while weakening anti-Russian coalitions. Russia can still play a niche political and economic role in the Middle East. Even if Russia's capacities to reach its goals are increasingly limited, the Middle East's importance for its greater aspirations will motivate Russia to try to punch far above its weight.

In order to preserve its position in the Middle East, Russia will make important revisions to its regional diplomacy, aiming to safeguard its achievements rather than seek out new gains. Russia's main efforts will also become more focused on areas of key importance. Another successful military adventure in the Middle East could help Moscow maintain its image as a regional broker. However, the Kremlin is not prepared for such a move; the costs and risks are high, and Moscow is only willing to accept them in order to protect its key regional allies, such as Assad. This does not mean a complete rejection of muscle-flexing in the Middle East if it does not incur much risk. Yet, overall, the Kremlin will try to make its presence in the region less risky and less costly by giving preference to diplomatic efforts over military adventures: hence, the partial military "withdrawal" from Libya and greater focus on diplomatic processes.

Meanwhile, Russia will try to optimize the use of its resources and efforts by focusing on those areas that are a priority for its national interests and security, such as conflict-settlement in Syria, cooperation within OPEC+, Iran's nuclear ambitions, preservation of its balancing act between key regional players, religious dialogue, and security cooperation. Russia will be more cautious about greater involvement in issues that are irrelevant for its key priorities or those that create extra risks, such as the Libyan conflict, the Israeli-Palestinian confrontation, or the war in Yemen.

The adoption of such a "defensive" strategy will not mean a "quieter" Russia in the Middle East. To defend its positions, Russia will stay active in the Middle East to demonstrate its importance and prevent the strategic initiative on issues such as the settlement of the Syrian conflict from falling into the hands of its opponents. Moscow has focused on regional diplomatic initiatives that do not require much material investment in order to demonstrate its importance and develop regional alliances. For instance, 2019 saw numerous multi-level visits by Russian officials to the Middle East and by Middle Eastern leaders to Russia. These were intended to demonstrate Moscow's leading role in the Middle East. In July 2019, the Russian Ministry of Foreign Affairs released its "Concept of collective security in the Persian Gulf." The Kremlin believes that the emergence of a new security system in the Gulf is inevitable, and Russia intends to be a participant. There are no illusions in Moscow that its concept document will be adopted by others: rather, its release was intended to secure Russia a seat at the table in any discussion on the future structure of international relations of the Gulf.

All in all, Russia should be considered a second-tier non-regional player in the Middle East, but one that can play the leading role in some cases, as in Syria. Russia has a wide agenda but limited capacity to pursue its interests or challenge either the interests of the regional states or Western powers. For the moment, Russia's capacity to broaden its position in the Middle East has probably reached its limits and there is little chance of further improvement. This does not mean that Russia has no options to further exploit the opportunities provided by its existing relations in the region. Russia's balancing strategy, its limited resources, and the complex relations of Middle Eastern countries with the United States and regional leaders like Iran, Saudi Arabia, Egypt, and Turkey exclude the formation of long-lasting, comprehensive alliances or cooperation on the majority of items on the regional agenda. But Russia can build up ad hoc, short-lived partnerships with some Gulf states regarding Libya to secure the interests of General Haftar; it can cooperate with Iran in Syria; and it can be silently supportive of the Saudi coalition in Yemen. Russia's capacity as a mediator capable of delivering messages between all Middle Eastern players also should not be ignored. In spite of potentially declining oil output, Russia will also remain one of the important players in the hydrocarbon markets, facing the same problems as the crude producers of the Gulf and looking for ways to handle them through cooperation with the GCC.

None of this means that Russia will not be able to secure its current gains in the Middle East through an active and, if necessary, aggressive foreign policy. In other words, the role of shaping developments in the region that Russia adopted after its military deployment in Syria may not look sustainable in the long run. However, its intent will endure in the active policy Russia will adopt to defend its gains in the Middle East.

NOTES

1. THE MIDDLE EAST IN RUSSIA'S FOREIGN POLICY, 1990–2020

1. This chapter cites a wide range of literature both in English and in Russian to illustrate the evolution of the Russian foreign policy discourse. Citation does not indicate the approval of or agreement with the points made in any particular publication.
2. For an overview, see Viacheslav Morozov, *Russia's Postcolonial Identity: A Subaltern Empire in a Eurocentric World* (Basingstoke, UK: Palgrave Macmillan, 2015).
3. Michael McFaul, "Is Putinism the Russian Norm or an Aberration?" *Current History* 117, no. 801 (2018): 251–7.
4. Richard Sakwa, *Russia against the Rest: The Post-Cold War Crisis of World Order* (Cambridge, UK: Cambridge University Press, 2017); Dmitri Trenin, *Novyi balans sil: Rossiia v poiskakh vneshnepoliticheskogo ravnovesiia* [A new balance of power: Russia seeking foreign policy equilibrium] (Moscow: Alpina, 2021).
5. For recent interventions, see e.g., Mark Kramer and Joshua R. Itzkowitz Shifrinson, "NATO Enlargement—Was There a Promise?" *International Security* 42, no. 1 (2017): 186–92; Kimberly Marten, "Reconsidering NATO Expansion: A Counterfactual Analysis of Russia and the West in the 1990s," *European Journal of International Security* 3, no. 2 (2018): 135–61.
6. Dmitry Gorenburg, "Circumstances Have Changed since 1991, but Russia's Core Foreign Policy Goals Have Not," *PONARS Eurasia Policy Memo* 560 (2019): 3–4, www.ponarseurasia.org/sites/default/files/policy-memos-pdf/Pepm560_Gorenburg_Jan2019_0.pdf.
7. Ministry of Foreign Affairs, Russia, "Foreign Policy Concept of the Russian Federation (approved by President of the Russian Federation Vladimir Putin on November 30, 2016)," December 1, 2016, www.mid.ru/en/foreign_policy/official_documents/-/asset_publisher/CptICkB6BZ29/content/id/2542248.
8. Igor Okunev, "Vneshniaia politika dlia bol'shinstva?" [Foreign policy for the majority?], *Rossiia v gobal'noi politike* 11, no. 2 (2013): 40–8.
9. Ministry of Foreign Affairs, Russia, "Foreign Policy Concept of the Russian Federation."

10. Tatiana Romanova, "O neoklassicheskom realisme i sovremennoi Rossii" [On the neoclassical realist and modern Russia], *Rossiia v gobal'noi politike* 10, no. 3 (2012): 8–21.

11. Sergei Dubinin and Evgenii Savostianov, "Ekonomicheskie determinanty i osnovy tselepolaganiia sovremennoi vneshnei politiki. Vyvody dlia Rossii" [Economic determinants and foundations of goal-setting in modern foreign policy. Conclusions for Russia], *Rossiia v gobal'noi politike*, June 15, 2020, https://globalaffairs.ru/articles/ekonomicheskie-determinanty.

12. Sergei Karaganov et al., *Zashchita mira, zemli, svobody vybora dlia vsekh stran: Novye idei dlia vneshnei politiki Rossii* [Protecting peace, land, freedom of choice for all countries: new ideas for Russian foreign policy], (Moscow: Izdatel'skii dom Vysshei shkoly ekonomiki, 2020), 31–2, 63–4; Leonid Issaev and Nikolay Kozhanov, "Diversifying Relationships: Russian Policy toward GCC," *International Politics* (2021), https://doi.org/10.1057/s41311–021–00286–4.

13. For a general historical overview, see Dmitry Trenin, *What Is Russia up to in the Middle East?* (Cambridge, UK: Polity, 2017), 12–52.

14. Deborah Welch Larson and Alexei Shevchenko, "Shortcut to Greatness: The New Thinking and the Revolution in Soviet Foreign Policy," *International Organization* 57, no. 1 (2003): 77–109.

15. For a detailed analysis, see Graham E. Fuller, "Moscow and the Gulf War," *Foreign Affairs* 70, no. 3 (1991): 55–76.

16. *Ibid.*, 69–70.

17. Mark N. Katz, "Comparing Putin's and Brezhnev's Policies toward the Middle East," *Society* 45, no. 2 (2008): 177–180.

18. Robert O. Freedman, "Russia, Israel and the Arab-Israeli Conflict: The Putin Years," *Middle East Policy* 17, no. 3 (2010): 51–63; Alek D. Epstein and Stanislav Kozheurov, *Rossiia i Izrail': trudnyi put' navstrechu* [Russia and Israel: a difficult path to meet], (Mocsow: Mosty kultury; Jerusalem: Gesharim, 2011).

19. Mark N. Katz, "Support Opposing Sides Simultaneously: Russia's Approach to the Gulf and the Middle East," *Al Jazeera Centre for Studies*, August 23, 2018, http://studies.aljazeera.net/en/reports/2018/08/support-opposing-sides-simultaneously-russias-approach-gulf-middle-east-180823104054250.html.

20. Rauf Mammadov, "Russia in the Middle East: Energy Forever?" in *Russia in the Middle East*, eds. Theodore Karasik and Stephen Blank (Washington, DC: Jamestown Foundation, 2018), 212–39.

21. Bobo Lo, *Russian Foreign Policy in the Post-Soviet Era: Reality, Illusion and Mythmaking* (Basingstoke, UK: Palgrave Macmillan, 2002), 42.

22. Trenin, *Novyi balans sil*, 162–80.

23. See, *Ibid.*, 40–65; Ted Hopf, *Social Origins of International Politics: Identities and Foreign Policies, Moscow, 1955 and 1999* (Ithaca, NY: Cornell University Press, 2002), 211–57; Andrei P. Tsygankov, *Russia's Foreign Policy: Change and Continuity in National Identity*, 3rd ed. (Lanham, MD: Rowman and Littlefield, 2013).

24. Timofei Bordachev, "Posledniaia imperiia i ee sosedi" [The last empire and its neighbors], *Rossiia v gobal'noi politike* 19, no. 2 (2021): 8–24.

25. Cf. Rogers Brubaker, *Nationalism Reframed: Nationhood and the National Question in the New Europe* (Cambridge, UK: Cambridge University Press, 1996).

26. Moritz Pieper, "*Russkiy Mir*: The Geopolitics of Russian Compatriots Abroad," *Geopolitics* 25, no. 3 (2020): 756–79.

27. Florent Marciacq, "Serbia: Looking East, Going West?" in *The Western Balkans in the World: Linkages and Relations with Non-Western Countries*, eds. Florian Bieber, Nikolaos Tzifakis (London: Routledge, 2019), 61–72.

28. See, e.g., Yevgeny M. Primakov, "International Relations on the Eve of XXI Century: Problems and Prospects," *International Affairs* 10, no. 10 (1996): 3–13.

29. Lo, *Russian Foreign Policy*, 133.

30. Mark N. Katz, "Primakov Redux? Putin's Pursuit of 'Multipolarism' in Asia," *Demokratizatsiya* 14, no. 1 (2006): 145–46.

31. Alexei Vassiliev, "Russia and Iraq," *Middle East Politics* 7, no. 4 (2000): 127–9.

32. Trenin, *Novyi balans sil*, 90–9.

33. Anatoly Reshetnikov, *The Evolution of Russia's Great Power Discourse: A Conceptual History of Velikaya Derzhava* (PhD Dissertation, Budapest: Central European University, 2018).

34. Viatcheslav Morozov, "Resisting Entropy, Discarding Human Rights. Romantic Realism and Securitization of Identity in Russia," *Cooperation and Conflict* 37, no. 4 (2002): 409–30.

35. Boris Kashnikov, "Chechenskii terrorizm. Vzlet i padenie" [Chechen terrorism. Rise and fall], *Rossiiskii nauchnyi zhurnal* no. 2 (2008): 70–6.

36. Robert H. Donaldson, Joseph L. Nogee, and Vidya Nadkarni, *The Foreign Policy of Russia: Changing Systems, Enduring Interests*, 5th ed. (New York, NY: Routledge, 2014), 369–70.

37. Yevgeny M. Primakov, *The World Challenged: Fighting Terrorism in the Twenty-First Century* (Washington, DC: Brookings Institution Press, 2004), 61–4.

38. Valerii Konyshev and Alexander Sergunin, "Perspektivy razvitiia natsional'noi sistemy protivoraketnoi oborony SShA" [Prospects for the development of the US national missile defense system], *Natsional'nye interesy: prioritety i bezopasnost'*, no. 33 (2015), 45–56.

39. Alexander Shumilin, "Problema Iraka v amerikano-rossiiskikh otnosheniiakh (2002–2006 gg.)" [The Iraqi problem in US-Russian pelations (2002–2006)], *SShA i Kanada: ekonomika, politika, kul'tura*, no. 10 (2006), 35–46.

40. Primakov, *The World Challenged*, 82–93.

41. Marten, "Reconsidering NATO Expansion."

42. Katz, "Primakov Redux?" 147.

43. Andrey Makarychev and Viatcheslav Morozov, "Multilateralism, Multipolarity, and Beyond: A Menu of Russia's Policy Strategies," *Global Governance* 17, no. 3 (2011): 353–73.

44. S. Neil MacFarlane, "The 'R' in BRICs: Is Russia an Emerging Power?" *International Affairs* 82, no. 1 (2006): 41–57.

45. Boris Kheifets, "Perspektivy institutsializatsii BRIKs" [Institutionalization perspectives of BRICs], *Voprosy ekonomiki*, no. 8 (2015): 25–42.

46. David Bdoyan, "Periody transformatsii rossiisko-turetskikh otnoshenii" [Periods of transformation of Russian-Turkish relations], *Vestnik MGIMO-Universiteta*, no. 4 (2017): 165–82.

47. Freedman, "Russia, Israel and the Arab-Israeli Conflict"; Philipp Casula and Mark N. Katz, "The Middle East," in *Routledge Handbook of Russian Foreign Policy*, ed. Andrei P. Tsygankov (London: New York: Routledge, 2018), 305; Roberto Mansilla Blanco, "Russia in Latin America: Geopolitics and Pragmatism," *Global Americans*, November 28, 2018, https://theglobalamericans.org/2018/11/russia-in-latin-america-geopolitics-and-pragmatism.

48. Robert Horvath, "Putin's 'Preventive Counter-Revolution': Post-Soviet Authoritarianism and the Spectre of Velvet Revolution," *Europe-Asia Studies* 63, no. 1 (2011): 1–25; Ilya Yablokov, *Fortress Russia: Conspiracy Theories in the Post-Soviet World* (Cambridge, UK: Polity Press, 2018).

49. Olga Malinova, "Constructing the 'Usable Past': the Evolution of the Official Historical Narrative in Post-Soviet Russia," in *Cultural and Political Imaginaries in Putin's Russia*, eds. Niklas Bernsand and Barbara Törnquist-Plewa (Leiden, Netherlands; Boston, MA: Brill, 2018), 85–104.

50. Aglaya Snetkov, *Russia's Security Policy under Putin: A Critical Perspective* (New York: Routledge, 2014).

51. Vladimir Putin, *Speech and the Following Discussion at the Munich Conference on Security Policy*, February 10, 2007, http://en.kremlin.ru/events/president/transcripts/24034.

52. His main doctrinal text was originally published in 2006: Vladislav Surkov, "Nationalization of the Future: Paragraphs *pro* Sovereign Democracy," *Russian Studies in Philosophy* 47, no. 4 (2009): 8–21. See also Richard Sakwa, "Developed Putinism: Change without Development," *Russian Analytical Digest* 127 (2013): 2–4.

53. Viatcheslav Morozov, "Sovereignty and Democracy in Contemporary Russia: A Modern Subject Faces the Post-Modern World," *Journal of International Relations and Development* 11, no. 2 (2008): 152–80.

54. Fareed Zakaria, "The Rise of Illiberal Democracy," *Foreign Affairs* 76, no. 6 (1997): 22–43; Lilia Shevtsova, "Ten Years after the Soviet Breakup: Russia's Hybrid Regime," *Journal of Democracy* 12, no. 4 (2001): 65–70.

55. "The Foreign Policy Concept of the Russian Federation, July 15, 2008, http://en.kremlin.ru/supplement/4116.

56. Kremlin, "Interview Given by Dmitry Medvedev to Television Channels Channel One, Rossia [sic], NTV," August 31, 2008, http://en.kremlin.ru/events/president/transcripts/48301. For analysis, see Jeffrey Mankoff, *Russian Foreign Policy: The Return of Great Power Politics* (Lanham, MD: Rowman & Littlefield, 2012), 39–40.

57. Bettina Renz, *Russia's Military Revival* (Cambridge, UK: Polity Press, 2018).

58. North Atlantic Treaty Organization (NATO), "Bucharest Summit Declaration," April 3, 2008, www.nato.int/cps/en/natolive/official_texts_8443.htm.

59. Licínia Simão, "Bringing 'the Political' Back into European Security: Challenges to

the EU's Ordering of the Eastern Partnership," *East European Politics* 33, no. 3 (2017): 338–54.

60. Vladimir Putin, "A New Integration Project for Eurasia: The Future in the Making," The Embassy of the Russian Federation to the United Kingdom of Great Britain and Northern Ireland, October 4, 2011, www.rusemb.org.uk/press/246.

61. Viacheslav Morozov, "The Normative Deadlock in EU-Russia Relations: Hegemony without Influence," in *The Routledge Handbook of EU-Russia Relations: Structures, Actors, Issues*, eds. Tatiana Romanova, Maxine David (London: Routledge, 2021), 50–2.

62. Karaganov et al., *Zashchita mira, zemli, svobody vybora*.

63. Some of the logic behind this thinking has been recently exposed by Surkov in his new programmatic article: Vladislav Surkov, "Dolgoe gosudarstvo Putina" [Putin's long state], *Nezavisimaia gazeta*, February 11, 2019, www.ng.ru/ideas/2019–02–11/5_7503_surkov.html.

64. Roy Allison, "Russia and the Post-2014 International Legal Order: Revisionism and *Realpolitik*," *International Affairs* 93, no. 3 (2017): 519–41.

65. I explore the issue of dependence and subalternity in a book-length format in Morozov, *Russia's Postcolonial Identity*.

66. Emil Souleimanov and Ondrej Ditrych, "The Internationalisation of the Russian-Chechen Conflict: Myths and Reality," *Europe-Asia Studies* 60, no. 7 (2008): 1199–222.

67. Yurii Morozov, "Problemy i perspektivy vzaimodeistviia v Afganistane zain-teresovannykh v etom gosudarstv i ikh soiuzov" [Problems and prospects of inter-ested states and their unions regarding interaction in Afghanistan], *Natsional'nye interesy: prioritety i bezopasnost'* 14, no. 5 (2018): 955–71.

68. Roy Allison, "Russia and Syria: Explaining Alignment with a Regime in Crisis," *International Affairs* 89, no. 4 (2013): 797–8; Casula and Katz, "The Middle East," 301 and 304–5.

69. Roy Allison, "Russian 'Deniable' Intervention in Ukraine: How and Why Russia Broke the Rules," *International Affairs* 90, no. 6 (2014): 1289–95; Andrej Krickovic, "Catalyzing Conflict: The Internal Dimension of the Security Dilemma," *Journal of Global Security Studies* 1, no. 2 (2016): 111–26; and see also Horvath, "Putin's 'Preventive Counter-Revolution.'"

70. Maksim Grigoriev, *Euromaidan* (Moscow: Kuchkovo pole, 2014).

71. Samuel Charap and Timothy J. Colton, *Everyone Loses: The Ukraine Crisis and the Ruinous Contest for Post-Soviet Eurasia* (London: International Institute for Strategic Studies, 2017).

72. Allison, "Russia's 'Deniable' Intervention," 1269–75.

73. Emma Ashford, "Not-So-Smart Sanctions: The Failure of Western Restrictions against Russia," *Foreign Affairs* 95, no. 1 (2016): 114–23.

74. Allison, "Russia's 'Deniable' Intervention."

75. Keir Giles, "Assessing Russia's Reorganized and Rearmed Military," Carnegie Endowment for International Pace, 2017, https://carnegieendowment.org/files/5.4.2017_Keir_Giles_RussiaMilitary.pdf.

76. Henry E. Hale, "How Crimea Pays: Media, Rallying Round the Flag, and Authoritarian Support," *Comparative Politics* 50, no. 3 (2018): 369–91.

77. Dmitry Gorenburg, "Russia's Naval Strategy in the Mediterranean," *Russian Military Reform*, September 18, 2019, https://russiamil.wordpress.com/2019/09/18/russias-naval-strategy-in-the-mediterranean.

78. Maria Khodynskaia-Golenishcheva, "Terrorizm v Sirii segodnia i zavtra" [Terrorism in Syria today and tomorrow], *Aziia i Afrika segodnia*, no. 1 (2016): 7–14.

79. Dmitry Adamsky, "Moscow's Syria Campaign: Russian Lessons for the Art of Strategy," *Russie.Nei.Visions* 109 (Paris: IFRI, 2018), www.ifri.org/sites/default/files/atoms/files/rnv_109_adamsky_moscow_syria_campaign_2018.pdf.

80. Viktor Nadein-Ranevskii, "Politika Turtsii na Blizhnem Vostoke" [Turkey's Middle East policy], *Puti k miru i bezopasnosti*, no. 1 (2020): 139–56; Trenin, *What Is Russia up to in the Middle East?*, 85–112.

81. Ministry of Foreign Affairs of the Russian Federation, "Russia's Security Concept for the Gulf Area," July 23, 2019, www.mid.ru/en/web/guest/foreign_policy/international_safety/conflicts/-/asset_publisher/xIEMTQ3OvzcA/content/id/3733575.

82. *Ibid.*

83. *Ibid.*

84. Emil Aslan Souleimanov, "Russia's Policy in the Libyan Civil War: A Cautious Engagement," *Middle East Policy* 26, no. 2 (2019): 95–103.

85. Andrej Krickovic and Yuval Weber, "Commitment Issues: The Syrian and Ukraine Crises as Bargaining Failures of the Post-Cold War International Order," *Problems of Post-Communism* 65, no. 6 (2018): 373–84.

2. DIFFERENT BUT SIMILAR: COMPARING MOSCOW'S MIDDLE EAST POLICIES IN THE COLD WAR AND PUTIN ERAS

1. Dmitri Trenin, *What Is Russia up to in the Middle East?* (Cambridge, UK: Polity, 2018), 12–19.

2. *Ibid.*, 20.

3. Rashid Khalidi, "Arab Views of the Soviet Role in the Middle East," *Middle East Journal* 39, no. 4 (1985): 718–21.

4. Robert O. Freedman, *Moscow and the Middle East: Soviet Policy since the Invasion of Afghanistan* (Cambridge, UK: Cambridge University Press, 1991), 71–80.

5. Trenin, *What Is Russia up to*, 34–8; Alexey Vasiliev, *Russia's Middle East Policy: From Lenin to Putin* (London: Routledge, 2018), 239–343.

6. Yevgeny Primakov, *Russia and the Arabs: Behind the Scenes in the Middle East from the Cold War to the Present*, trans. Paul Gould (New York: Basic Books, 2009), 57–73.

7. Vasiliev, *Russia's Middle East Policy*, 29–60.

8. The Soviet-style state-controlled economic model did not appeal just to Arab nationalists, but to revolutionaries throughout the "Third World" during the Cold War era. Forest D. Colburn, *The Vogue of Revolution in Poor Countries* (Princeton, NJ: Princeton University Press, 1994), 49–62.

9. Galia Golan, *Soviet Policies in the Middle East from World War Two to Gorbachev* (Cambridge, UK: Cambridge University Press, 1990), 13–14; Efraim Karsh, *The Soviet Union and Syria: The Asad Years* (London: Royal Institute of International Affairs/Routledge, 1988), 73; Christopher Harmer, "Russian Naval Base Tartus," Institute for the Study of War, July 31, 2012, www.understandingwar.org/sites/default/files/Backgrounder_Russian_NavalBaseTartus.pdf.

10. Mohrez Mahmoud El Hussini, *Soviet-Egyptian Relations, 1945–85* (London: Macmillan, 1987).

11. Primakov, *Russia and the Arabs*, 260; Clyde Haberman, "Israel and Soviets Restore Full Relations," *New York Times*, October 19, 1991, www.nytimes.com/1991/10/19/world/israel-and-soviets-restore-full-relations.html.

12. Stephen Page, *The Soviet Union and the Yemens: Influence in Asymmetrical Relationships* (New York: Praeger, 1985), 4–5; Mark N. Katz, *Russia and Arabia: Soviet Foreign Policy toward the Arabian* Peninsula (Baltimore, MD: Johns Hopkins University Press, 1986), 162–71; Yahia Zoubir, "Soviet Policy toward the Western Sahara Conflict," *Africa Today* 34, no. 3 (1987): 22–5; Directorate of Intelligence, "Jordan's Soviet Option," Central Intelligence Agency, November 1988, www.cia.gov/library/readingroom/document/cia-rdp89s01450r000600620001–3; and Golan, *Soviet Policies in the Middle East from World War Two to Gorbachev*, 178–80.

13. Katz, *Russia and Arabia*, 103–56 and 171–83.

14. This was told to me repeatedly during my visits to Oman in December 1982 and Saudi Arabia in April 1984, as well as in conversations with Arab Gulf diplomats in Washington, DC, during the early and mid-1980s.

15. Richard Pearson, "Ali Sabry, Former Egyptian Vice President," *Washington Post*, August 5, 1991, www.washingtonpost.com/archive/local/1991/08/05/ali-sabry-former-egyptian-vice-president/30e8be47–87ca-4ce0–99f4–92ebf319f7dc/?utm_term=.890931a6da83.

16. Eric Pace, "Sudan Ousts 2 Communist Diplomats, Charging Link to Plotters," *New York Times*, August 3, 1971,www.nytimes.com/1971/08/03/archives/sudan-ousts-2-communist-diplomats-charging-link-to-plotters.html. According to Primakov, Moscow was not involved in the Sudanese Communist Party's coup attempt, and its leaders had "kept their intentions hidden" from Moscow. See Primakov, *Russia and the Arabs*, 80.

17. Galia Golan noted, "This rift led to a sharp deterioration in relations and open polemics. Oddly enough it did not lead to a break in relations or even to the suspension of arms supplies." See Golan, *Soviet Policies in the Middle East*, 172. According to Primakov, even as he was executing Iraqi communists, "Saddam never stopped insisting that the leadership in Baghdad had established and would maintain close relations with those … communists who had opted to cooperate with the regime." Quoted in Primakov, *Russia and the Arabs*, 307.

18. Katz, *Russia and Arabia*, 90–5; Mark N. Katz, "Civil Conflict in South Yemen," *Middle East Review* 19, no. 1 (1986): 7–13.

19. Bruce D. Porter, *The USSR in Third World Conflicts: Soviet Aims and Diplomacy in Local Wars, 1945–1980* (Cambridge, UK: Cambridge University Press), 182–215.

20. Oles M. Smolansky and Bettie M. Smolansky, *The USSR and Iraq: The Soviet Quest for Influence* (Durham, NC: Duke University Press, 1991), 230–79; Vasiliev, *Russia's Middle East Policy*, 285–97.

21. Vasiliev, *Russia's Middle East Policy*, 228–9.

22. Director of Central Intelligence, National Intelligence Estimate, "Soviet Forces and Capabilities in the Southern Theater of Military Operations," Central Intelligence Agency, December 1983, 13, www.cia.gov/library/readingroom/document/0000278543; Panagiotis Dimitrakis, "The Soviet Invasion of Afghanistan: International Reactions, Military Intelligence and British Diplomacy," *Middle Eastern Studies* 48, no. 4 (2012): 524.

23. Nadav Safran, *Saudi Arabia: The Ceaseless Quest for Security* (Ithaca, NY: Cornell University Press, 1988), 320.

24. See, for example, the chapter titled, "Cursed Nineties" in Vasiliev, *Russia's Middle East Policy*, 303–43.

25. Talal Nizameddin, *Russia and the Middle East: Towards a New Foreign Policy* (New York: St. Martin's Press, 1999), 71–107.

26. Mark N. Katz, "Saudi-Russian Relations in the Putin Era," *Middle East Journal* 55, no. 4 (2001): 612–17.

27. Trenin, *What Is Russia up to*, 113–33.

28. Mark N. Katz, "Saudi-Russian Relations since 9/11," *Problems of Post-Communism* 51, no. 2 (2004): 7–9.

29. Christopher Phillips, *The Battle for Syria: International Rivalry in the New Middle East* (New Haven, CT: Yale University Press, 2016), 92–9.

30. Phillips, *The Battle for Syria*, 213–23.

31. Mark N. Katz, "Russia and the Arab Spring," Middle East Institute, April 3, 2012, www.mei.edu/publications/russia-and-arab-spring.

32. Dimitar Bechev, "Russia and Turkey: The Promise and the Limits of Partnership," in *Russia's Return to the Middle East: Building Sandcastles?* eds. Nicu Popescu and Stanislav Secrieru, Chaillot Paper no. 114 (Paris: European Union Institute for Security Studies, 2018), 95–101; Pavel Baev, "Russia and Turkey: Strategic Partners and Rivals," IFRI, May 3, 2021, www.ifri.org/sites/default/files/atoms/files/baev_turkey_russia_2021.pdf.

33. Carlotta Gall and Patrick Kingsley, "Turkey Halts Syrian Incursion, Hours after Deal with Russia," *New York Times*, October 23, 2019, www.nytimes.com/2019/10/23/world/middleeast/turkey-russia-syria.html.

34. James Sladden et al., "Russian Strategy in the Middle East," RAND Corporation, 2017, 6–7, www.rand.org/pubs/perspectives/PE236.html; Mark N. Katz, "What Do They See in Him? How the Middle East Views Putin and Russia," *Russian Analytical Digest*, no. 219, May 3, 2018, 2–4, www.css.ethz.ch/content/dam/ethz/special-interest/gess/cis/center-for-securities-studies/pdfs/RAD219.pdf.

35. Mark N. Katz, "The Arab Spring and Russian Foreign Policy toward the Middle East," *Routledge Handbook of International Relations in the Middle East*, ed. Shahram Akbarzadeh (London: Routledge, 2019), 158–60; Wolfgang Mühlberger, "Arab

Public Opinion: The View on Russia's Foreign Policy," in *Forward to the Past: New/Old Theatres of Russia's International Projection*, eds. Aldo Ferrari and Eleonora Tafuro Ambrosetti (Milan, Italy: ISPI, 2020), 87–107.

36. Amir Asmar, "Why Would Arab Leaders Pursue Strategic Partnerships with Russia?" Council on Foreign Relations, November 5, 2019, www.cfr.org/blog/why-would-arab-leaders-pursue-strategic-partnerships-russia.

37. Carole Nakhle, "Russia's Energy Diplomacy in the Middle East," in *Russia's Return to the Middle East: Building Sandcastles?* eds. Nicu Popescu and Stanislav Secrieru, Chaillot Paper no. 114 (Paris: European Union Institute for Security Studies, 2018), 32.

38. Joshua Yaffa, "How the Russian-Saudi Oil War Went Awry—For Putin Most of All," *The New Yorker*, April 15, 2020, www.newyorker.com/news/dispatch/how-the-russian-saudi-oil-war-went-awry-for-putin-most-of-all; Sergey Sukhankin, "Contextualizing the Russia-KSA Oil Deal: Can It Last?" Gulf International Forum, May 12, 2021, https://gulfif.org/contextualizing-the-russia-ksa-oil-deal-can-it-last.

39. Marcin Kaczmarski, "Russia-China Relations in Central Asia: Why Is There a Surprising Absence of Rivalry?" The Asan Forum, April 19, 2019, www.theasanforum.org/russia-china-relations-in-central-asia-why-is-there-a-surprising-absence-of-rivalry.

40. Ali Hussein Bakeer and Giorgio Cafiero, "Bashar al-Assad and the Greater Arab World," Atlantic Council, February 8, 2019, www.atlanticcouncil.org/blogs/syriasource/bashar-al-assad-and-the-greater-arab-world; Liz Sly, "Assad Wants to Be Back in the Arab Fold. The U.S. Stands in the Way," *Washington Post*, March 3, 2019, www.washingtonpost.com/world/assad-wants-to-be-back-in-the-arab-fold-the-us-stands-in-the-way/2019/03/03/eb10c5e8-18e3-11e9-b8e6-567190c2fd08_story.html?utm_term=.c1472c00db17.

41. Mark N. Katz, "Russia and Israel: An Improbable Friendship," in *Russia's Return to the Middle East: Building Sandcastles?* eds. Nicu Popescu and Stanislav Secrieru, Chaillot Paper no. 114 (Paris: European Union Institute for Security Studies, 2018), 103–8.

42. Alexei Khlebnikov, "Trump's Decision on Jerusalem Might Open the Door for Russia," *Moscow Times*, December 12, 2017, www.themoscowtimes.com/2017/12/12/trumps-decision-on-jerusalem-might-open-door-for-russia-oped-a59908; Radio Free Europe/Radio Liberty, "Russia, Iran, Arab States Reject 'Unlawful' U.S. Decision on Golan Heights," March 26, 2019, www.rferl.org/a/russia-iran-arab-states-reject-unlawful-us-decision-on-golan-heights/29843054.html.

43. Marianna Belenkaya, "Russia's Timid Approach to the Israeli-Palestinian Conflict," *Moscow Times*, May 18, 2021, www.themoscowtimes.com/2021/05/18/russias-timid-approach-to-the-israeli-palestinian-conflict-a73930.

44. David Welna, "U.S.-Turkey Standoff over F-35 Escalates as Each Side Waits for the Other to Blink," National Public Radio, April 3, 2019, www.npr.org/2019/04/03/709222963/u-s-turkey-standoff-over-f-35-escalates-as-each-side-waits-for-the-other-to-blin; Menkse Tokyay, "US Formally Excludes Turkey

from F-35 Consortium, *Arab News*, April 22, 2021, www.arabnews.com/node/1847266/middle-east.

45. Michael Peck, "Israel vs. Russia: The Middle East War That Could Become a Nuclear Train Wreck," *National Interest*, May 19, 2019, https://nationalinterest.org/blog/buzz/israel-vs-russia-middle-east-war-could-become-nuclear-train-wreck-58482.

46. "Russian Expert Shumilin: 'Iran Is No Longer the Ally of Russia,'" February 8, 2019, https://middleeasttransparent.com/en/russian-expert-shumilin-iran-is-no-longer-the-ally-of-russia; Nicole Grajewski, "Friends or Frenemies? How Russia and Iran Compete and Cooperate," Foreign Policy Research Institute, March 12, 2020, www.fpri.org/wp-content/uploads/2020/03/rfp-1-grajewski-final.pdf.

47. Sebastien Roblin, "Israeli F-16s Smashed a Syrian Missile Complex (and Russia's Missiles Didn't Strike)," *National Interest*, May 13, 2019, https://nationalinterest.org/blog/buzz/israeli-f-16s-smashed-syrian-missile-complex-and-russia%E2%80%99s-missiles-didn%E2%80%99t-strike-57247.

48. This was the theme that Russian speakers emphasized at the Valdai Discussion Club conference on "Russia in the Middle East: Playing on All Fields," Valdai Discussion Club, Moscow, February 19–20, 2018, https://valdaiclub.com/events/posts/articles/russia-middle-east—valdai-speakers. For a firsthand account, see Mark N. Katz, "Can Russia Succeed Where America Failed in the Middle East?" LobeLog, February 23, 2018, http://lobelog.com/can-russia-succeed-where-america-failed-in-the-middle-east.

49. Krishnadev Calamur, "No One Wants to Help Bashar al-Assad Rebuild Syria," *The Atlantic*, March 15, 2019, www.theatlantic.com/international/archive/2019/03/where-will-money-rebuild-syria-come/584935.

50. Samy Akil, "Why China Will Not Rebuild Syria," East Asia Forum, May 8, 2021, www.eastasiaforum.org/2021/05/08/why-china-will-not-rebuild-syria.

51. Julien Barnes-Dacey, "Russia and the 'Resistance Axis,'" in *Russia's Return to the Middle East: Building Sandcastles?* eds. Nicu Popescu and Stanislav Secrieru, Chaillot Paper no. 114 (Paris: European Union Institute for Security Studies, 2018), 67.

52. Mark N. Katz, "The Gulf and the Great Powers: Evolving Dynamics," *Middle East Policy* 24, no. 2 (2017): 102–9; Ben Hubbard and Javier C. Hernández, "Amid Trouble with the West, Saudi Arabia Looks East," *New York Times*, February 20, 2019, www.nytimes.com/2019/02/20/world/middleeast/saudi-arabia-pakistan-india-china.html.

3. DOMESTIC FACTORS IN RUSSIA'S MIDDLE EAST POLICY

1. Alexey Vasiliev, *Russia's Middle East Policy: From Lenin to Putin* (London: Routledge, 2018), 388.

2. Vasiliev, *Russia's Middle East Policy*, 417.

3. D. V. Streltsov, ed., *Rossiya i strany vostoka v post-bipolyarnom mire: uchebnik* [Russia and the East in the post-bipolar period: textbook] (Moscow: Aspect Press, 2014), 54–5.

4. Yevgeny M. Primakov, *Konfidencialno: Blizhnii Vostok na scene i za kulisami* [Confidential: The Middle East on stage and behind the scenes] (Moscow: Rossiyskaya Gazeta, 2006), 329. Henceforth, all original quotes in the Russian language have been translated into English by the author.

5. Dmitry Travin, *Will Putin's System Last until 2024?* (Saint Petersburg: Norma, 2016), 85.

6. Maxim Ivanov, "Vzlety i padeniya reitinga Putina [Ups and downs of Putin's ratings]," *Vedomosti*, August 19, 2019, www.vedomosti.ru/politics/articles/2019/08/13/808697-vzglyad-snizu.

7. Yegor Gaidar and Anatoly Chubais, *Ekonomicheskie zapiski* [Economy notes] (Moscow: ROSSPEN: 2008), 45–6.

8. Travin, *Will Putin's System Last until 2024?* 57.

9. Askar Akaev et al., "Technological Development and Protest Waves: Arab Spring as a Trigger of the Global Phase Transition?" *Technological Forecasting and Social Change* 116 (2017): 316–21.

10. See, Sharon Erickson Nepstad, "Nonviolent Resistance in the Arab Spring: The Critical Role of Military–Opposition Alliances," *Swiss Political Science Review* 17, no. 4 (2011): 485–91.

11. See, Andrey Korotayev and Julia Zinkina, "Egyptian Revolution: A Demographic Structural Analysis," *Entelequia: Revista Interdisciplinar* 13, no. 2011 (2011): 139–69; L. Grinin, L. M. Issaev, and A. Korotayev, *Revolutsii i nestabilnost na Blizhnem Vostoke* [Revolutions and instability in the Middle East] (Moscow: Uchitel, 2015); and Andrey Korotayev, Leonid Issaev, and Alisa Shishkina, "Egyptian Coup of 2013: An 'Econometric' Analysis," *Journal of North African Studies* 21, no. 3 (2016): 341–56.

12. See, Jack A. Goldstone, "Understanding the Revolutions of 2011: Weakness and Resilience in Middle Eastern Autocracies," *Foreign Affairs* 3, no. 90 (2011): 8–16; Colin J. Beck, "Reflections on the Revolutionary Wave in 2011," *Theory and Society* 43, no. 2 (2014): 197–223; and Andrey Korotayev, "Developing the Methods of Estimation and Forecasting the Arab Spring," *Central European Journal of International and Security Studies* 7, no. 4 (2013): 28–58.

13. While in 2010 CNTS registered only five major anti-government demonstrations in the Middle East, in 2011 this number rocketed up to 307.

14. Reuters, "Iran Says New U.S. Sanctions Violate Nuclear Deal, Vows 'Proportional Reaction,'" August 2, 2017, www.reuters.com/article/us-iran-nuclear-usa-sanctions-idUSKBN1AI2N0.

15. Travin, *Will Putin's System Last until 2024?* 138.

16. Ministry of Foreign Affairs of the Russian Federation, "O godovshchine nachala revolyutsionnykh preobrazovaniy v Yegipte" [On the Anniversary of the Start of Revolutionary Transformations in Egypt], January 25, 2012, www.mid.ru/web/guest/maps/eg/-/asset_publisher/g1LePFf60C7F/content/id/173682.

17. Ministry of Foreign Affairs of the Russian Federation, "Interv'yu zamestitelya Ministra inostrannykh del Rossii M. Bogdanova agentstvu 'Interfaks'" [Interview of Deputy Minister of Foreign Affairs of Russia M. Bogdanov to Interfax News

Agency, Moscow], July 5, 2011, www.mid.ru/web/guest/foreign_policy/news/-/asset_publisher/cKNonkJE02Bw/content/id/200982.

18. Vladislav Vorobiev, "SSSR: fantomnye boli [USSR: Phantom Pains]," RG.RU, February 13, 2013, https://rg.ru/2013/02/12/karasin-site.html.

19. Vasiliev, *Russia's Middle East Policy*, 520.

20. Travin, *Will Putin's System Exist until 2024?* 237.

21. See, for example: Dmitry Travin and L. Gudkov, *After the Crimea: Opinion Polls in 2017* (Moscow: Levada Center, 2018).

22. Travin, *Will Putin's System Exist until 2024?* 66.

23. Federal News Agency, "Rossiya spasla Siriyu i ves' Blizhniy Vostok ot 'rakovoy opukholi' IG" [Russia saved Syria and the entire Middle East from the "cancer" of the IGIL], April 24, 2019, https://riafan.ru/1173122-rossiya-spasla-siriyu-i-ves-blizhnii-vostok-ot-rakovoi-opukholi-ig.

24. Kremlin, "70-ya sessiya General'noy Assamblei OON" [70th session of the UN General Assembly], September 28, 2015, http://kremlin.ru/events/president/news/50385.

25. *TASS Russian News Agency*, "Lavrov: deystviya rossiyskikh VKS pomogli perelomit' situatsiyu v Sirii" [Lavrov: The actions of the Russian VKS helped to turn the tide in Syria], January 26, 2016, https://tass.ru/politika/2614526.

26. Kremlin, "Vladimir Putin posetil aviabazu Khmeymim v Sirii" [Vladimir Putin visited Khmeimim airbase], December 11, 2017, http://kremlin.ru/events/president/news/56351.

27. Alexey Pushkov, Twitter, May 25, 2019, https://twitter.com/Alexey_Pushkov/status/1132155927069642752.

28. Kremlin, "70-ya sessiya General'noy Assamblei OON."

29. Travin, *Will Putin's System Exist until 2024?* 254.

30. *BBC News*, "Putin poprosil oppozitsiyu 'ne raskachivat' lodku'" [Putin asked the opposition "not to rock the boat"], November 23, 2011, www.bbc.com/russian/russia/2011/11/111123_putin_duma.

31. Kremlin, "Zasedaniye Soveta po razvitiyu grazhdanskogo obshchestva i pravam cheloveka" [Meeting of the Council for Civil Society Development and Human Rights], December 11, 2018, http://kremlin.ru/events/president/news/59374.

32. *Regnum*, "Vladimir Putin: 'Kollaps SSSR—krupneishaya geopoliticheskaya katastrofa veka' [Vladimir Putin: 'The Collapse of the USSR—The Largest Geopolitical Catastrophe of the Century'"], April 25, 2005, https://regnum.ru/news/444083.html.

33. Grigory Golosov, "Fortunato Putin: pochemu Putinu vezet i chto imenno on vyigryvayet" [Fortunato Putin's voices: Why Putin is lucky and what exactly he wins], *Republic*, August 21, 2014, https://republic.ru/posts/l/1146025.

34. Consultant.ru, "Postanovlenie Syezda Narodnykh Deputatov SSSR ot 24.12.1989 N 982–1 'O politicheskoy otsenke resheniya o vvode sovetskikh voysk v Afganistan v dekabre 1979 goda'" [Statement of the Congress of People's Deputies of the Soviet Union N 982–1 24.12.1989 "On the state assessment of the decision on the intro-

duction of Soviet troops in Afghanistan in December 1979"], www.consultant.ru/cons/cgi/online.cgi?req=doc&base=ESU&n=3113#09208851373960383.

35. Denis Volkov, "Foreign Policy Fatigue," *Riddle*, September 4, 2018, www.ridl.io/en/foreign-policy-fatigue.

36. See, for example, *Svoboda*, "Putin prikazal voyennym nachat' vyvod osnovnoy chasti sil Rossii iz Sirii" [Putin ordered the military to begin withdrawing the main part of the Russian forces from Syria], March 14, 2016, www.svoboda.org/a/27611079.html; *Svoboda*, "Putin zayavil o skorom zavershenii" [Putin announced the imminent completion of the military operation in Russia in Syria], November 21, 2017, www.svoboda.org/a/28865958.html; and Kremlin, "Vladimir Putin posetil aviabazu Khmeymim v Sirii."

37. Public Opinion Foundation (FOM), "Vneshnyaya politika: monitoring" [Foreign policy: Monitoring], June 20, 2019, https://fom.ru/Politika/14223; Public Opinion Foundation (FOM), "Interes k vneshney politike. Uspekhi i neudachi" [Interest in foreign policy. Successes and failures], May 20, 2019, https://fom.ru/Politika/14209.

38. *Ibid.*

39. *Ibid.*

40. Pavel Aptekar, "Kak rossiyane ustali ot vneshney politiki" [How Russians became tired of foreign policy], Vedomosti, June 21, 2019, www.vedomosti.ru/opinion/articles/2019/06/21/804715-rossiyane-ustali.

41. Kremlin, "Zasedaniye diskussionnogo kluba 'Valday'" [The Valdai Discussion Club meeting], October 18, 2018 http://kremlin.ru/events/president/news/58848.

42. "Ryabkov okharakterizoval kurs RF v otnoshenii SSHA kak 'strategicheskoye terpeniye'" [Ryabkov described the course of the Russian Federation towards the United States as "strategic patience"], Interfax, February 20, 2019, www.interfax.ru/russia/651314.

43. Vasiliev, *Russia's Middle East Policy*, 377.

4. RUSSIAN LEGAL AND NORMATIVE CLAIMS FOR ITS INTERVENTION IN THE SYRIAN CONFLICT SINCE 2015

1. Russian military specialists unsurprisingly present the operation as a successful case of power projection. See, for example, Anatoly Tsyganok, *Voyna v Sirii i ee posledstviya dlya Blizhnego Vostoka, Kavkaza i Tsentral'noy Azii: russkiy vzglyad* [The war in Syria and its consequences for the Middle East, the Caucasus, and Central Asia: A Russian perspective] (Moscow: AIRO-XXI, 2016), 196–256.

2. Interview for Interfax, *BBC Monitoring Online*, Moscow, February 10, 2013.

3. See Walid al-Moualem, Syrian Arab Republic, Deputy Prime Minister, Minister of Foreign Affairs and Expatriates, "Statement at 70th Session of the U.N. General Assembly," October 2, 2015, https://gadebate.un.org/sites/default/files/gastatements/70/70_SY_en.pdf.

4. Interfax—Kazakhstan news agency, Almaty, *BBC*, October 21, 2015.

5. Ministry of Foreign Affairs, Russia, "Press Release on Sergey Lavrov's Press Conference Following Russia's Presidency of the UN Security Council, New York, October 1, 2015," www.mid.ru/en/foreign_policy/news/-/asset_publisher/cKNonkJE02Bw/content/id/1825252. From September 2014 the US-led coalition was termed the Global Coalition to Defeat ISIS, with the US military operational name "Operation Inherent Resolve."

6. *Ibid.*

7. Jon Sharman, "Russia and Iran Warn US They Will 'Respond with Force' if Red Lines Crossed in Syria Again," *Independent*, April 9, 2017, www.independent.co.uk/news/world/middle-east/russia-iran-us-america-syria-red-lines-respond-with-force-aggressor-air-strikes-war-latest-a7675031.html.

8. Carol Morello and David Filipov, "Tillerson Brings Tough Line to Moscow over Russia's Backing for Syrian Regime," *Washington Post*, April 11, 2017, www.washingtonpost.com/world/in-moscow-tillerson-seeks-to-move-russia-away-from-syrian-alliance/2017/04/11/adb6f8ed-4712-493e-927e-40574ab3cdb6_story.html.

9. Konstantin Kozachev, Interfax news agency, Moscow, *BBC*, February 5, 2016.

10. Boris Dolgov, senior researcher at the Russian Academy of Sciences Centre for Arab and Islamic Studies, cited in "What Does Turkey's Syria Offensive Mean For Russia," *The Moscow Times*, October 10, 2018, www.themoscowtimes.com/2019/10/10/what-does-turkeys-syria-offensive-mean-for-russia-a67678.

11. The Ministry of Foreign Affairs of the Russian Federation, "Foreign Minister Sergey Lavrov's statement and answers to media questions at a joint news conference following talks with Minister of Foreign Affairs of Iran Mohammad Javad Zarif, Moscow, June 16, 2020," June 16, 2020, www.mid.ru/en/web/guest/adernoenerasprostranenie/-/asset_publisher/JrcRGi5UdnBO/content/id/4166214.

12. Yuri Kochetkov, "Russia, Iran Agree on Role of International Law in Syria," TeleTrader, June 16, 2020, www.teletrader.com/russia-iran-agree-on-role-of-international-law-in-syria/news/details/52429995?ts=1622806011330.

13. This is summarized in Laura Visser, "Russia's Intervention in Syria," *EJIL: Talk! Blog of the European Journal of International Law*, November 25, 2015, www.ejiltalk.org/russias-intervention-in-syria.

14. For a summary presentation of this position, see Research Services, Deutscher Bundestag, "Assessment of Russian, US and Israeli Involvement in Syria in the Light of International Law," WD 2—3000—029/18, 2018, https://neu-alexander.de/files/2018/07/Assessment-of-Russian-US-and-Israeli-involvement-in-the-conflict-in-Syria-in-the-light-of-international-law.pdf.

15. International Court of Justice, "Military and Paramilitary Activities in and against Nicaragua (Nicaragua v. United States of America)," Judgment of June 22, 1986, www.icj-cij.org/en/case/70/judgments. For analysis see, for example, Dapo Akande, "The Contribution of the International Court of Justice to the Law on the Use of Force," November 18, 2011, *EJIL: Talk! Blog of the European Journal of International Law*, www.ejiltalk.org/the-contribution-of-the-international-court-of-justice-and-the-law-of-the-use-of-force.

16. As analyzed by Chris Borgen, "Parsing the Syrian-Russian Agreement Concerning Russia's Deployment," *OpinioJuris*, January 18, 2016, http://opiniojuris.org/2016/01/18/32350.

17. International lawyers cited in Ziyad Hayatli, "Russia's Intervention in Syria: A Legal Perspective," *The New Jurist*, August 28, 2016, http://newjurist.com/russia's-intervention-in-syria-a-legal-perspective.html.

18. A question addressed by Gregory H. Fox, "Intervention by Invitation," *Wayne State University Law School Research Paper* no. 2014–04, http://ssrn.com/abstract=2407539. Also in Marc Weller, ed., *The Oxford Handbook on the Use of Force* (Oxford, UK: Oxford University Press, 2015).

19. Marc Weller, "Russia Says Its Airstrikes in Syria Are Perfectly Legal. Are They?" *Huffington Post*, January 3, 2017, www.huffingtonpost.co.uk/entry/russia-airstrikes-syria-international-law_us_560d6448e4b0dd85030b0c08?ec_carp=4661581491607029201.

20. *Ibid.* In August 2011, the UK, France, and Germany stated that Assad had lost all legitimacy and could no longer claim to lead the country. This kind of assessment was more a political and pragmatic analytical assessment, however, than a legal evaluation.

21. Marc Weller, "Islamic State Crisis: What Force Does International Law Allow," *BBC*, September 25, 2014, www.bbc.co.uk/news/world-middle-east-29283286.

22. Weller, "Russia Says Its Airstrikes in Syria Are Perfectly Legal. Are They?"

23. Visser, "Russia's Intervention in Syria."

24. *Washington Post*, "Read Putin's U.N. General Assembly Speech," September 28, 2015, www.washingtonpost.com/news/worldviews/wp/2015/09/28/read-putins-u-n-general-assembly-speech.

25. "Read Putin's U.N. General Assembly Speech."

26. Ministry of Foreign Affairs, Russia, "Press Release on Sergey Lavrov's Press Conference."

27. Ministry of Foreign Affairs, Russia, "Foreign Minister Sergey Lavrov's Interview with NTV's Programme Pozdnyakov," October 13, 2015, www.mid.ru/en/web/guest/meropriyatiya_s_uchastiem_ministra/-/asset_publisher/xK1BhB2bUjd3/content/id/1846271.

28. *Ibid.*

29. Kiril Avramov and Ruslan Trad, "An Experimental Playground: The Footprint of Russian Private Military Companies in Syria," *The Defense Post*, February 17, 2018, https://thedefensepost.com/2018/02/17/russia-private-military-contractors-syria.

30. *Associated Press (AP)*, "The Latest: Russian Private Military Contractors in Syria," June 20, 2019, https://apnews.com/61b26d25e24e4115873b39a8de8dcf32.

31. Andrew Linder, "Russian Private Military Companies in Syria and Beyond," Center for Strategic and International Studies (CSIS), 2018, https://csis-prod.s3.amazonaws.com/s3fs-public/181017_RussianPrivateMilitary.pdf; Neil Hauer, "The Rise and Fall of a Russian Mercenary Army," *Foreign Policy*, October 8, 2019,

https://foreignpolicy.com/2019/10/06/rise-fall-russian-private-army-wagner-syrian-civil-war.

32. Kurt Nimmo, "Putin Says U.S. Proxy War in Syria Violates International Law," Infowars.com, September 27, 2015, www.infowars.com/putin-says-u-s-proxy-war-in-syria-violates-international-law.

33. Olivier Corten, *The Law against War: The Prohibition on the Use of Force in Contemporary International Law* (Oxford, UK: Oxford University Press, 2010).

34. International Court of Justice (ICJ), *Legality of the Threat or Use of Nuclear Weapons. Reports of Judgments, Advisory Opinions and Orders* (The Hague, Netherlands: ICJ, July 8, 1996), 35, www.icj-cij.org/files/case-related/95/095-19960708-ADV-01-00-EN.pdf.

35. Deborah Haynes and Lucy Fisher, "Barbaric Bombing of Aleppo is 'Like Nazi Horrors at Guernica,'" *The Times*, October 12, 2016, www.thetimes.co.uk/article/barbaric-bombing-of-aleppo-is-like-nazi-horrors-at-guernica-xn9jk9m9j; Michael R. Gordon, "Report Rebuts Russia's Claims of Restraint in Syrian Bombing Campaign," *New York Times*, February 12, 2017, www.nytimes.com/2017/02/12/us/politics/russia-syria-aleppo-bombing-campaign-restraint.html?_r=0.

36. Amnesty International, "Syria: Putin Takes Hypocrisy to a New Level with Remarks on Raqqa Civilian Deaths," July 17, 2018, www.amnesty.org/en/latest/news/2018/07/syria-putin-takes-hypocrisy-to-a-new-level-with-remarks-on-raqqa-civilian-deaths.

37. Tim Ripley, "Russia Learns Military Lessons in Syria," *Jane's Intelligence Review*, 2017, www.janes.com/images/assets/758/69758/Russia_learns_military_lessons_in_Syria.pdf.

38. James Kearney, "An Assessment of Russia's Rules of Engagement," Action on Armed Violence (AOAV), March 14, 2019, https://aoav.org.uk/2019/an-assessment-of-russias-roe.

39. United Nations Security Council, "7560th Meeting," November 16, 2015, 12, www.un.org/en/ga/search/view_doc.asp?symbol=S/PV.7560.

40. Human Rights Watch, "Russia/Syria: Flurry of Prohibited Weapons Attacks," June 3, 2019, www.hrw.org/news/2019/06/03/russia/syria-flurry-of-prohibited-weapons-attacks.

41. Liz Sly, "U.N. to Investigate Accusations That Russia, Syria Are Deliberately Targeting Hospitals," *Washington Post*, August 1, 2019, www.washingtonpost.com/world/middle_east/un-to-investigate-accusations-that-russia-syria-are-deliberately-targeting-hospitals/2019/08/01/efa6461a-b478-11e9-acc8-1d847bacca73_story.html. These attacks occurred despite "deconfliction" under which the UN supplies the coordinates of hospitals, schools, bakeries, and other civilian infrastructure to Russia, Turkey, and the United States, with the intention of preventing attacks on them.

42. *Radio Free Europe*, "EU's Mogherini Condemns Attacks on Civilians by Syria, Russia in Idlib Province," November 23, 2019, www.rferl.org/a/eu-mogherini-condemns-civilian-attacks-syria-russia/30287850.html.

43. Richard Spencer, "Syria: Assad Used Chemical Attacks to Drive Wedge between Civilians and Rebels," *The Times*, April 14, 2020, www.thetimes.co.uk/article/syria-assad-used-chemical-attacks-to-drive-wedge-between-civilians-and-rebels-bqh336v0x.

44. Assessment of Justin Bronk, air combat specialist at the Royal United Services Institute, as cited in Kearney, "An Assessment of Russia's Rules of Engagement."

45. As concluded also by a study of the Global Public Policy Institute in Berlin, as cited in Spencer, "Syria: Assad Used Chemical Attacks to Drive Wedge Between Civilians and Rebels."

46. *Ibid.*

47. Roy Allison, "Russia and the Post-2014 International Legal Order: Revisionism and *Realpolitik*," *International Affairs* 93, no. 3 (2017): 527–8.

48. Kearney, "An Assessment of Russia's Rules of Engagement."

49. Amnesty International, "Syria: Putin Takes Hypocrisy to a New Level."

50. For example, Mohammed Nuruzzaman, "Rethinking Foreign Military Interventions to Promote Human Rights: Evidence from Libya, Bahrain and Syria," *Canadian Journal of Political Science* 48, no. 3 (2015): 531–552.

51. Ryan Goodman, "Is the US-Russia Pact in Syria Barred by International Law?" *Just Security*, September 20, 2016, www.justsecurity.org/33058/us-russia-pact-syria-international-law.

52. Monika Hakimi, "US Responsibility Arising from Russian Violations of the Law of Armed Conflict," *Just Security*, September 21, 2016, www.justsecurity.org/33075/u-s-responsibility-arising-russian-violations-law-armed-conflict.

53. Julian Borger, "Russia Says Ceasefire at Risk after US Bombing of Syrian Troops," *The Guardian*, September 18, 2016, www.theguardian.com/world/2016/sep/18/us-accuses-russia-of-grandstanding-over-deadly-syria-air-strikes.

54. *Radio Free Europe*, "UN Creates Body to Prepare Syrian War Crimes Cases over Russian Objections," December 22, 2016, www.rferl.org/a/un-creates-body-prepare-syria-war-crimes-cases-over-russian-objections/28190272.html.

55. Gennady Gatilov, "The Humanitarian Crisis in Syria: How Human Tragedies Are Used for Political Purposes," *International Affairs* 62, no. 6 (2016): 2.

56. Shanghai Cooperation Organization Secretariat, "Joint Communique on the Results of the Meeting of Defence Ministers of SCO Member States," April 29, 2019, http://eng.sectsco.org/news/20190430/533861.html.

57. Roy Allison, "Russia and Syria: Explaining Alignment with a Regime in Crisis," *International Affairs* 89, no. 4 (2013): 808–10.

58. Gatilov, "The Humanitarian Crisis in Syria," 3–4.

59. Statement by Vassily Nebenzia, at United Nations, "Security Council Rejects 2 Draft Resolutions Authorizing Cross-Border, Cross-Line Humanitarian Access in Syria," Security Council 8697th Meeting, December 20, 2019, www.un.org/press/en/2019/sc14066.doc.htm.

60. Gatilov, "The Humanitarian Crisis in Syria," 6.

61. Gatilov, "The Humanitarian Crisis in Syria," 6–8. On the Russar (Russian-Arab) Foundation, see www.frussar.com.

62. TASS, "Patriarch Vows Russian Orthodox Church Will Continue to Render Assistance to Syria," December 5, 2017, https://tass.com/society/979113.

63. Amie Ferris-Rotman, "During Easter, Some Russians Look to Strengthen Bonds with Syria's Embattled Christians," *Washington Post*, April 20, 2019, www.washingtonpost.com/world/2019/04/20/during-easter-season-some-russians-look-strengthen-bonds-with-syrias-embattled-christians.

64. *Rossiyskaya Gazeta* website October 12, 2012, 8, as cited in *BBC* Monitoring online October 12, 2012.

65. Gatilov, "The Humanitarian Crisis in Syria," 9 and 11.

66. Yuliya Nikitina, "Russia's Policy on International Interventions," *PONARS Eurasia Policy Memo*, no. 312, February 2014, www.ponarseurasia.org/sites/default/files/policy-memos-pdf/Pepm_312_Nikitina_Feb2014.pdf.

67. Mikhail Margelov, chair of the Federation Council's International Affairs Committee, interview on *Ekho Moskvy* radio, Interfax news agency, Moscow, *BBC*, July 9, 2012.

68. The Ministry of Foreign Affairs of the Russian Federation, "Speech and Answers to the Media Questions by the Minister of Foreign Affairs of the Russian Federation Sergey V. Lavrov after Negotiations with the Joint Special Representative of the UN and LAS Lakhdar Brahimi for Syria," October 29, 2012, www.mid.ru/en/foreign_policy/news/-/asset_publisher/cKNonkJE02Bw/content/id/137246.

69. Sergei Konovalov, "Syrian Vector for Russian Paratroops" [in Russian], *Nezavisimaya Gazeta*, June 6, 2012; Pavel Felgenhauer, "Russian Military Prepares Expeditionary Forces, Allegedly for Deployment to Syria," *Eurasia Daily Monitor* 9, no. 113 (2012), https://jamestown.org/program/the-russian-military-prepares-expeditionary-forces-allegedly-for-deployment-to-syria.

70. Uran Botobekov, "Russia Wants CSTO Allies to Deploy to Syria," *Eurasia Daily Monitor* 14, no. 89 (2017), https://jamestown.org/program/russia-wants-csto-allies-deploy-syria.

71. See Amanda Guidero and Maia C. Hallward, "International Laws and Norms and Intervention in Syria and Yemen," in *Global Responses to Conflict and Crisis in Syria and Yemen* (Basingstoke, UK: Palgrave Pivot, 2019), 15–29.

72. See Justin Morris, "Libya and Syria: R2P and the Spectre of the Swinging Pendulum," *International Affairs* 89, no. 5 (2013): 1265–83.

73. Roy Allison, *Russia, the West, and Military Intervention* (Oxford, UK: Oxford University Press, 2013), 195–9.

74. For analyses of the Russian approach to R2P, see Vladimir Baranovsky and Anatoly Mateiko, "Responsibility to Protect: Russia's Approaches," *The International Spectator* 51, no. 2 (2016): 49–69; Natasha Kuhrt, "Russia, the Responsibility to Protect and Intervention," in *The Responsibility to Protect and the Third Pillar: Legitimacy and Operationalization*, eds. Daniel Fiott and Joachim Koops (Oxford, UK: Oxford University Press, 2015), 97–114; and Allison, *Russia, the West, and Military Intervention*, 64–8.

75. See Paul R. Williams, J. Trevor Ulbrick, and Jonathan Worboys, "Preventing Mass

Atrocity Crimes: The Responsibility to Protect and the Syria Crisis," *Case Western Journal of International Law* 45, no. 1–2 (2012): 473–503.

76. For a discussion of this point and the wider context of Russian normative response to R2P in the Syrian conflict, see Derek Averre and Lance Davies, "Russia, Humanitarian Intervention and the Responsibility to Protect: The Case of Syria," *International Affairs* 91, no. 4 (2015): 813–34.

77. A point stressed by Russian Foreign Minister Sergei Lavrov, see interview in Susan B. Glasser, "'The Law of Politics' According to Sergei Lavrov," *Foreign Policy*, April 29, 2013, https://foreignpolicy.com/2013/04/29/the-law-of-politics-according-to-sergei-lavrov.

78. Joseph Lutta, "How Russian Intervention in Syria Redefined the Right to Protect in Armed Conflict," *Russian Law Journal* 6, no. 2 (2018): 25–6, and 36.

79. For a full discussion, see Fiott and Koops, *The Responsibility to Protect*.

80. Lutta, "How Russian Intervention in Syria Redefined the Right to Protect in Armed Conflict," 25–6, and 36.

81. Kremlin, "Valdai International Discussion Club," October 3, 2019, http://en.kremlin.ru/events/president/news/61719.

82. Kremlin, "Statement by President of Russia Vladimir Putin," April 14, 2018, http://en.kremlin.ru/events/president/news/57257; Sewell Chan, "U.N. Security Council Rejects Russian Resolution Condemning Syrian Strikes," *New York Times*, April 14, 2018, www.nytimes.com/2018/04/14/world/middleeast/un-security-council-syria-airstrikes.html.

83. See Amichai Cohen and Elena Chachko, "The Israel-Iran-Syria Clash and the Law on Use of Force," *Lawfare*, February 14, 2018, www.lawfareblog.com/israel-iran-syria-clash-and-law-use-force.

84. Allison, "Russia and the Post-2014 International Legal Order," 531–2.

85. Mark N. Katz, "What Do They See in Him? How the Middle East Views Putin and Russia," *Russian Analytical Digest*, no. 219 (2018): 2–4, https://css.ethz.ch/content/dam/ethz/special-interest/gess/cis/center-for-securities-studies/pdfs/RAD219.pdf.

86. *Ibid.*, 3.

87. Declaration by Putin after meeting Bashar al-Assad on May 17, 2018, and Russian Presidential Envoy to Syria Alexander Laverentiev. Raz Zimmt, "Russian Declarations Regarding Removal of Foreign Forces from Syria Encounter Greater Criticism in Iran," The Meir Amit Intelligence and Terrorism Information Center, May 24, 2018, www.terrorism-info.org.il/app/uploads/2018/05/E_134_18.pdf.

88. The Ministry of Foreign Affairs of the Russian Federation, "Joint Statement by the Representatives of Iran, Russia and Turkey on the International Meeting on Syria in the Astana format, Sochi, 16–17 February 2021," February 17, 2021, www.mid.ru/en/foreign_policy/news/-/asset_publisher/cKNonkJE02Bw/content/id/4576121.

89. Lieutenant General Sergei Chvarkov, in *RIA Novosti*, 2016, as cited in Vladimir Sazhin, "Russia and Iran in Syria," *Modern Diplomacy*, November 9, 2020, www.moderndiplomacy.eu/2020/11/09/russia-and-iran-in-syria.

90. James Zogby, Elizabeth Zogby, and Sarah Hope Zogby, "Sir Bani Yas Forum: Public Opinion 2017," Zogby Research Services, August 24–September 19, 2017, www. aaiusa.org/sir_bani_yas_poll_public_opin.

91. *Ibid.*

5. RUSSIA AND IRAN: STRATEGIC PARTNERS OR PROVISIONAL COUNTERWEIGHTS?

1. Dominic Lieven, "Dilemmas of Empire 1850–1918: Power, Territory, Identity," *Journal of Contemporary History* 34, no. 2 (1999): 180.

2. See Ghoncheh Tazmini, "'To Be or Not To Be' (like the West): Modernisation in Russia and Iran," *Third World Quarterly* 39, no. 10 (2018): 1998–2015.

3. Richard Sakwa, "Beyond the Impasse," Dialogue of Civilizations Research Institute Expert Comment, 2018, 25, https://doc-research.org/wp-content/uploads/2018/10/Beyond-the-impasse_Download-file.pdf.

4. Trine Flockhart, "The Coming Multi-Order World," *Contemporary Security Policy* 37, no. 1 (2016): 5.

5. See Amitav Acharya and Barry Buzan, *The Making of Global International Relations: Origins and Evolution of IR at Its Centenary* (Cambridge, UK: Cambridge University Press, 2019), 3; *Non-Western International Relations Theory: Perspectives on and beyond Asia* (London: Routledge, 2010).

6. Acharya and Buzan, *The Making of Global International Relations*, 317.

7. *Ibid.*, 303.

8. See, for example, John W. Parker, "Russia-Iran: Strategic Partners or Competitors?" Baker Institute for Public Policy *Working Paper*, 2016, www.bakerinstitute.org/files/10480; *Tehran Times*, "Rouhani and Putin: Iran and Russia are 'Strategic Partners,'" November 1, 2017, www.tehrantimes.com/news/418142/Rouhani-and-Putin-Iran-and-Russia-are-strategic-partners; and Vladimir Sazhin, "Iran-Russia Strategic Partnership at the New Stage: What Could We Propose to Each Other?" in *Russia-Iran Partnership: an Overview and Prospects for the Future*, ed. Igor Ivanov (Moscow: The Institute for Iran-Eurasia Studies, 2016), 9–21, http://iras.ir/images/docs/files/000002/nf00002517–1.pdf.

9. Hossein Aghaie Joobani and Mostafa Mousavipour, "Russia, Turkey, and Iran: Moving towards Strategic Synergy in the Middle East?" *Strategic Analysis* 39, no. 2 (2015): 142.

10. *France 24*, "Why They Are Chanting 'Death to Russia' in Tehran," July 21, 2009, https://observers.france24.com/en/20090721-why-tehran-protestors-chant-death-russia-putin-ahmadinejad.

11. Oliver Carroll, "Russia and Saudi Arabia 'Sign $3bn Arms Deal' as King Salman Visit Shows How Much Relations Have Changed," *The Independent*, October 5, 2017, www.independent.co.uk/news/world/europe/russia-king-salman-visit-saudi-arabia-moscow-vladimir-putin-a7985161.html.

12. Adam Tarock, "Russo-Iranian Relations in the Post-Soviet Era," *Diplomacy and Statecraft* 28, no. 3 (2017): 518–37.
13. Ghoncheh Tazmini, "Russian-Iranian Relations in the Context of the Tehran Declaration," *Iranian Review of Foreign Affairs* 1, no. 3 (2010): 7–32.
14. See Mark N. Katz, "Can Russian-US Relations Improve?" *Strategic Studies Quarterly* 8, no. 2 (2014): 129–41.
15. Anton Khlopkov and Anna Lutkova, "The Bushehr NPP: Why Did It Take So Long?" Center for Energy and Security Studies, August 21, 2010, http://ceness-russia.org/data/doc/TheBushehrNPP-WhyDidItTakeSoLong.pdf.
16. *The Moscow Times*, "Bushehr Nuclear Plant Sees More Delays," August 8, 2011, www.themoscowtimes.com/2011/08/08/bushehr-nuclear-plant-sees-more-delays-a8755.
17. *Ibid.*
18. Khlopkov and Lutkova, "The Bushehr NPP," 5–6.
19. Alexander A. Pikayev, "Why Russia Supported Sanctions against Iran," James Martin Center for Nonproliferation Studies (CNS), June 23, 2010, www.nonproliferation.org/why-russia-supported-sanctions-against-iran.
20. Pavel Felgenhauer, "The 'Unravelling Relationship' between Russia and Iran," *BBC News*, July 25, 2010, www.bbc.com/news/world-europe-10684110.
21. Tazmini, "Russian-Iranian Relations," 7–32.
22. Pikayev, "Why Russia Supported Sanctions against Iran."
23. Military Watch, "Iran May Have the S-400 in All but Name; What Russia Really Delivered in 2016 and Why It Matters," March 24, 2018, https://militarywatchmagazine.com/article/iran-may-have-the-s-400-in-all-but-name-what-russia-really-delivered-in-2016-and-why-it-matters.
24. Michael Eisenstadt and Brenda Shaffer, "Russian S-300 Missiles to Iran: Groundhog Day or Game-Changer?" The Washington Institute *Policy Watch* 2482, September 4, 2015, www.washingtoninstitute.org/policy-analysis/view/russian-s-300-missiles-to-iran-groundhog-day-or-game-changer.
25. Maysam Behravesh, "Will Russia Let Iran Down to Win the US Over?" *Al Jazeera*, June 20, 2018, www.aljazeera.com/indepth/opinion/russia-iran-relations-1806 19125816399.html.
26. Steven Rosefielde and Stefan Hedlund, *Russia since 1980* (New York: Cambridge University Press, 2009), 211–230.
27. Mohammad Ali Hozbabri, "Iran-Russia Relations within the Framework of 'Prisoner's Dilemma,'" *Mehr News*, July 3, 2019, https://en.mehrnews.com/news/147137/Iran-Russia-relations-within-the-framework-of-Prisoner-s-Dilemma.
28. Sam Meredith, "Iran Warns 'Unilateralism' between Saudi Arabia and Russia Could Lead to the Death of OPEC," *CNBC*, July 1, 2019, www.cnbc.com/2019/07/01/iran-warns-unilateralism-could-lead-to-the-death-of-opec-oil-minister.html.
29. David Brennan, "Russia and Saudi Arabia Hold 'Catholic Marriage' with Poem and Badges, Form Enormous Oil Cartel," *Newsweek*, July 3, 2019, www.newsweek.com/russia-saudi-arabia-opec-oil-catholic-marriage-poem-1447301.

30. *Financial Times*, "Iran Warns OPEC Might Die Due to Russia-Saudi Domination," July 1, 2019, www.ft.com/content/6f8ce486-9bda-11e9-b8ce-8b459ed04726.

31. *Ibid.*

32. Brennan, "Russia and Saudi Arabia Hold 'Catholic Marriage.'"

33. Hozhabri, "Iran-Russia Relations within the Framework of Prisoner's Dilemma."

34. TASS, "Russia, Saudi Arabia Prepare Dozens of New Projects, says Russia's Energy Minister," September 11, 2019, https://tass.com/economy/1077686.

35. *Al Jazeera*, "Putin Visits Saudi Arabia in Sign of Growing Ties," October 14, 2019, www.aljazeera.com/news/2019/10/putin-visits-saudi-arabia-sign-growing-ties-191014171206513.html.

36. *Reuters*, "Russia's Putin Says No Proof Iran Was Behind Saudi Attacks," October 2, 2019, www.reuters.com/article/us-saudi-aramco-attacks-putin/russias-putin-says-no-proof-iran-was-behind-saudi-attacks-idUSKBN1WH196.

37. *Al Jazeera*, "Saudi Arabia, Iran Take Steps towards Indirect Talks," October 5, 2019, www.aljazeera.com/news/2019/10/saudi-arabia-iran-steps-indirect-talks-nyt-191005171357718.html.

38. Sinan Hatahet, *Russia and Iran: Economic Influence in Syria* (London: Chatham House, the Royal Institute of International Affairs, 2019), www.chathamhouse.org/sites/default/files/publications/research/2019–03–08RussiaAndIranEconomicInfluenceInSyria.pdf.

39. Michel Duclos, "Russia and Iran in Syria—A Random Partnership or an Enduring Alliance?" Atlantic Council Rafik Hariri Center for the Middle East *Interim Report*, June 2019, www.atlanticcouncil.org/wp-content/uploads/2019/06/Russia_and_Iran_in_Syria_a_Random_Partnership_or_an_Enduring_Alliance.pdf.

40. Hatahet, "Russia and Iran: Economic Influence in Syria."

41. Natasha Turak, "Iran Just Struck a Hoard of Deals with Iraq, and Washington Isn't Happy," *CNBC*, March 20, 2019, www.cnbc.com/2019/03/20/iran-just-struck-several-deals-with-iraq-and-washington-isnt-happy.html.

42. Frederick Kempe and Giampiero Massolo, "Preface," *The MENA Region: A Great Power Competition*, eds. Karim Mezran and Arturo Varvelli (Milan, Italy: ISPI and Atlantic Council, Ledizioni Ledi Publishing, 2019), 11.

43. Xinhua, "Iraq, Russia to Widen Cooperation in all Fields," February 4, 2019, www.xinhuanet.com/english/2019–02/04/c_137799183.htm.

44. Abbas Kadhim, "Iraqi-Russian Relations amidst US Security-Focused Engagement," *The MENA Region: A Great Power Competition*, eds. Karim Mezran and Arturo Varvelli (Milan, Italy: ISPI and Atlantic Council, Ledizioni Ledi Publishing, 2019), 79.

45. Dmitry Zhdannikov, "Iraq Resists U.S. Pressure to Reduce Iranian Gas Imports," *Reuters*, September 10, 2019, www.reuters.com/article/us-iraq-iran-power/iraq-resists-u-s-pressure-to-reduce-iranian-gas-imports-idUSKCN1VV0T3.

46. Shi Yinglun, "Russia's Oil and Gas Investments in Iraq Exceed 10 bln USD," *Xinhua*, February 27, 2019, www.xinhuanet.com/english/2019–02/27/c_137854984.htm.

47. *Shafaaq News*, "Russia Consolidating Its Position in Iraq amid Anti-Iran Sanctions,"

April 30, 2019, www.shafaaq.com/en/world/russia-consolidating-its-position-in-iraq-amid-anti-iran-sanctions.

48. *VOA News*, "Putin Says Iran Should Stay in Nuclear Deal," May 15, 2019, www.voanews.com/world-news/middle-east/putin-says-iran-should-stay-nuclear-deal.

49. PressTV, "Putin: Russia Regrets Seeing Iran Nuclear Deal Unravel, Done Enough to Save it," May 15, 2019, www.presstv.com/detail/2019/05/15/596048/putin-russia-fire-brigade-regret-iran-nuclear-deal-unraveling.

50. *Tehran Times*, "Russian Diplomat Urges Europe to Save Nuclear Deal," July 10, 2019, www.tehrantimes.com/news/437987/Russian-diplomat-urges-Europe-to-save-nuclear-deal.

51. The Instrument in Support of Trade Exchanges (INSTEX) is a European special-purpose vehicle (SPV) established in January 2019. Its mission is to facilitate non-USD and non-SWIFT transactions with Iran to avoid breaking US sanctions. INSTEX is a payment system that works like barter, and its basic premise is that there should be no cross-border payments between Iran and the European Union. As no money is transferred across borders, the sanctions in place are not violated. See Management Study Guide, "The Instex Payment System," 2020, www.managementstudyguide.com/instex-payment-system.htm.

52. Valdai Club, "Opening of the Third Russia-Iran Dialogue (in Farsi)," *YouTube*, June 26, 2019, www.youtube.com/watch?v=rvhQcpUX5QQ.

53. PressTV, "Russian Railways Launches €1.2 Billion Project in Iran," July 3, 2019, www.presstv.com/Detail/2018/07/03/566891/Iran-railway-Russia-investment-US-sanctions-Trump.

54. Joobani and Mousavipour, "Russia, Turkey, and Iran," 143.

55. Rizal Abdul Kadir, "Convention on the Legal Status of the Caspian Sea," *International Legal Materials* 58, no. 2 (2019): 399–413.

56. Omid Shokri Kalehsar, "Challenges and Opportunities toward Iran in the Convention on the Legal Status of the Caspian Sea," United World, September 19, 2019, https://uwidata.com/5358-challenges-and-opportunities-toward-iran-in-the-convention-on-the-legal-status-of-the-caspian-sea.

57. *IRNA*, "پانزدهمین اجلاس کمیسیون مشترک همکاری اقتصادی ایران و روسیه آغاز شد" (The 15th meeting of the Iran-Russia Joint Economic Cooperation Commission begins), June 16, 2019.

58. PressTV, "Iran, Russia Square Up to US Sanctions with 12 Accords," June 19, 2019, www.presstv.com/Detail/2019/06/19/598880/Iran-Russia-energy-Novak-US-sanctions-railway-oil-gas.

59. *Ibid.*

60. *Ibid.*

61. *IRNA*, "عضویت ایران در اتحادیه اوراسیا برگ برنده تهران است" [Iran's membership in the Eurasian Union is Tehran's trump card], February 27, 2021.

62. Bourse & Bazaar, "Iran Trade Deal with Russia-Led Bloc Warrants Cautious Optimism," October 22, 2019, www.bourseandbazaar.com/articles/2019/10/21/iran-joins-russian-led-trade-bloc-with-cautious-optimism.

63. The Society for Worldwide Interbank Financial Telecommunication (SWIFT) "is

a global member-owned cooperative and the world's leading provider of secure financial messaging services," 2020, www.swift.com/about-us/discover-swift.

64. *IRNA*, "سوئیفت روسی؛ جایگزینی برای سوئیفت اروپایی" [Russian SWIFT: An alternative to European SWIFT], July 20, 2020.

65. *Islamic Republic News Agency*, "Iranian Banks on Way to Join Russian SWIFT," September 14, 2019, https://en.irna.ir/news/83475187/Iranian-banks-on-way-to-join-Russian-SWIFT.

66. Richard Sakwa, *Russia against the Rest: The Post-Cold War Crisis of World Order* (Cambridge, UK: Cambridge University Press, 2017).

67. See Bobo Lo, *Russia and the New World Disorder* (Baltimore, MD: Brookings Institution Press, 2017).

68. Martin Smith, *Russia and NATO since 1991: From Cold War through Cold Peace to Partnership?* (London: Routledge, 2006), 1–26.

69. Donette Murray, *US Foreign Policy and Iran: American-Iranian Relations since the Islamic Revolution* (London: Routledge, 2009).

70. Sakwa, "Beyond the Impasse," 4–5.

71. *Ibid.*

6. THE DRIVERS OF RUSSIA-GCC RELATIONS

1. Leonid Issaev and Alisa Shishkina, "Russia in the Middle East: In Search of Its Place," in *Political Narratives in the Middle East and North Africa*, eds. Wolfgang Muhlberger and Toni Alaranta (Dordrecht, Netherlands: Springer, 2020), 95–144.

2. Eugene Rumer, *Russian Foreign Policy beyond Putin* (London: Routledge, 2017); Eugene Rumer, *Russia in the Middle East: Jack of All Trades, Master of None* (Washington: CEIP, 2019).

3. Theodore Karasik, "Russia's Financial Tactics in the Middle East," in *Russia in the Middle East*, eds. Theodore Karasik and Stephen Blank (Washington, DC: Jamestown Foundation, 2018), 240–64.

4. Dmitri Kozlov, "Korolyam Tut ne Mesto" [There is no place for kings], *Kommersant*, March 16, 2020, www.kommersant.ru/doc/4290336.

5. Margarita Shpilevskaya, "Glava RFPI: Sotrudnichestvo s Saudovskoy Araviey i OAE na Bespretcedentno Vysokom Urovne" [Head of the RDIF: Cooperation with Saudi Arabia and the UAE has reached an unprecedented level], TASS, October 28, 2019, https://tass.ru/interviews/7050882.

6. Kiril Dmitriev, "RF i Saudovskaya Araviya Prodolzhat Razvivat Investpartnerstvo" [Russia and Saudi Arabia will continue investment cooperation], *RDIF*, March 11, 2020, https://rdif.ru/fullNews/4921.

7. *Vedomosti*, "Saudi Aramco Mozhet Sozdat Sovmestnyye Predpriyatiya s Rosneftyu i Lukoilom" [Saudi Aramco may set up joint ventures with Rosneft and Lukoil], October 22, 2018, www.vedomosti.ru/business/news/2018/10/22/784264-saudi.

8. *Ibid.*

9. Author interviews with Russian economic experts, Institute of Oriental Studies under the Russian Academy of Science, Moscow, Russia, December 2018.

10. *RIA Novosti*, "Putin: Rossiya Tcenit Vklad Korolya Saudovskoy Aravii v Sotrudnichestvo" [Putin: Russia appreciates the Saudi King's input in cooperation], October 14, 2019, https://ria.ru/20191014/1559769929.html.

11. Author interview with a Russian oil market expert, Doha, Qatar, April 2019.

12. *Al Arab*, "Rossiya Obeshchayet Saudovskoy Aravii Obuzdat Iran v Sirii" [Russia promises Saudi Arabia to curb Iran in Syria], *Inosmi*, January 24, 2019, https://inosmi.ru/politic/20190124/244448534.html.

13. Maaz Bilalov, "Chechenskiy Desant Putina" [Chechen breakthrough with Putin], *Kavkaz. Realii*, October 17, 2019, www.kavkazr.com/a/30219599.html; *RIA Novosti*, "V Saudovskoy Aravii Vysoko Otcenili Uroven Religioznykh Svobod v Rossii" [Saudi Arabia highly praised the level of religious freedoms in Russia], January 21, 2019, https://ria.ru/20190121/1549665385.html; Information also gathered from author interviews with a Russian diplomat, Doha, Qatar, March 2019, and with a Russian expert on the GCC countries, Higher School of Economics, Moscow, Russia, June 21, 2020.

14. *RIA Novosti*, "V Saudovskoy Aravii Vysoko Otcenili Uroven Religioznykh Svobod v Rossii" [Saudi Arabia praised the level of religious freedom in Russia], January 21, 2019, https://ria.ru/20190121/1549665385.html.

15. Author interview with a Russian diplomat, Doha, Qatar, March 2019.

16. Issaev and Shishkina, "Russia in the Middle East," 95–144.

17. *Novaya Gazeta*, "Levada Tsentr Soobshchil o Padenii Reytinga Putina do 25%" [Levada Center reported on the fall of Putin's ratings to 25%], May 30, 2020, https://novayagazeta.ru/news/2020/05/30/161906-levada-tsentr-soobschil-o-padenii-reytinga-putina-do-25.

18. Rumer, *Russia in the Middle East*.

19. Nicole Grajewsky, *Friends or Frenemies? How Russia and Iran Compete and Cooperate* (Philadelphia, PA: Foreign Policy Research Institute, 2020); Nikolay Kozhanov, "Russia's Difficult Balancing Act between Iran and Israel," *Al Jazeera*, February 1, 2020, www.aljazeera.com/indepth/opinion/russia-difficult-balancing-act-iran-israel-200129193640167.html.

20. Aleksei M. Vasiliev et al., "Libya and Interests of Russia," *Asia and Africa Today* 6 (2020): 4–13.

21. Leonid Issaev and Aleksey Korotayev, "Russia's Policy towards the Middle East: The Case of Yemen," *International Spectator* 55, no. 3 (2020): 132–47.

22. Nikolay Kozhanov and Leonid Issaev, "Russian Influence in the Gulf Has Its Limits," *Al Jazeera*, April 5, 2019, www.aljazeera.com/indepth/opinion/russian-influence-gulf-limits-190404133832327.html.

23. Milan Czerny, "Russia's Security Mirage in the Gulf," *Riddle*, April 30, 2021, www.ridl.io/en/russia-s-security-mirage-in-the-gulf.

24. Author interview with a Russian expert on the GCC countries, Higher School of Economics, Moscow, Russia, June 21, 2020; Bilalov, "Chechenskiy Desant Putina."

25. Author interviews with Russian experts on the Gulf, Higher School of Economics,

Institute of the World Economy and International Relations (IMEMO) under the Russian Academy of Science, Moscow, Russia, May 2019, December 2019.

26. Author interviews with Russian experts on the Gulf, Higher School of Economics, Institute of the World Economy and International Relations (IMEMO) under the Russian Academy of Science, Moscow, Russia, May 2019, December 2019.

27. Author interviews with Lebanese and US experts on US foreign policy in the Middle East, Carnegie Middle East Center, Beirut, Lebanon, May 5, 2015.

28. Author interview with a Saudi official, London, UK, October 1, 2015; Author interview with Qatari diplomats, Doha, Qatar, March 2019.

29. Author interview with a US official, Washington DC, May 2, 2012.

30. Author interview with a Saudi official, London, UK, October 1, 2015.

31. *Ibid.*; Brad Plumer, "China Now Gets More Oil from the Middle East Than the US Does," *Vox*, September 3, 2014, www.vox.com/2014/9/3/6101885/middle-east-now-sells-more-oil-to-china-than-to-the-us.

32. Daniel Benaim and Jake Sullivan, "America's Opportunity in the Middle East," *Foreign Affairs*, May 22, 2020, www.foreignaffairs.com/articles/middle-east/2020-05-22/americas-opportunity-middle-east; John Hannah and Bradley Bowman, "The Pentagon Tries to Pivot Out of the Middle East—Again," *Foreign Policy*, May 19, 2020, https://foreignpolicy.com/2020/05/19/military-pivot-middle-east-saudi-arabia; Multiple author interviews with US experts on American foreign policy in the Middle East, July 16, 2020, The Middle East Institute, Washington DC; Author interview with an official from the Department of State, Washington DC, May 2020.

33. For more details see Nikolay Kozhanov, *Russian Policy across the Middle East: Motivations and Methods* (London: Chatham House, 2018).

34. *RIA Novosti*, "Peskov ne Vidit Osnovaniy ne Verit' Saudovskoy Storone po Povodu Khashugdzhi" [Peskov sees no reason not to believe the Saudi side about Khashoggi], October 26, 2018, https://ria.ru/20181026/1531538985.html.

35. Author interview with a Russian expert on the Middle East, Institute of the World Economy and International Relations (IMEMO) under the Russian Academy of Science, Moscow, Russia, December 19, 2018.

36. Aleksandr Gostev, "Bolshaya Liviyskaya Sdelka Kremlya. Kto Kogo Podderzhivayet v Novoy Voyne" [Big Libyan deal of the Kremlin. Who supports whom in a new war], *Svoboda*, April 10, 2019, www.svoboda.org/a/29872791.html.

37. Issaev and Shishkina, "Russia in the Middle East."

38. Author interview with a Russian expert on the Middle East, Higher School of Economics, Moscow, Russia, September 19, 2018.

39. Marianna Belenkaya, "Yemen Poprosil u Rossii Zerno i Prizval Ee Okazat Davleniye na Iran" [Yemen asked Russia for grain and urged her to put pressure on Iran], *Kommersant*, January 23, 2018, www.kommersant.ru/doc/3527227.

40. Author interview with a Russian expert on the Middle East, Higher School of Economics, Moscow, Russia, September 19, 2018.

41. *RIA Novosti*, "Lavrentyev Peredal Sirii Poslaniye ot Saudovskoy Aravii, Soobshchil

Istochnik" [Lavrentiev conveyed a message from Syria to Syria, a source said], April 20, 2019, https://ria.ru/20190420/1552878420.html.

42. Author interviews with Russian experts on the Middle East, Moscow, Russia, September, December 2018.

43. Author interview with a Russian expert on the Middle East, Higher School of Economics, Moscow, Russia, September 19, 2018.

44. *Ibid.*

45. Author interviews with Qatari diplomats, Doha, Qatar, March 2019.

46. Kozhanov and Issaev, "Russian Influence in the Gulf Has Its Limits."

47. *Ibid.*

48. Author interviews with the representatives of Russian business, Saint Petersburg, Russia, April 24–6, 2019.

49. *Znak*, "Arktik SPG-2 Mozhet Stat Chastyu Gazovoy Strategii Saudi Aramco" [Arctic LNG-2 may become part of Saudi Aramco's gas strategy], February 14, 2018, www.znak.com/2018–02–14/arktik_spg_2_mozhet_stat_chastyu_gazovoy_strategii_saudi_aramco.

50. Author interview with a Russian oil market expert, Doha, Qatar, April 2019.

51. "Novak i MEA Otcenili Dokhody Rossii ot Sdelki OPEK v 2019 godu" [Novak and IEA estimated Russia's incomes from the OPEC deal in 2019], *InvestFuture*, November 15, 2019, https://investfuture.ru/news/id/novak-i-mea-ocenili-dohody-rossii-ot-sdelki-opek-v-2019-godu; Russian Ministry of Finance, *Budgetniy Prognoz Rossiyskoy Federatcii na Period do 2036 goda* [Budget forecast of the Russian Federation until 2036] (Moscow: Russian Ministry of Finance, 2019), www.min-fin.ru/common/upload/library/2019/04/main/Budzhetnyy_prognoz_2036.pdf; Author interviews with Russian experts on oil and gas markets in Doha, Qatar, February, 2020, and at the Institute of the World Economy and International Relations under the Russian Academy of Science, Moscow, Russia, March 2020, and in Moscow, Russia, May 2020.

52. *Noviye Izvestiya*, "Chernoye Uzhe ne Zoloto" [Black is no longer gold], October 4, 2019, https://newizv.ru/article/general/04–10–2019/chernoe-uzhe-ne-zoloto-neft-stanovitsya-nerentabelnoy-ne-tolko-v-rossii-no-i-v-ssha; Author interviews with Russian experts on oil and gas markets, Doha, Qatar, February, 2020, and at the Institute of the World Economy and International Relations under the Russian Academy of Science, Moscow, Russia, March 2020; Moscow, Russia, May 2020.

53. *RNS*, "Rossiya Vistupayet za Sokhraneniye Dobychi Nefti na Urovne i Kvartala" [Russia calls to keep oil production at the level of the 1st quarter], March 11, 2020, https://rns.online/energy/Rossiya-vistupaet-za-sohranenie-dobichi-nefti-na-urovne-I-kvartala—2020–03–11/?fbclid=IwAR1lwoJK_ZurL1xMk-ok-m-bDa-8x1LjX1L6fgeszKWUvTRVDjw7dgWhAGk.

54. Yuri Barsukov, "Kak Son Pustoy" [Like empty dreams], *Kommersant*, March 2, 2021, www.kommersant.ru/doc/4711116.

55. *Ibid.*

56. Kozlov, "Korolyam Tut ne Mesto."

57. *Al Jazeera*, "Pompeo Calls for Gulf Unity at Start of Middle East Tour," March 20, 2019, www.aljazeera.com/news/2019/03/pompeo-calls-gulf-unity-start-middle-east-tour-190320093357748.html.

58. *Al Jazeera*, "Russian Foreign Minister Sergey Lavrov to Hold Talks in Qatar," March 4, 2019, www.aljazeera.com/news/2019/03/russian-foreign-minister-sergey-lavrov-hold-talks-qatar-190304070458781.html.

59. Kozhanov and Issaev, "Russian Influence in the Gulf has its Limits."

60. Author interview with Qatari diplomats, Doha, Qatar, March 2019.

61. *Ibid.*

62. Konstantin Simonov, "Vremya otrezvleniya. Ostanovyat li rossiyskiye neftegazovyye kompanii svoyu ekspansiyu na Blizhniy Vostok?" [Sobering time. Will Russian oil and gas companies stop their expansion in the Middle East?], *ValdaiClub*, February 27, 2019, http://ru.valdaiclub.com/a/highlights/vremya-otrezvleniya/?sphrase_id=91293.

7. RUSSIA AND THE YEMENI CIVIL WAR

1. Norman Cigar, "South Yemen and the USSR: Prospects for the Relationship," *Middle East Journal* 39, no. 4 (1985): 775.

2. Yevgeny Primakov, *Russia and the Arabs: Behind the Scenes in the Middle East from the Cold War to the Present*, trans. Paul Gould (New York, NY: Basic Books, 2009), 85.

3. President of Russia, "Meeting with President of Yemen Abd Rabbuh Mansour Hadi," April 2, 2013, http://en.kremlin.ru/events/president/news/17787.

4. Southern Transitional Council European Union (STC-EU), "STC High Level Visit to Moscow Intensifies International Focus on 'Southern Issue,'" March 24, 2019, https://stc-eu.org/en/stc-high-level-visit-to-moscow-intensifies-international-focus-on-southern-issue.

5. Ministry of Foreign Affairs of the Russian Federation, "Press Release on Deputy Foreign Minister Mikhail Bogdanov's Telephone Conversation with President of the Southern Transitional Council of Yemen Aidarus al-Zubaidi," April 28, 2020, www.mid.ru/en/foreign_policy/news/-/asset_publisher/cKNonkJE02Bw/content/id/4107592.

6. Michelle Nichols, "U.S. Threatens Action against Iran after Russia U.N. Veto," *Reuters*, February 27, 2018, www.reuters.com/article/us-yemen-security-un/u-s-threatens-action-against-iran-after-russia-u-n-veto-idUSKCN1GA2QT.

7. Michael Makovsky, Blaise Misztal, and Jonathan Ruhe, "Fragility and Extremism in Yemen: A Case Study of the Stabilizing Fragile States Project," Bipartisan Policy Center, January 2011, 36, https://bipartisanpolicy.org/wp-content/uploads/2019/03/Yemen-Final-Report.pdf.

8. Richard Connolly and Cecilie Sendstad, *Russia's Role as an Arms Exporter: The Strategic and Economic Importance of Arms Exports for Russia*, Chatham House, Russia and Eurasia Programme *Research Paper*, March 2017, 18, www.chathamhouse.org/sites/default/files/publications/research/2017-03-20-russia-arms-exporter-connolly-sendstad.pdf.

9. President of Russia, "Beginning of Meeting with President of the Republic of Yemen Ali Abdullah Saleh," February 25, 2009, http://en.kremlin.ru/events/president/transcripts/48385#sel=4:1:Z6u,8:19:yU3.

10. The specific areas of the Red Sea littoral region which are of particular interest to Russia are the Gulf of Aden, Bab el-Mandeb Strait, and its adjacent territories on the Horn of Africa. Although Russia's ambitions on the Red Sea are not codified in its foreign policy concept or defense doctrines, and official statements on this issue remain ambiguous, Moscow's more frequent engagements with the STC, Sudan, and Somalia have been cited as evidence of Russia's desire to expand its influence in the Red Sea and corresponding trade routes that pass through the Bab el-Mandeb Strait. See "Does Russia Seek Return of Independent South Yemen?" *Al-Monitor*, April 11, 2019, www.almonitor.com/pulse/originals/2019/04/russia-south-yemen-uae-prospects.html, and Andrew McGregor, "Will Khartoum's Appeal to Putin for Arms and Protection Bring Russian Naval Bases to the Red Sea?" Jamestown Foundation, *Eurasia Daily Monitor* 14, no. 158 (December 6, 2017), https://jamestown.org/program/will-khartoums-appeal-putin-arms-protection-bring-russian-naval-bases-red-sea.

11. Robert O. Freedman, *Moscow and the Middle East: Soviet Policy since the Invasion of Afghanistan* (Cambridge, UK: Cambridge University Press, 1991), 331.

12. Feliks Gromov quoted in Sergey Aksensov, "Ostrov Sokotra Snova Zhdet Nashikh Korableh" [Socotra Island is waiting for our ships again], *Svobodnaya Pressa*, August 7, 2017, https://svpressa.ru/war21/article/178556.

13. "Russia Set to Establish Naval Logistics Base in Sudan," TASS, November 11, 2020, https://tass.com/defense/1222673.

14. TASS, "Lavrov: US Shows Double Standards by Supporting Yemen's Fleeing President," March 26, 2015, https://tass.com/world/785269.

15. *Ibid.*

16. TASS, "Russian Lawmaker Compares Situation in Yemen to Ukrainian Developments," March 27, 2015, https://tass.com/world/785371.

17. Nikolay Patrushev quoted in *Izvestiya*, "Kampaniya v Yyemene Podtverdila Krizis Mezhdunarodnykh Organizatsiy" [The campaign in Yemen confirmed the crisis of international organizations], April 13, 2015, https://iz.ru/news/585305.

18. Anton Vernitsky, "Saudovskaya Arabiya Vmeste s Soyuznikami Nachala Voyennuyu Operatsiyu Protiv Myatezhnikov v Yyemene" [Saudi Arabia, together with its allies, launched a military operation against the rebels in Yemen], *Channel One Russia*, March 26, 2015, www.1tv.ru/news/2015–03–26/22072-saudovskaya_araviya_vmeste_s_soyuznikami_nachala_voennuyu_operatsiyu_protiv_myatezhnikov_v_yemene.

19. *RIA Novosti*, "SB OON obsudit oruzheynoye embargo v otnoshenii povstantsev v Yyemene" [UN Security Council to Discuss Arms Embargo against the Rebels in Yemen], April 14, 2015, https://ria.ru/20150414/1058386982.html.

20. *Izvestiya*, "Kampaniya v Yyemene Podtverdila Krizis Mezhdunarodnykh Organizatsiy."

21. Oleg Filimonov, "Kriziz v Yyemene: Perspektivy Rossiyskoy Diplomatiy?" [The

crisis in Yemen: Prospects for Russian diplomacy?], Russian International Affairs Council, March 9, 2017, https://russiancouncil.ru/analytics-and-comments/analytics/krizis-v-yemene-perspektivy-dlya-rossiyskoy-diplomatii.

22. Barbara Bodine, telephone interview by author, July 2, 2019.

23. *RT Arabic*, "Rusia takshif 'an al-dawr alladhi tal'abuh fi-l-yaman" [Russia reveals the role it plays in Yemen], October 5, 2018, https://arabic.rt.com/russia/974369-.

24. *Sputnik*, "UN Special Envoy Griffiths Notes Progress in Yemeni Peace Process," January 12, 2019, https://sputniknews.com/interviews/201901121071419618-yemen-un-special-envoy-interview.

25. Ahmed Eleiba, "Will Russia Step in to Yemen?" *Al-Ahram Weekly*, March 2, 2018, http://english.ahram.org.eg/NewsContent/2/8/292011/World/Region/Will-Russia-step-in-to-Yemen-.aspx.

26. *Sputnik*, "Russia to Continue Evacuating Civilians from Yemen—Foreign Ministry," April 5, 2015, https://sputniknews.com/middleeast/201504051020494564.

27. *RT*, "US, UK Thank Russia for Evacuation of Their Citizens from Yemen," April 13, 2015, www.rt.com/news/249345-yemen-evacuation-russia-gratitude.

28. *RIA Novosti*, "Rossiya Prizyvayet k Srochnoy Guamanitarnoy Pomoshchi Yyemenu" [Russia calls for urgent humanitarian assistance to Yemen], April 25, 2017, https://ria.ru/20170425/1493101997.html?in=t.

29. Stephanie Nebehay, "U.N., Russia Warn against Assault on Main Yemeni Port," *Reuters*, April 25, 2017, https://uk.reuters.com/article/uk-yemen-security-un/u-n-russia-warn-against-assault-on-main-yemeni-port-idUKKBN17R18M.

30. The Embassy of the Russian Federation to the United Kingdom of Great Britain and Northern Ireland, *Press Release on the Delivery of Humanitarian Aid to Yemen*, July 25, 2017, www.rusemb.org.uk/fnapr/6178.

31. "Russia Earmarks $4mln to Provide Food Assistance to Yemen," TASS, June 3, 2020, https://tass.com/politics/1163577.

32. Yulia Kiseleva, "Russia's Soft Power Discourse: Identity, Status and the Attraction of Power," *Politics* 35, no. 3–4 (2015): 316.

33. Stephen Blank, "Russia and Yemen's Agony," *Eurasia Daily Monitor* 12, no. 68 (2015), https://jamestown.org/program/russia-and-yemens-agony.

34. TASS, "Situation in Yemen Shows US Reluctance to End Conflict—Russian Foreign Ministry," November 10, 2018, https://tass.com/politics/1030197.

35. Evgeny Shestakov, "Kto Khochet Unichtozhit Yyemen?" [Who wants to destroy Yemen?], *Rossiskaya Gazeta*, March 30, 2015, https://rg.ru/2015/03/30/yemen.html.

36. Leonid Savin, "Voyna v Yyemene: Podderzhit li Vashington Zakhvat Porta Khodeyda?" [The war in Yemen: Will Washington support the seizure of Hodeidah Port?], *Fondsk*, May 5, 2017, www.fondsk.ru/news/2017/05/05/vojna-v-jemene-podderzhit-li-vashington-zahvat-porta-hodejda-43925.html.

37. Anna Borshchevskaya and Catherine Cleveland, *Russia's Arabic Propaganda: What It Is, Why It Matters*, Washington Institute for Near East Policy, Policy Notes 57, December 2018, 5–6, www.washingtoninstitute.org/uploads/Documents/pubs/PolicyNote57-BorshchevskayaCleveland.pdf.

38. Emad Tufalli, "Khabirun: Nantazir Mubadaratan Rusiatan Jadatan Liwaqf Alharb fi Alyaman" [Expert: We are waiting for a serious Russian initiative to stop the war in Yemen], *Sputnik Arabic*, May 26, 2021, https://arabic.sputniknews.com/radio_world/202105261049080717-اليمن-في-الحرب-لوقف-جدية-روسية-مبادرة-بانتظار-نحن-خبير-/

39. Even though Russia officially recognizes the Hadi government as Yemen's sole legitimate authority, discussions between Russian and Houthi officials have occurred periodically. On September 7, 2018, Russian Ambassador to Yemen Vladimir Dedushkin stated that Russia had been maintaining "contact with both delegations," which included the Houthis (See TASS, "Houthis' Absence from Consultations on Yemen Points to Lack of Trust—Russian Ambassador," September 7, 2018, https://tass.com/politics/1020573). Russian Deputy Foreign Minister Mikhail Bogdanov has also met with the Houthis on several occasions, with an August 27–9, 2019 trip to Oman acting as one example (See TASS, "Russian Diplomat Meets with Yemeni Politicians, Public Figures in Oman," August 29, 2019, https://tass.com/politics/1075583).

40. Brian M. Perkins, "Yemen: Between Revolution and Regression," *Studies in Conflict & Terrorism* 40, no. 4 (2016): 312.

41. Grigory Kosach quoted in Nikolay Surkov, "Yemen: Yet Another Friction Point in the Russia-West Relationship?" Russia Beyond the Headlines, April 21, 2015, www.rbth.com/international/2015/04/21/yemen_yet_another_friction_point_in_the_russia-west_relationshi_45419.html.

42. Alexander Bratersky, "Yyemen Stal Polem Bitvy za Vliyaniye na Blizhnem Vostoke" [Yemen has become a battleground for influence in the Middle East], *Gazeta*, March 27, 2015, www.gazeta.ru/politics/2015/03/27_a_6616477.shtml. Although Iran officially denies military involvement in Yemen, there is substantial evidence that Tehran has provided financial and military support to Houthi rebel forces. In January 2018, a UN Panel of Experts concluded that Iran had violated the arms embargo in Yemen. See *New York Times*, "Iran Violated Yemen Arms Embargo, U.N. Experts Say," January 12, 2018, www.nytimes.com/2018/01/12/world/middleeast/iran-yemen-saudi-arabia-arms-embargo-un.html.

43. Hamidreza Azizi, email interview by author, June 21, 2019.

44. *Ibid.*

45. Mehr News, "Iran, Russia Discuss Developments in Syria, Yemen," November 6, 2018, https://en.mehrnews.com/news/139379/Iran-Russia-discuss-developments-in-Syria-Yemen.

46. *Tasnim*, "No-Fly Zone in Yemen against Int'l Law: Iranian Official," April 30, 2015, www.tasnimnews.com/en/news/2015/04/30/726837/no-fly-zone-in-yemen-against-int-l-law-iranian-official.

47. Louis Charbonneau, "Iran Submits Four-Point Yemen Peace Plan to United Nations," *Reuters*, April 17, 2015, www.reuters.com/article/us-yemen-security-iran/iran-submits-four-point-yemen-peace-plan-to-united-nations-idUSKBN0N823820150417.

48. Fyodor Lukyanov, "US-Russian Meeting on Iranian Nuclear Issue," PIR Center

Policy Memo, Gstaad, Switzerland, January 27–9, 2013, http://pircenter.org/media/content/files/12/13903835392.pdf.

49. "Thewal S300 bh aaran bedwen delal naset. Rews ha m'eteqdend keh bheran amen bh jengua mesteqam ban aaran w'erebsetan s'eweda tebdal khewahed shed" [Delivery of S-300 to Iran is not without reason; The Russians believe that the Yemeni crisis will turn into a direct war between Iran and Saudi Arabia], *Entekhab*, April 27, 2015, www.entekhab.ir/fa/news/199394/تحویل-s300-نیست-دلیل-بی-ایران-به

روس-ها-معتقدند-بحران-یمن-به-جنگ-مستقیم-ایران-و-عربستان-تبدیل-می-شود

50. United Nations Security Council, *The Situation in the Middle East*, 8190th Meeting, S/PV 8190, February 26, 2018, 3, www.un.org/en/ga/search/view_doc.asp?symbol=S/PV.8190.

51. *Ibid.*, 5.

52. *RIA Novosti*, "Delegatsiya Khuti i Pomoschchnik Ministra Inostrannykh Del Irana Obsudili Krizis v Yyemene" [Houthi delegation and assistant foreign minister of Iran discussed the crisis in Yemen], February 12, 2018, https://ria.ru/20180212/1514483776.html.

53. *Tasnim*, "Russia to Veto Western Bid to Condemn Iran at UN over Yemen," February 26, 2018, www.tasnimnews.com/en/news/2018/02/26/1666716/russia-to-veto-western-bid-to-condemn-iran-at-un-over-yemen.

54. Azizi, interview. For a counterargument that emphasizes the instrumentality of Russia's veto and claims that missiles used by the Houthis were shipped by Moscow to Saleh's government: "Th amena kes aas' peret af a lergur senaraw tew pewet pereswer awen" [The Yemeni case is part of a larger scenario to put pressure on Iran], *Iranian Diplomacy*, March 30, 2018, www.irdiplomacy.ir/fa/news/1975734/پرونده-یمن-بخشی-از-یک-سناریوی-بزرگ-تر-برای-فشار-به-ایران-است

55. Pavel Aptekar, "Zachem Saudovskoy Aravii Voyna v Yyemene" [Why Saudi Arabia is at war with Yemen], *Vedomosti*, March 30, 2015, www.vedomosti.ru/opinion/articles/2015/03/31/zachem-saudovskoi-aravii-voina-v-iemene.

56. *Ibid.*

57. Sergey Serebrov, "The Yemen Trap: No End in Sight for a Major Geopolitical Game," Valdai Discussion Club, October 17, 2016, https://valdaiclub.com/a/highlights/the-yemen-trap-no-end-in-sight-for-a-major-geopoli.

58. Aptekar, "Zachem Saudovskoy."

59. Yevgeny Satanovsky quoted in *Kommersant*, "Yesli Tegeran i Er-Riyad Vser'yez Nachnut Voynu, Neft' Vzletit Vser'yez i Nadolgo" [If Tehran and Riyadh seriously start a war, oil will take off seriously and for a long time], March 27, 2015, www.kommersant.ru/doc/2695149.

60. Bruce Riedel, "Saudi's Star Prince Keeps Rising, Visits Putin in St. Petersburg," *Markaz*, Brookings Institution, June 19, 2015, www.brookings.edu/blog/markaz/2015/06/19/saudis-star-prince-keeps-rising-visits-putin-in-st-petersburg.

61. Leonid Issaev and Nikolay Kozhanov, "The Russian-Saudi Rapprochement and Iran," *Al Jazeera*, August 24, 2017, www.aljazeera.com/indepth/opinion/2017/08/russian-saudi-rapprochement-iran-170817154056810.html.

62. TASS, "Russian, Saudi Leaders Discuss Situation in Middle East—Lavrov," October 5, 2017, https://tass.com/politics/969226.
63. Kirill Semenov, "Saudis Could Seek Russian Bailout in Yemen," *Al-Monitor*, October 9, 2017, www.al-monitor.com/pulse/originals/2017/10/saudi-arabia-bail-out-yemen-conflict-mediation.html.
64. *Ibid.*
65. Mark N. Katz, "Yemen's President Invites Closer Ties with Russia," *Arab Gulf States Institute in Washington*, August 3, 2017, https://agsiw.org/yemens-president-invites-closer-ties-russia.
66. Ahmed Salem al-Wahishi, personal interview with author, Moscow, September 25, 2018.
67. *Middle East Monitor*, "Kuwait Objects to British Draft Resolution on Yemen," December 19, 2018, www.middleeastmonitor.com/20181219-kuwait-objects-to-british-draft-resolution-on-yemen.
68. *RIA Novosti*, "Zamglavy MID Rossii Obsudil s Predstavitelyami OAE Situatsiyu v Sirii i Yyemene" [Russian deputy foreign minister discusses the situations in Syria and Yemen with UAE representatives], December 7, 2016, https://ria.ru/201 61207/1483045249.html.
69. Marcelle Wahba, telephone interview by author, June 26, 2019.
70. Mohammad Ali, "Absence of Southern Transitional Council Destined Yemen Consultations to Failure—Source," Urdu Point, September 8, 2018, www.urdupoint.com/en/world/absence-of-southern-transitional-council-dest-428176.html.
71. Andrew Korybko, "Yemen's Socotra: The UAE's 'Eighth Emirate'?" *Sputnik*, May 12, 2018, https://sputniknews.com/radio_trendstorm/201805121064330710-yemen-socotra-the-uae-eighth-emirate.
72. STC official, telephone interview with author, October 30, 2019.
73. Marianna Belenkava and Elizaveta Naumova, "Saudovskaya Araviya i OAE Stolknulis' v Adene" [Saudi Arabia and the UAE clash in Aden], *Kommersant*, August 8, 2019, www.kommersant.ru/doc/4054811.
74. UN Web TV, "Dmitry Polyanskiy (Russia) on the Situation in Yemen—Security Council Media Stakeout," August 10, 2019, http://webtv.un.org/watch/dmitry-polyanskiy-russia-on-the-situation-in-yemen-security-council-media-stakeout-10-august-2019/6071548097001/?lan=original.
75. Andrei Baklanov, email interview by author, August 17, 2019.
76. "Yemen Separatists Seize $225M in Russian-Printed Cash," *The Moscow Times*, June 18, 2020, www.themoscowtimes.com/2020/06/18/yemen-separatists-seize-225m-in-russian-printed-cash-a70610.
77. "Diblumasiun saeudi: al'iimarat takhununa fi alyaman bidhariet al'iikhwan" [The UAE is betraying us in Yemen under the pretext of the brotherhood), *Al-Khaleej*, September 4, 2019, https://alkhaleejonline.net/سياسة/دبلوماسي-سعودي-الإمارات-تخوننا-فياليمن-بحجة-الإخوان
78. TASS, "Russia Concerned by UAE Airstrikes on Yemen—Foreign Ministry," August 31, 2019, https://tass.com/world/1075858.

79. Saudi Press Agency, "Russia Welcomes Signing of Riyadh Agreement Document between Yemeni Legitimate Government and Southern Transitional Council," November 7, 2019, www.spa.gov.sa/viewfullstory.php?lang=en&newsid=199 5427.

80. Nikolay Surkov quoted in Vostokoved Rasskazal, "Chto Pomozhet Reshit Konflikt v Yyemene" [Orientalist said that he would help resolve the conflict in Yemen], *RIA Novosti*, March 21, 2018, https://ria.ru/20180321/1516934893.html.

81. Alexander Vladimirovich Frolov, "Yyemen Marginalnaya Voyna?" [Yemen: Marginal war?], IMEMO RAN, December 10–11, 2017, www.imemo.ru/files/File/ru/Articles/2017/Frolov_Observer122017.pdf.

82. *Middle East Monitor*, "Russia Receives Yemen Houthi Delegation," December 15, 2016, www.middleeastmonitor.com/20161215-russia-receives-yemen-houthi-delegation.

83. Sergey Serebrov quoted in Andrey Onitkov, "Khusity Budut Zashchishchat Rossiyshkih Diplomatov" [Houthis will protect Russian diplomats], *Izvestiya*, December 20, 2017, https://iz.ru/683375/andrei-ontikov/khusity-zashchitiat-rossiiskikh-diplomatov.

84. Mareb Alward, email interview by author, November 21, 2018.

85. "Albakhiti yuhadhir rusia min altadakhul aleaskarii fi alyaman" [Al-Bukhaiti warns Russia against military intervention in Yemen], Yemen Press Agency, May 2, 2020, www.ypagency.net/256262.

86. "Alhuthi: nurahib bijawlat mufawadat fi rusia bayn aljumhuria alyamania wadual aleudwan" [Al-Houthi: We welcome a round of negotiations between the Republic of Yemen and the countries of aggression], *Sputnik Arabic*, March 2, 2021, https://arabic.sputniknews.com/arab_world/202103021048256441-بجولة-نرحب-الحوثي-علي / .مفاوضات-في-روسيا-بين-الجمهورية-اليمنية-ودول-العدوان /

87. Abdulsalam Mohammed, email interview by author, January 8, 2019.

88. Viacheslav Matuzov, telephone interview by author, January 5, 2019.

89. Grigory Lukyanov quoted in *RIA Novosti*, "Eksperty Govoril o Khode Proti-vostoyaniya Koalitsii i Gusitov v Yyemene" [Experts talked about the course of the opposition of the coalition and the Houthis in Yemen], March 26, 2019, https://ria.ru/20190326/1552106413.html.

8. MAKING UP FOR LOST TIME: RUSSIA AND CENTRAL MAGHREB

1. Oren Kessler and Boris Zilberman, "Russia's Charm Offensive in North Africa: Its Growing Economic and Military Influence in the Region," *Foreign Affairs*, April 3, 2017, www.foreignaffairs.com/articles/north-africa/2017–04–03/russia-s-charm-offensive-north-africa.

2. Anna Borshchevskaya, "From Moscow to Marrakech: Russia Is Turning Its Eyes to Africa," *The Hill*, September 21, 2017, https://thehill.com/opinion/international/351684-from-moscow-to-marrakech-russia-is-turning-to-africa.

3. Sarah Feuer and Anna Borshchevskaya, "Russia Makes Inroads in North Africa," *The Washington Institute Policy Watch* 2884, November 2, 2017, www.washingtoninstitute.org/policy-analysis/view/russia-makes-inroads-in-north-africa.

4. Stephen Blank, "Moscow's Competitive Strategy," American Foreign Policy Council, July 2018, 6, www.lexingtoninstitute.org/wp-content/uploads/2018/07/7.25.18-Moscows-Competitive-Strategy.pdf; Mihai Chihaia, "North Africa—A Gateway for Russia's Involvement," *Global Policy Journal*, March 7, 2018, www.globalpolicyjournal.com/blog/07/03/2018/north-africa---gateway-russia's-involvement; Anna Borshchevskaya, "Russia's Growing Influence in North Africa," *Atlantic Community*, February 26, 2019, https://atlantic-community.org/russias-growing-influence-in-north-africa.

5. Lisa Watanabe, "Russia's Renaissance in the Arab World," *Center for Security Studies* (CSS), May 24, 2019, https://css.ethz.ch/en/services/digital-library/articles/article.html/2187a66b-3d59–410d-9106–249a7ab65cd5. See also Ekaterina Stepanova, "Does Russia Have a Grand Plan for the Middle East?" *Politique étrangère* 2, (2016): 23–35.

6. Yahia H. Zoubir, "Soviet Policy in the Maghreb," *Arab Studies Quarterly* 9, no. 4 (1987): 399–421.

7. Yahia H. Zoubir, "The United States, the Soviet Union, and the Maghreb: Prospects for the Future," *The Maghreb Review* 15, nos. 3–4 (1990): 164–87.

8. Yahia H. Zoubir, "China's Relations with Algeria: From Revolutionary Friendship to Comprehensive Strategic Partnership," in *China and North Africa: Between Economics, Politics and Security*, ed. Adel Abdel-Ghafar (London: I. B. Tauris, 2021). While their policies differ, both China and Russia decided to extend their relations in the region. China began significant economic ties with Algeria in the early 2000s, while Russia reactivated its relations with Algeria, its traditional partner in the Maghreb, through massive arms sales. Later, Russia revamped its ties with Morocco and Tunisia.

9. Watanabe, "Russia's Renaissance in the Arab World," 66.

10. In late September 2011, the Algerian prime minister told this author that Western powers orchestrated the Arab Spring to induce regime change and redesign the MENA region. See also Dmitri Trenin, "Russia in the Middle East: Moscow's Objectives, Priorities, and Policy Drivers," *Carnegie Endowment for International Peace*, March 25, 2016, https://carnegieendowment.org/files/03–25–16_Trenin_Middle_East_Moscow_clean.pdf.

11. Borshchevskaya, "Russia's Growing Influence in North Africa."

12. Carol Saivetz, ed., *The Soviet Union in the Third World* (Cambridge, MA: Harvard University Russian Research Center, 1989); Jeffrey Hough, *The Struggle for the Third World: Soviet Debates and American Options* (Washington, DC: Brookings Institution, 1986). The Soviet Union provided support to most national liberation, anti-colonialist movements in Africa, Asia, and Latin America.

13. For instance, after the Arab defeat in 1967, Algerian President Houari Boumediène urged the Soviets to "assume their full responsibilities" to defend a progressive country that had fallen victim to imperialist aggression. *Le Monde*, "L'Algérie veut obte-

nir des éclaircissements sur la politique Soviétique au Moyen-Orient" [Algeria wants to get clarifications on the Soviet foreign policy in the Middle East], June 13, 1967, www.lemonde.fr/archives/article/1967/06/13/l-algerie-veut-obtenir-des-eclaircissements-sur-la-politique-sovietique-au-moyen-orient_2635 768_1819218.html.

14. William T. Shinn, Jr., "'The National Democratic State': A Communist Program for the Less-Developed Areas," *World Politics* 15, no. 3 (1963): 382–3. See also Robert O. Freedman, *Soviet Foreign Policy toward the Middle East Since 1970*, 3rd ed. (New York, NY: Praeger, 1982), 17. For deeper discussion, see Jerry F. Hough, *The Struggle for the Third World: Soviet Debates and American Options* (Washington, DC: Brookings Institution, 1986), esp. 156.

15. Yahia H. Zoubir, "Russia and Algeria: Reconciling Contrasting Interests," *Maghreb Review* 36, no. 2 (2011): 99–126.

16. Nicole Grimaud, *La Politique extérieure de l'Algérie* [Algeria's foreign policy] (Paris: Karthala, 1984), 147.

17. David Ottaway and Marina Ottaway, *Algeria: The Politics of a Socialist Revolution* (Berkeley, CA: University of California Press, 1970), 158. In fact, the US decision not to offer Algeria a Military Assistance Program (MAP) had been made the previous year. American policymakers believed that Algeria should address its request to France, and, if France refused, "We should urge them [Algerians] to limit their military program to one oriented toward civic action, progressive reduction of armed forces, and internal security, and offer to help them along these lines." US National Archives, "U.S. Policy toward Algeria," *National Security Action Memorandum* no. 211, December 14, 1962, declassified document (author's personal file).

18. M. J. V. Bell, "Military Assistance to Independent African States," *Adelphi Papers*, no. 15 (1964): 8. The major deliveries, however, did not begin until 1964 and 1966.

19. Irina Gridan, Gaëlle Le Boulanger, "Les relations militaires entre l'Algérie et la Russie, de l'indépendance aux années 1970," [Military relations between Algeria and Russia, from independence to the 1970s], *Outre-Mers. Revue d'histoire*, nos. 334–5 (2007): 40.

20. Saphia Arezki, *De l'ALN à l'ANP: la construction de l'armée algérienne, 1954–1991* [From the ALN to the ANP: the construction of the Algerian army, 1954–1991] (Algiers: Barzakh, 2018), 243–9.

21. Daniel Volman, "The Role of Foreign Military in the Western Sahara War," in *International Dimensions of the Western Sahara Conflict*, eds. Yahia H. Zoubir and Daniel Volman (Westport, CT: Praeger Publishers, 1993), 159.

22. Anonymous sources told the author that Russia has reiterated this request for the naval base in recent years.

23. Yahia H. Zoubir, "Soviet Policy in the Maghreb," *Arab Studies Quarterly* 9, no. 4 (1987): 399–421.

24. For detailed analysis, see Yahia H. Zoubir, "Moscow, the Maghreb, and Conflict in the Western Sahara," in *International Dimensions of the Western Sahara Conflict*, eds.

Yahia H. Zoubir and Daniel Volman (Westport, CT: Praeger Publishers, 1993), 103–125.

25. In 1975, Morocco invaded Western Sahara, a former Spanish colony. The national liberation movement POLISARIO Front opposed Morocco's irredentist claims and its illegal occupation of the former colony. The Algerian-backed POLISARIO and Morocco fought a war from 1976 until a UN-brokered ceasefire was proclaimed in September 1991. The UN was to organize a referendum for self-determination, but Morocco has opposed its holding despite the existence of a UN mission (MINURSO) set up for that purpose. See Yahia H. Zoubir, "Stalemate in Western Sahara: Ending International Legality," *Middle East Policy* 14, no. 4 (2007–8), 158–77.

26. Robert Śmigielski, "The Role of Arms Exports in the Foreign Policy of the Russian Federation," *Bulletin of the Polish Institute of Foreign Affairs* 54, no. 130 (2010): 248.

27. Antonio Sánchez Andrés, "Political-Economic Relations between Russia and North Africa," Real Instituto Elcano *Working Paper* 22/2006, November 7, 2006, 5, www.files.ethz.ch/isn/31874/WP%2022,%202006.pdf.

28. See the interview of Russian Ambassador to Algeria in Achira Mammeri, "L'Algérie achète nos Migs pour se protéger" [Algeria buys our Migs to protect itself], *L'Expression*, September 15, 2009, https://algeria-watch.org/?p=42007.

29. Derek Lutterbeck and Georgij Engelbrecht, "The West and Russia in the Mediterranean: Towards a Renewed Rivalry?" *Mediterranean Politics* 14, no. 3 (2009): 385–406.

30. Andrés, "Political-Economic Relations between Russia and North Africa."

31. Author interviews in 1996–1998 with senior military officers who recounted how they sought spare parts for Soviet equipment from the former Soviet republics or in Eastern Europe.

32. "Russia's Military Involvement in the Middle East," *Middle East Review of International Affairs (MERIA)* 5, no. 1 (2001); Interview with senior military officers in Algeria and abroad in the 1990s.

33. Oksana Antonenko, "Russia's Military Involvement in the Middle East."

34. These figures have been calculated from SIPRI reports by Lutterbeck and Engelbrecht, "The West and Russia in the Mediterranean," 395.

35. Bruno Etienne and Maurice Flory, "Chronique diplomatique," in *Annuaire de l'Afrique du Nord 1966*, vol. 5 (Paris: CNRS, 1967), 282, http://aan.mmsh.univ-aix.fr/Pdf/AAN-1966-05_11.pdf. On the terms of the economic agreement, see Charles Debbasch and Bruno Etienne, *Annuaire de l'Afrique du Nord 1967*, vol. 6 (Paris: CNRS, 1968).

36. John Waterbury, "The Soviet Union and North Africa," in *The Soviet Union and the Middle East*, eds. Ivo Lederer and Wayne Vucinich (Stanford, CA: Hoover Institution Press, 1974), 86.

37. Africa Confidential, "Morocco: Soviet-American Rivalry," *Africa Confidential* 19, no. 20 (1978): 5; *Archives Larousse: Journal de l'Année, Edition 1978*, www.larousse.fr/archives/journaux_annee/1978/96/afrique.

38. *Middle East Economic Digest* (hereafter *MEED*), March 17, 1978, p. 32.

39. Tony Hodges, *Western Sahara: The Roots of a Desert War* (Westport, CT: Laurence Hill, 1983), 354. This is apparently the "largest commercial deal ever concluded [by the Soviets] with a Third World country"; see John Damis, *Conflict in Northwestern Africa: The Western Sahara Dispute* (Stanford, CA: Hoover Institution Press, 1983), 131.

40. For good perspectives on Russian policy in the MENA, see Nikolay Kozhanov, "Russian Policy across the Middle East: Motivations and Methods," Chatham House *Russia and Eurasia Programme Research Paper*, February 2018, www.chathamhouse. org/sites/default/files/publications/research/2018–02–21-russian-policy-middle-east-kozhanov.pdf; Dmitri Trenin, *What Is Russia up to in the Middle East?* (Cambridge, UK: Polity, 2018).

41. Vassily Kuznetsov, Erik Burgos, and Clément Therme, "La politique étrangère russe au Maghreb: Entre commerce et sécurité" [Russian foreign policy in the Maghreb: Between commerce and security], *Confluences Méditerranée*, no. 104 (2018): 85–95.

42. Yahia H. Zoubir, "The Protracted Civil War in Libya: The Role of Outside Powers," *Turkey Insight* 22, no. 4 (2020): 11–27.

43. Dmitri Trenin, *Russia's Policy in the Middle East: Prospects for Consensus and Conflict with the United States* (New York: The Century Foundation, 2010), https://carnegieendowment.org/files/trenin_middle_east.pdf.

44. Zvi Magen and Olena Bagno-Moldavsky, "New Directions in Russia's Foreign Policy: Implications for the Middle East," *Strategic Assessment* 13, no. 4 (2011): 78.

45. Carole Nakhle, "Russia's Energy Diplomacy in the Middle East," in *Russia's Return to the Middle East: Building Sandcastles?* eds. Nicu Popescu and Stanislav Secrieru, Chaillot Paper no. 114 (Paris: European Union Institute for Security Studies, 2018), 29–35.

46. Aomar Baghzouz, "Algeria–France: Permanent Normalization," in *The Politics of Algeria: Domestic Issues and International Relations*, ed. Yahia H. Zoubir (London & New York: Routledge, 2020), 181–95; Yahia H. Zoubir, "The United States and Maghreb–Sahel Security," *International Affairs* 85, no. 5 (2009): 977–95.

47. Yahia H. Zoubir, "The Dialectics of Algeria's Foreign Relations from 1990 to the Present," in *Algeria in Transition—Reforms and Development Prospects*, ed. Ahmed Aghrout (London: Routledge, 2004), 151–82.

48. Yahia H. Zoubir, "The United States and Morocco: The Long-Lasting Alliance," in *Handbook on US Middle East Relations*, ed. Robert Looney (Oxon, UK; New York: Routledge, 2009), 237–48.

49. Author interviews with Algerian high-ranking officers.

50. Mansouria Mokhefi, "Alger-Moscou: Évolution et limites d'une relation privilégiée" [Algiers-Moscow: Evolution and limits of a privileged relationship], *Politique étrangère*, no. 3 (2015): 57.

51. Dmitry Bokarev, "Russia and Algeria: Decades of Friendship and Military and Technical Cooperation," *New Eastern Outlook*, September 24, 2019, https://journal-neo.org/2019/09/24/russia-and-algeria-decades-of-friendship-and-military-and-technical-cooperation.

52. Russian Ambassador to Algeria, cited in *El Moudjahid*, April 6, 2001 (not available online; author's personal file).

53. Fayçal Oukaci, "En échange de contrats d'armement de 4 milliards de dollars— Moscou efface la dette" [In exchange for $4 billion in arms contracts—Moscow clears debt], *L'Expression*, March 11, 2006, www.lexpressiondz.com/nationale/moscou-efface-la-dette-32527.

54. Cited in Mouloud Aït-Chaâlal, "Algérie-Russie: Un contrat militaire pour 2,5 milliards de dollars" [Algeria-Russia: A military contract worth 2.5 million dollars], *Le Jeune Indépendant*, April 5, 2001, www.algeria-watch.org/farticle/russie.htm.

55. Alexander's Oil and Gas Connections, "Algeria and Russia to Develop Bilateral Cooperation in All Spheres," May 27, 2001, www.gasandoil.com/news/2001/07/ntr12717.

56. *Jane's Defense Weekly*, "Russia to Help Algeria Update Forces," June 6, 2001, http://articles.janes.com/articles/Janes-Defence-Weekly-2001/Russia-to-help-Algeria-update-forces.html.

57. Aït-Chaâlal, "Algérie-Russie: Un contrat militaire pour 2,5 milliards de dollars."

57. Alexander's Oil and Gas Connections, "Algeria and Russia to Develop Bilateral Cooperation."

58. Algérie Presse Service (APS), "Le président Poutine souligne l'excellence des relations entre l'Algérie et la Russie" [President Putin highlights the excellent relations between Algeria and Russia], March 13, 2005 (author's personal file).

59. "Signature de quatre protocoles d'accord de coopération" [Signing of four cooperation agreements], Algérie Presse Service (APS), March 10, 2006 (author's personal file).

60. N. Ryad, "Après l'effacement des créances militaires russes: Le grand flou sur le nouveau volume de la dette extérieure algérienne" [After the write-off of Russian military claims: The great blur on the new volume of the Algerian external debt], *Liberté*, March 12, 2006, www.djazairess.com/fr/liberte/54022.

61. Richard Connolly and Cecilie Sendstad, "Russia's Role as an Arms Exporter: The Strategic and Economic Importance of Arms Exports for Russia," Chatham House, Russia and Eurasia Programme *Research Paper*, March 17, 2017, www.chathamhouse.org/sites/default/files/publications/research/2017-03-20-russia-arms-exporter-connolly-sendstad.pdf. See also Timofey Borisov, "Russian Arms Exports in the Middle East," in *Russia's Return to the Middle East Building Sandcastles?* eds. Nicu Popescu and Stanislav Secrieru, Chaillot Paper no. 114 (Paris: European Union Institute for Security Studies, 2018), 37–43.

62. *Sputnik* (in French), "Algeria Could Become Russia's Main Military Partner," March 29, 2007, http://en.rian.ru/russia/20070329/62781987.html.

63. *Sputnik* (in French), "La Russie rachète 24 chasseurs algériens (Ivanov)" [Russia bought back 24 Algerian fighters (Ivanov)], February 9, 2009, https://fr.sputniknews.com/international/20090209120048679/.

64. Guy Martin, "Algerian Navy Purchases Two Tiger Corvettes from Russia," *Defence Web*, July 1, 2011, www.defenceweb.co.za/sea/sea-sea/algerian-navy-purchases-two-tiger-corvettes-from-russia.

65. *Sputnik* (in French), "Russia to Build Two Tiger Corvettes for Algerian Navy," June 30, 2011, http://en.rian.ru/russia/20110630/164924783.html.

66. Bokarev, "Russia and Algeria: Decades of Friendship."

67. *Ibid.*

68. Mokhefi, "Alger-Moscou: Évolution et limites d'une relation privilégiée," 63.

69. Pieter D. Wezeman et al., "Trends in International Arms Transfers, 2018," *SIPRI Fact Sheet*, March 2019, 2 and 6, www.sipri.org/sites/default/files/2019–03/fs_1903_at_2018.pdf.

70. Kuznetsov, Burgos, and Therme, "La politique étrangère russe au Maghreb," 91. Since 2015, various newspaper publications have announced official discussions regarding Algeria's acquisition of the S-400s (*The New Defence Order Strategy [DFNC]*), "L'Algérie aurait commencé à déployer des S 400" [Algeria reportedly started deploying S400s], July 14, 2015, www.menadefense.net/algerie/lalgerie-aurait-commence-a-deployer-des-s-400) and that they have already been deployed on the territory (*Sputnik*, "Algérie: Des blogueurs publient les images des S-400 livrés au pays" [Algeria: Bloggers publish images of S-400s delivered to the country], July 27, 2015, https://fr.sputniknews.com/defense/201507211017136748). However, an Algerian military official told the author on July 23, 2019, that there has been no such procurement (yet?). In August 2019, a Russian expert in military affairs told the author that the issue of the S-400s is kept so secret that no one knows for sure whether there has really been discussion on their purchase by Algerians because both sides are so secretive about such matters; however, he suspected that such talks did take place.

71. "L'Algérie serait le premier client export pour le Su-57 et le Su-34" [Algeria might be the first export customer for Su-57 and Su-34], *Menadefense*, December 27, 2019, www.menadefense.net/algerie/lalgerie-serait-le-premier-client-export-pour-le-su-57-et-le-su-34.

72. Aaron Mehta, "Morocco cleared for massive F-16 fighter buy," *Defense News*, March 26, 2019, https://www.defensenews.com/global/mideast-africa/2019/03/25/morocco-cleared-for-massive-f-16-fighter-buy.

73. Eric Brothers, "Lockheed Martin delivers 123 F-35s in 2020," Aerospace and Manufacturing Design, December 29, 2020, https://www.aerospacemanufactur-inganddesign.com/article/lockheed-martin-delivers-123-f35s-2020. Algeria's reaction to those purchases and its subsequent decision were confirmed to the author in an anonymous interview with an Algerian military officer soon after the publication of this information.

74. Email interview on June 4, 2021, with Akram Kharief, director of the well-informed, Algiers-based MENADEFENSE, https://www.menadefense.net/fr/

75. "Le Su 34E bientôt réceptionnés par l'Algérie," MENADEFENSE, March 12, 2021, https://www.menadefense.net/algerie/le-su-34e-bientot-receptionnes-par-lal-gerie.

76. "The first Russian-Algerian military exercise will be held in North Ossetia," Ministry of Defence of the Russian Federation, April 21, 2021, https://eng.mil.ru/en/news_page/country/more.htm?id=12357191@egNews.

77. Algérie Presse Service (APS), "Relations algéro-russes: un 'véritable partenariat' en construction, relève le MAE" [Algerian-Russian relations: A 'true partnership' under construction, notes the MAE], March 8, 2006 (author's personal files).

78. Olivia Marsaud, "Algérie: La Russie efface la dette algérienne" [Algeria: Russia expunges Algeria's debt], *RFI* (Radio France Internationale), March 10, 2006, www1.rfi.fr/actufr/articles/075/article_42379.asp.

79. *Ibid*.

80. Algérie Presse Service (APS), "Signature d'un protocole d'accord de coopération entre Sonatrach et Loukoïl" [Signing of a cooperation agreement between Sonatrach and Lukoil], August 4, 2006 (author's personal file); Agence France Presse (AFP), "Loukoïl et Sonatrach vont coopérer dans les hydrocarbures" [Lukoil and Sonatrach to cooperate in the oil and gas sector], August 4, 2006, www.lapresse.ca/affaires/economie/200901/06/01–679996-loukoil-et-sonatrach-vont-cooperer-dans-les-hydrocarbures.php.

81. Claude Mandil, "Sécurité énergétique et Union Européenne: Propositions pour la présidence française" [Energy security and the European Union: Proposals for the French presidency], Vie Publique, April 21, 2008, 16, www.vie-publique.fr/sites/default/files/rapport/pdf/084000245.pdf.

82. Hakim Darbouche, "Russian-Algerian Cooperation and the 'Gas OPEC': What's in the Pipeline?" *CEPS Policy Brief*, no. 123 (2007): 3, www.files.ethz.ch/isn/32622/pb123.pdf.

83. Mark N. Katz, "Analysis: Russia, Algeria and Gas to Europe," *United Press International, Middle East Times*, November 28, 2006, www.algeria-watch.org/en/articles/2006/russia_algeria.htm.

84. RT.com, "Algeria Invites Gazprom, Lukoil to Jointly Develop Oil and Gas," February 18, 2014, http://rt.com/business/algeria-gazprom-lukoil-oil-532.

85. Kuznetsov, Burgos, and Therme, "La politique étrangère russe au Maghreb," 90.

86. *World Nuclear News (WNN)*, "Algeria May Get Russian Reactor," September 4, 2014, www.world-nuclear-news.org/NN-Algeria-may-get-Russian-reactor-0409201401.html.

87. "Algeria, Russia ink five cooperation agreements," APS, October 10, 2017, https://www.aps.dz/en/economy/20532-algeria-russia-ink-five-cooperation-agreements.

88. For instance, in 2012, only Algeria and Syria itself voted against the decision to expel Syria from the Arab League. The Arabs had openly criticized Russia for supporting the Assad regime. See Alexey Malashenko, "Russia and the Arab Spring," *Carnegie Moscow Center*, October 2013, https://carnegieendowment.org/files/russia_arab_spring2013.pdf.

89. Anna Borshchevskaya, "The Tactical Side of Russia's Arms Sales to the Middle East," in *Russia in the Middle East*, eds. Theodore Karasik and Stephen Blank (Washington, DC: The Jamestown Foundation, 2018), 197.

90. Алжир: «антикризисный» партнер России в арабском мире [Algeria: Russia's "anti-crisis" partner in the Arab world], РСМД [Russian International Affairs Council], March 1, 2016, https://russiancouncil.ru/analytics-and-comments/analytics/alzhir-antikrizisnyy-partner-rossii-v-arabskom-mire.

91. *Sputnik*, "Bientôt, les produits laitiers et de la viande bovine russes dans les assiettes des Algériens" [Soon, dairy products and Russian beef on the plates of Algerians], June 5, 2019, https://fr.sputniknews.com/afrique/201906051041349432-produits-laitiers-viande-bovine-russes-assiettes-algeriens.

92. Zhor Hadjam, "Exportations de céréales vers l'Algérie: La Russie tente à nouveau de se placer—Durant la campagne céréalière 2018/2019, l'Algérie a importé pas moins de 4,6 millions de tonnes de blé tendre de la France," *El Watan*, January 22, 2020, www.elwatan.com/edition/economie/exportations-de-cereales-vers-lalgerie-la-russie-tente-a-nouveau-de-se-place-22-01-2020.

93. Daniel Workman, "Wheat Imports by Country," *World's Top Exports*, October 19, 2019, www.worldstopexports.com/wheat-imports-by-country.

94. Россия и Алжир разыграют дорожную карту [Russia and Algeria to play the road map], *Kommersant*, January 24, 2019, www.kommersant.ru/doc/3862040.

95. "Covid-19: l'Algérie va produire en septembre le vaccin russe Spoutnik V" [Covid-19: Algeria will produce Russian vaccine Sputnik V in September], *Le Figaro & AFP*, April 7, 2021, www.lefigaro.fr/flash-actu/covid-19-l-algerie-va-produire-en-septembre-le-vaccin-russe-spoutnik-v-20210407?web=1&wdLOR=c72251AFB-F8BB-4C2C-941C-D83E726F5024.

96. Adlène Meddi, "Vaccination anti-Covid-19: pourquoi l'Algérie a choisi le Spoutnik-V" [Anti-Covid-19 vaccination: why Algeria chose Sputnik-V], *Le Point*, December 31, 2020, www.lepoint.fr/afrique/vaccination-anti-covid-19-pourquoi-l-algerie-a-choisi-le-spoutnik-v-31-12-2020-2407751_3826.php.

97. Cited in Vasily Kuznetsov, "Moscow Monitors Situation in Algeria as Protests Continue," *Al-Monitor*, March 14, 2019, www.al-monitor.com/pulse/originals/2019/03/russia-algeria-protests.html.

98. *Ibid.*

99. Moscow denied supporting the regime as the regime's party FLN had claimed. See Skander Salhi, "Exclusif. Pourquoi les Russes ne soutiennent pas Ahmed Gaid Salah" [Exclusive. Why the Russians do not support Ahmed Gaid Salah], *Maghreb Intelligence*, September 9, 2019, www.maghreb-intelligence.com/exclusif-pourquoi-les-russes-ne-soutiennent-pas-ahmed-gaid-salah.

100. Cited in Kaci Haidar, "Vladimir Poutine souhaite "sincèrement" à l'Algérie de 'surmonter ses difficultés et de renforcer sa souveraineté'" [Vladimir Putin "sincerely" wishes for Algeria to "overcome its difficulties and to reinforce its sovereignty"], *Algérie 1*, October 24, 2019, www.algerie1.com/actualite/vladimir-poutine-souhaite-laquo-nbsp-sincerement-nbsp-raquo-a-lalgerie-de-surmonter-ses-difficultes-et-de-renforcer-sa-souverainete.

101. Saïd N., "L'ambassadeur de Russie à Alger dévoile la manipulation du FLN" [Russian ambassador in Algiers reveals the manipulation of the FLN], *Algérie Patriotique*, September 2, 2019, www.algeriepatriotique.com/2019/09/02/lambassadeur-de-russie-a-alger-devoile-la-manipulation-du-fln.

102. *The Moscow Times* (*Reuters*), "Russia Backs Algerian Government Plan for Talks with Opposition," March 19, 2019, www.themoscowtimes.com/2019/03/19/russia-backs-algerian-government-plan-for-talks-with-opposition-a64867.

103. A. B., "Réactions internationales à l'élection du 12 décembre: La Russie, les Etats-Unis et les pays arabes félicitent Tebboune" [International reactions to the December 12 election: Russia, the United States and the Arab countries congratulate Tebboune], *El Watan*, December 15, 2019, www.elwatan.com/edition/actualite/reactions-internationales-a-lelection-du-12-decembre-la-russie-les-etats-unis-et-les-pays-arabes-felicitent-tebboune-15–12–2019.

104. Cited in *Radio Algérienne*, "Le président russe Vladimir Poutine: 'nous soutenons la politique internationale et régionale équilibrée prônée par l'Algérie,'" [Russian President Vladimir Putin: 'we support Algeria's balanced international and regional policy'] February 5, 2020, www.radioalgerie.dz/news/fr/article/202 00205/189314.html.

105. Cited in Algérie Presse Service (APS), "L'Algérie aspire à renforcer ses relations avec la Russie pour les hisser au niveau de l'entente politique" [Algeria aspires to strengthen its relations with Russia to bring them up to the level of political understanding], February 22, 2020, www.aps.dz/algerie/102005-president-tebboune-l-algerie-aspire-a-renforcer-ses-relations-avec-la-russie-pour-les-hisser-au-niveau-de-l-entente-politique.

106. Cited in Левон Арутюнян [Levon Harutyunyan], "Реванш исламистов: радикалы захватывают мирный протест в Алжире" [Islamist revenge: Radicals take over peaceful protest in Algeria], Газета, April 16, 2021, www.gazeta.ru/politics/2021/04/16_a_13561550.shtml.

107. Abdallah Saaf, *La Russie et le Maghreb* (Rabat, Morocco: OCP Policy Center, 2016), 17. Sergey Lavrov visited Morocco in 2005, while Putin did so in 2006.

108. Feuer and Borshchevskaya, "Russia Makes Inroads in North Africa."

109. Western Sahara Resource Watch, "Russia Once Again Violates Its Own Fish Deal with Morocco," April 26, 2013, www.wsrw.org/a217x2576. See also, Western Sahara Resource Watch, "Un bateau frigo norvégien navigue dans la tanière des lions" [A Norwegian refrigerator boat sails in the den of lions], January 23, 2019, www.wsrw.org/a111x4426.

110. Laila Zerrour, "Maroc-Russie: Un partenariat 'win-win'" [Morocco-Russia: A "win-win" partnership], *Aujourd'hui le Maroc*, October 12, 2017, http://aujourd-hui.ma/actualite/maroc-russie-un-partenariat-win-win. During his visit to the region in October 2017, the Russian prime minister signed eleven agreements with Morocco, which covered a number of areas.

111. *Morocco World News*, "Minister: Agriculture Represents 77% of Moroccan Exports to Russia," October 7, 2018, www.moroccoworldnews.com/2018/10/254749/agriculture-represents-morocco-russia.

112. *Ministry of Agriculture of the Russian Federation*, "Russia and Morocco Strengthen Economic Cooperation," October 24, 2019, http://mcx.ru/en/news/Russia-and-Morocco-Strengthen-Economic-Cooperation.

113. "Российские туристы стали чаще посещать Марокко," [Russian tourists began to visit Morocco more often], РИА Новости, December 17, 2018, https://ria.ru/20210607/fsb-1735945179.html

114. Zerrour, "Maroc-Russie: Un partenariat 'win-win.'"

115. Christopher Woody, "The US and Russia Are Dominating the Global Weapons Trade," *Business Insider*, December 28, 2016, www.businessinsider.com/us-russia-global-arms-sales-2016–12.

116. *Algérie-Patriotique*, a well-informed newspaper on military affairs, affirms that while Morocco is the party that claimed not to be interested in purchasing S-400s, it was in fact the Russians who refused to sell them to Morocco. Karim B., "Le mensonge du Makhzen sur la non-acquisition du système russe S-400" [Makhzen's lie on the non-acquisition of the Russian system S-400], *Algérie Patriotique*, May 29, 2019, www.algeriepatriotique.com/2019/05/29/le-mensonge-du-makhzen-sur-la-non-acquisition-du-systeme-antiaerien-russe-s-400. The author interviewed numerous Russian and Algerian academics and officials regarding the sale of the S-400, but none seems to have concrete evidence. Both the Algerian and Russian governments are opaque on such matters.

117. *Voice of America*, "Russian Prime Minister Strikes Energy Deals in Morocco," October 11, 2017, www.voanews.com/world-news/middle-east-dont-use/russian-prime-minister-strikes-energy-deals-morocco.

118. *Business Times Africa*, "Morocco, Russia to Build Refinery," October 24, 2019, http://mail.businesstimesafrica.net/index.php/business/item/5241-morocco-russia-to-build-refinery.

119. Larbi Arbaoui, "Morocco to Train Russian Imams," *Morocco World News*, March 19, 2016, www.moroccoworldnews.com/2016/03/182434/182434.

120. Stephen Zunes and Jacob Mundy, *Western Sahara: War, Nationalism, and Conflict Irresolution* (Syracuse, NY: Syracuse University Press, 2010).

121. United Nations Security Council, "8387th Meeting," S/PV.8387, October 31, 2018, https://undocs.org/en/S/PV.8387.

122. "Россия не поддержала резолюцию Совбеза ООН по Западной Сахаре" [Russia did not support UN Security Council resolution on Western Sahara], РИА Новости, October 31, 2018, https://ria.ru/20181031/1531900151.html.

123. "Западная Сахара—бунтарь с ангельским лицом?" [Western Sahara—a rebel with an angel's face?], РСМД, March 23, 2015, https://russiancouncil.ru/analytics-and-comments/interview/zapadnaya-sakhara-buntar-s-angelskim-litsom/?sphrase_id=28291547.

124. Habibulah Mohamed Lamin, "How Polisario Front Hopes to Partner with Russia in Western Sahara," *Al-Monitor*, April 11, 2017, www.al-monitor.com/pulse/originals/2017/04/western-sahara-polisario-sell-russia-moscow-visit.html.

125. Tamba François Koundouno, "Morocco-Russia Intensify Relations as Strategic Interests Converge," *Morocco World News*, December 31, 2019, www.moroccoworldnews.com/2019/12/290187/morocco-russia-relations-strategic-interests.

126. Feuer and Borshchevskaya, "Russia Makes Inroads in North Africa."

127. Mohammed Issam Laaroussi, "Russia's Search for Strategic Partnerships in North Africa: Balancing Algeria and Morocco," Washington Institute for Near East Policy, February 19, 2019, www.washingtoninstitute.org/fikraforum/view/russias-search-for-strategic-partnerships-in-north-africa-balancing-algeria.

128. Sánchez Andrés, "Political-Economic Relations between Russia and North Africa."

129. Борис Макаренко [Boris Makarenko], "Тунисский сценарий для России?" [A Tunisian scenario for Russia?], *Vedomosti*, January 20, 2011, www.vedomosti. ru/politics/articles/2011/01/20/tunisskij_scenarij_dlya_rossii.

130. Tobias Schumacher and Cristian Nitoiu, "Russia's Foreign Policy towards North Africa in the Wake of the Arab Spring," *Mediterranean Politics* 20, no. 1 (2015): 99.

131. Jake Rudnitsky and Samer Al-Atrush, "Russia Lobbies Tunisia to Support Syria's Arab League Return," Bloomberg, January 26, 2019, www.bloomberg.com/ news/articles/2019–01–26/russia-lobbies-tunisia-to-support-syria-s-return-to-arab-league.

132. Cited in *ibid.*

133. Schumacher and Nitoiu, "Russia's Foreign Policy towards North Africa," 101.

134. Oscar Nkala, "Russia Promises Helicopters, Gear for Tunisia's Anti-Terrorism Fight," *Defense News*, March 24, 2016, www.defensenews.com/global/mideast-africa/2016/03/24/russia-promises-helicopters-gear-for-tunisia-s-anti-terror-ism-fight.

135. *Tass Russian News Agency* (in French), "Russia and Tunisia Boost Cooperation on Anti-Terrorism, Says Lavrov," January 26, 2019, https://tass.com/politics/ 1041929.

136. *World Nuclear News (WNN)*, "Russia and Tunisia Sign Nuclear MOU," June 2, 2015, www.world-nuclear-news.org/NP-Russia-and-Tunisia-sign-nuclear-MOU-02061503.html.

137. *Nuclear Street News*, "Russia and Tunisia Agree on Legal Foundation for Nuclear Power Cooperation," September 26, 2016 https://nuclearstreet.com/nuclear_ power_industry_news/b/nuclear_power_news/archive/2016/09/26/russia-and-tunisia-agree-on-legal-foundation-for-nuclear-power-cooperation-092601#. XoBaZIgzZPY.

138. Feuer and Borshchevskaya, "Russia Makes Inroads in North Africa."

139. "Tunisia Seeks Strategic Partnership with Russia—Minister," TASS, February 27, 2018, https://tass.com/society/991822.

140. Nadia Dejoui, "800.000 touristes russes sont attendus en Tunisie cette année" [800,000 Russian tourists are expected in Tunisia this year], *L'Economiste maghrébin*, June 13, 2019, www.leconomistemaghrebin.com/2019/06/13/800-000-tour-istes-russes-attendus-tunisie.

141. Yahia H. Zoubir, "Expanding Sino–Maghreb Relations Morocco and Tunisia," Chatham House Research Paper (February 2020): 1–26, www.chathamhouse. org/sites/default/files/CHHJ7839-SinoMaghreb-Relations-WEB.pdf; Zoubir, "Les relations de la Chine avec les pays du Maghreb," 91–103.

142. See, for example, Borshchevskaya, "From Moscow to Marrakech."

INDEX

Note: Page numbers followed by "*n*" refer to notes, "*f*" refer to figures.

277

INDEX

coup d'etat (Sanaa), 165, 166, 171
COVID-19 pandemic, 174, 159, 216
  Sputnik-V (vaccine), 211
Crimea, 32, 78
  annexation of, 26, 31, 35, 70, 84, 111
CSTO. *See* Collective Security Treaty Organization (CSTO)
Currie, Kelley Eckels, 179
Czech Republic, 123

Damascus. *See* Syria; Syria: Russia military operation in; Syrian conflict: Russian legal and normative claims
"Davos in the desert" (Riyadh, 23 Oct 2018), 152
"deal of the century", 150
Dedushkin, Vladimir, 182, 183, 261n39
democratic legitimacy principles, 90–5, 111, 112
Democratic Republic of Yemen (DRY). *See* Yemen; Yemeni civil war: Russia's role in
Dengov, Lev, 7
Dmitriev, Kirill, 149
Doha. *See* Qatar
domestic factors: Russian foreign policy, 2, 3–4, 30, 61–81, 227
  domestic policy actors, emergence of, 6–8
  domestic unrest (2011–12), 59, 66–7, 69, 71
  Middle East agenda for internal political objectives, 61–2
  patriotic mobilization, wave of, 70–1, 71f
  Putin's domestic popularity, 64, 70, 76–7
  ruling elite, conflict inside, 70

Russian people's growing scepticism, 77–8, 78f, 79, 79f
  as "superpower", 74–5, 74f, 76
  See also Arab uprisings/Arab Spring (2011)
Donbas war (Ukraine), 26, 31, 35, 67, 77
Dostoyevsky, Fyodor, 117
Dremov, Oleg, 186

Egypt, 39, 41, 42, 43, 47
  Arab Spring assessment, 67–8
  Arab Spring, starting of, 65
  Camp David agreement, 55
  economic cooperation with Moscow, 143–4
  effective control principle, 90
  Obama administration and Mubarak fall, 49
  USSR alliance, end of, 40, 54
Egyptian-Israeli peace agreement, 42
elections (2011–12), 27, 30
Ennahda party, 219
Erdoğan, Recep Tayyip, 48, 52, 87
Ethiopia, 44
Eurasian Economic Union (EEU), 30, 132, 135, 138
Eurasianism, 71–3, 80
Euro-Atlantic liberal hegemony, 138
Eurocentrism, 27
Euromaidan revolution (Ukraine, Nov 2013), 30–2
European colonization, 40
European Union (EU), 2, 19, 22, 23, 31, 62, 137, 142, 191, 203, 218, 221, 222
  Eastern Partnership, 27
  EU-Algerian-EU relations, 208–9